SADLIER FAITH AND WITNESS

CREED

A Course on Catholic Belief Part II

Annotated Edition

Guide Writer
Trudy S. White

Text Authors
Norman F. Josaitis, S. T. D.
Rev. Michael J. Lanning, O. F. M.

William H. Sadlier, Inc.
9 Pine Street
New York, New York 10005-1002
http://www.sadlier.com

Acknowledgments

Scripture selections are taken from the *New American Bible with Revised New Testament and Psalms* Copyright © 1991, 1986, 1970 Confraternity of Christian Doctrine, Inc., Washington, DC. Used with permission. All rights reserved. No part of the *New American Bible* may be reproduced in any form without permission in writing from the copyright holder.

Excerpts from the English translation of the *Catechism of the Catholic Church* for use in the United States of America, Copyright © 1994, United States Catholic Conference, Inc.—Libreria Editrice Vaticana.

Excerpts from the English translation of *The Roman Missal* © 1973, International Committee on English in the Liturgy, Inc. (ICEL); excerpts from the English translation of *Order of Christian Funerals* © 1985, ICEL; excerpts from the English translation of *Rite of Penance* © 1974, ICEL; excerpts from the English translation of *A Book of Prayers* © 1982, ICEL. All rights reserved.

The English translation of the Our Father, the Nicene Creed, the Apostle's Creed, and the Gloria Patri by the International Consultation on English Texts (ICET).

Reprinted from *More Dreams Alive,* edited by Carl Koch. Excerpt written by Jonathan Huth, Saint John High School, Gulfport MS. Used by permission of the publisher (Saint Mary's Press, Winona, MN). All rights reserved.

Reprinted from *Praying with Hildegard of Bingen* by Durka (Saint Mary's Press, Winona, MN). Used with permission of the publisher. All rights reserved.

Excerpt from *Saints for All Seasons* by John J. Delaney. Copyright © 1978 by John J. Delaney. Used by permission of Doubleday, a division of Bantam Doubleday Dell Publishing Group Inc.

Excerpt from "As Kingfishers Catch Fire," from *Poems of Gerard Manley Hopkins,* 3d. ed., edited by W.H. Gardner, (New York and London: Oxford University Press, 1948).

General Consultant for Texts
Rev. Joseph A. Komonchak, Ph.D.

Official Theological Consultant for Texts
Most Rev. Edward K. Braxton, Ph.D., S.T.D.
Auxiliary Bishop of St. Louis

Publisher
Gerard F. Baumbach, Ed.D.

Editor in Chief
Moya Gullage

Pastoral Consultant
Rev. Msgr. John F. Barry

Scriptural Consultant
Rev. Donald Senior, C.P., Ph.D., S.T.D.

General Editors
Norman F. Josaitis, S.T.D.
Rev. Michael J. Lanning, O.F.M.

Catechetical and Liturgical Consultants
William Sadlier Dinger
Eleanor Ann Brownell, D. Min.
Joseph F. Sweeney
Helen Hemmer, I.H.M.
Mary Frances Hession
Maureen Sullivan, O.P., Ph.D.
Don Boyd

"The Ad Hoc Committee to Oversee the Use of the Catechism,
National Conference of Catholic Bishops,
has found the doctrinal content of this teacher's manual to be in
conformity with the *Catechism of the Catholic Church*."

Home Office:
9 Pine Street
New York, NY 10005–1002

ISBN: 0–8215–5663–0
123456789/98

A Course on Catholic Belief

Part II: The Church and the Holy Spirit

Sadlier's new FAITH AND WITNESS PROGRAM is a creative response to the needs of adolescents in the Catholic Church. It is rooted in a desire to serve effectively these young people, as well as those adults who teach, guide, and parent them on their faith journey.

It is shaped by an awareness of the multiple challenges and rewards of working with this vulnerable age group, which has been described as having one foot in childhood and the other groping toward adulthood.

At the heart of **Faith and Witness** is "a Person, the Person of Jesus of Nazareth, the only Son from the Father." And its aim is to draw adolescents into "communion with Jesus Christ." (*Catechism of the Catholic Church*, 426)

Just as Jesus himself related to and communicated with people "on their own level," so this program respects and responds to the adolescent's urgent questions: Who am I? Where am I going? What is my purpose in life?

Research done by the Carnegie Council on Adolescent Behavior verifies that many adolescents in our society have not been receiving the kind of guidance and support they need to thrive during this difficult period of metamorphosis. The Council's report warns that youth between ten and fourteen have become "a neglected generation." It notes alarming increases in adolescent suicide, firearm use, smoking, drug and alcohol addiction, pregnancy, and poor grades. Its recommendations stress that schools should create programs better suited to adolescents' developmental needs, and parents should be

INTRODUCING

FAITH AND WITNESS

A Five-Course Program for Junior High Students

encouraged to become more involved in their young people's lives.

Sadlier's new **Faith and Witness Program** endeavors to meet these goals through an integration of the specific social, intellectual, religious, and spiritual needs of youth. It addresses "the desire for God [that] is written in the human heart" (*Catechism*, 27) as well as the Church's pastoral mission. Particular attention is paid to the following aspects of that mission: examining the reasons for belief, celebrating the sacraments, being integrated into the faith community, providing and calling forth gospel witness (*Catechism*, 6).

The semester courses that together comprise the program draw young people into relationship with Jesus and the New Testament, Liturgy and Worship, Church History, Morality, and the Creed. Each course invites young people to venture further into the mystery of faith and the challenge of discipleship. Through shared study, reflection, prayer, and action in response to God's word, young people experience themselves as a small faith community within the larger community of the parish and the Church itself.

We asked the writers of the courses to share with you, in a few sentences, their response to the following question:

What hopes do you have for the young people who will use your book?

Creed

"We know what a privilege and a challenge it is to share with young people the dynamic teachings of our Catholic faith. Moreover it is important to share that faith in a clear and meaningful way with the next generation of believers. We do this in two parts: Creed Part I, covering faith and revelation; Creed Part II, covering the Church and the Holy Spirit. Our hope is that young people will come to love Jesus and his Church ever more and take their place in society as committed evangelizers."

**Dr. Norman F. Josaitis, S.T.D., and
Rev. Michael J. Lanning, O.F.M., authors**

Liturgy and Worship

"We all know that it takes a lot more knowledge and skill to do something than to watch something. I hope that this book will provide the students—the next generation of young Catholics—with the help they need to celebrate the sacraments intelligently, joyfully, and fruitfully."

**Rev. Thomas Richstatter, O.F.M., S.T.D.,
author**

New Testament

"The purpose of this book is to provide an introduction to the New Testament that will offer young people a mature appreciation of their faith. Knowing all about the good news of Jesus Christ is more than the work of one lifetime. But it is our hope that this book will help young people to become more committed disciples of Jesus and stronger members of his Church."

**Dr. Norman F. Josaitis, S.T.D., and
Rev. Michael J. Lanning, O.F.M., authors**

"This introduction, I hope, will make accessible to young people twenty centuries of Christian reflection on the New Testament."

**Dr. Mary Ann Getty, S.T.D.,
special consultant**

Morality

"Too many people think of morality as something negative and limiting. But the truth is that Christian morality is an invitation to become part of the most graced and promising life possible. Morality is all about authentic happiness and rich, lasting loves. My hope with this book is that students will discover that God loves them and wants the best for them, and that people who care for them will always challenge them to be good."

Rev. Paul J. Wadell, Ph.D., C.P., author

Church History

"I love Church history and agree with Cicero who said: 'To know nothing of what happened before you were born is to remain ever a child.' The same is true of Catholics who are unaware of our own religious heritage. The history of the Catholic Church is a marvelous story of saints and sinners, successes and failures, hopes and disappointments. For a person of faith, it is not only a human story but also a divine drama of God's grace at work in our world."

Rev. Thomas J. Shelley, Ph.D., author

You Are a Catechist

Grace and peace to you! You have been called to be a catechist, a faith-filled minister of the word to adolescents. The aim of your ministry is to bring young people into intimate communion with Jesus Christ, and to draw them more deeply into the faith life of the Church. Think for a moment:

◆ Why do you think you were invited to do this work with young people?
◆ What gifts, talents or experiences do you bring to this ministry?

Ministry to the Needs of Youth

Ministry to young people has two main goals:

• to contribute to the personal and spiritual growth of each young person in your care;

• to invite young people into responsible participation in the life, mission, and work of the faith community. The components of your ministry include:

Evangelization—reaching out to young people who are uninvolved in the life of the Church and inviting them into a relationship with Jesus and the Catholic community.

Catechesis—promoting a young person's growth in the Catholic faith through a teaching process that emphasizes understanding, reflection, and conversation.

Prayer and Worship—guiding young people in developing their relationship with Jesus through personal prayer; drawing them more deeply into the sacramental life of the Church; involving them in a variety of prayer and worship experiences to celebrate their friendship with Jesus in a faith community of their peers.

Community Life—forming young people into the Christian community through programs and relationships that promote openness, trust, respect, cooperation, honesty, responsibility, and willingness to serve; creating a climate where young people can grow and share their struggles, questions, and joys with other young people and feel they are valued members of the Church.

Justice, Peace, and Service—giving direction to young people as they develop a Christian social consciousness and a commitment to a life of justice and peace by providing opportunities for service.

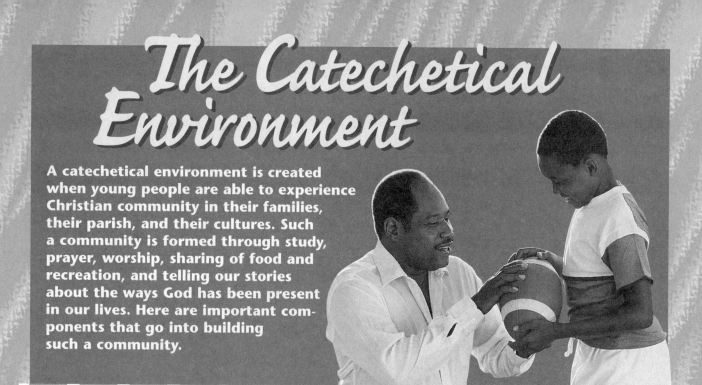

The Catechetical Environment

A catechetical environment is created when young people are able to experience Christian community in their families, their parish, and their cultures. Such a community is formed through study, prayer, worship, sharing of food and recreation, and telling our stories about the ways God has been present in our lives. Here are important components that go into building such a community.

Knowing the Young People

The environment and practices in the home and neighborhood have had, and continue to have, a powerful influence on the faith development of the young people in your group. It is important to be aware of the world the young people inhabit. Here are ways to develop that awareness.

◆ Be sure that your consistency, dependability, and fairness are such to win their confidence.

◆ Review the information you have been given regarding each young person.

◆ Become familiar with where and with whom each young person lives and who has legal custody.

◆ Make sure you are aware of young people who may be neglected or who come from homes that appear to be unhappy.

◆ Be available for private conferences with parents or family members, even if it means rearranging your schedule to meet their employment or family obligations.

◆ Be mindful of and sensitive to the language spoken in the home and the religious affiliation of parent(s) or guardians.

◆ Be alert to the general health and well-being of the young person.

Getting Families Involved

The mission of Catholic education is to support, develop, enhance, and encourage the positive learning that takes place within the home. It is essential, therefore, to involve the family in the catechetical process. Encourage them to participate fully in ongoing religious development of the young person. Regular family conversations about God and religion have a tremendous positive effect on a young person's faith attitudes and practices.

◆ Welcome the families when the program begins. Explain the catechetical program and invite their participation.

◆ Introduce them to the courses. The table of contents for each course provides an excellent overview of what the young people will be expected to learn about our Catholic faith during the program.

◆ Encourage a conversation about ways they can share with their son or daughter the *You Are My Witnesses* page. Duplicate and send home *Highlights for Home* from each chapter of the guide.

◆ Make positive telephone calls to parents. Conversations can be barrier-breakers, and from them catechists can gain great parental support and insight.

◆ Make a "Parents' Day" part of your yearly tradition so that the parents are given the opportunity to share their hopes and dreams for their daughters and sons.

Knowing the Neighborhood

◆ Become aware of the out-of-school activities both of the young people and of those with whom they frequently associate. If possible, attend some of their athletic or musical events.

◆ Be available and willing to listen to the young people without suggesting cures. When necessary, suggest that they seek professional advice as to how to deal with any unhealthy behaviors. Discuss these with the parents as well as any neighborhood influences and/or friends who are adversely affecting the young people's social, emotional, and spiritual development.

◆ Invite professionals to help the young people learn ways to cope with social pressures and problems such as alcohol, drugs, and peer pressure.

Sadlier's **Faith and Witness Program** is designed to nurture in young people a wholesome sense of self and a secure relationship with God in the context of the faith community. By integrating the teaching of Jesus and of the Church with the realities of their lives, they will be better prepared to minister to a world in which secular values often oppose the good news.

Making Discipline Positive

Positive discipline entails creating a climate in which young people feel secure, accepted, and supported. Here are suggestions for establishing and maintaining positive discipline in the group setting.

◆ Establish a sense of order immediately. Clearly and briefly explain to the young people what is expected of them. Rules should be few and easy to remember.

◆ Use affirmation; acknowledge the young people and remember to praise and affirm good behavior.

◆ Provide activities that build healthy self-esteem.

◆ Respect their thoughts and ideas, and expect them to do the same with you and their peers.

◆ Provide activities that challenge them to cooperate with one another.

◆ Deal with those who act inappropriately in a way that will calm them; set aside a space where they can think quietly about their actions and the consequences of them. If correcting is necessary, do it one-to-one, never publicly.

Developing Multicultural Awareness

True Christian community takes place within the context of the cultural heritage and the identity of the young people we teach.

◆ Be aware of and sensitive to ethnic and cultural diversity.

◆ Encourage the young people to express their cultural uniqueness through art, music, dance, food, and dress.

◆ Send communications home in the languages of the families, if possible.

◆ Invite families to share their cultural symbols and food at celebrations.

◆ Be aware of possible conflicts because of ethnic or cultural diversity among young people.

Youth With Special Needs

In recent years, the bishops of the United States have encouraged religious educators to pay particular attention to those young people who have special needs and to integrate these young people, when possible, into regular programs of religious education.

There are many different kinds of special needs. Some young people have *physical* needs that must be taken into consideration. Physical needs may involve any of the five senses, as well as special motor needs. Some have *emotional* needs that require our recognition, attention, and consideration. Still others have *special learning* needs. Learn about the special needs of these young people from the trained professionals who have dealt with them and their families.

Try to ascertain what adjustments or adaptations need to be made for your group. Be aware also of any adaptations necessary to enable the young people to profit from their religion materials. Plan the seating arrangement so that each person feels part of the group. Be sure that the group is aware of and sensitive to the special needs of all.

Recognize how all of us need to receive from as well as give to those who are disabled or challenged in any way. Jean Vanier, founder of the L'Arche communities in which people with disabilities and their caregivers live together, observes that those who are "broken" can reveal to us our own spiritual or psychological "brokenness." By this mutuality, we are strengthened, reconciled, and healed.

Understanding the Adolescent

Adolescence—the period that normally covers the years between eleven and fifteen—is a time of major change, development, and sometimes upheaval in the young person's life. To the young person everything seems to be in flux, in motion—physical development, emotions, ideas, relationships. It is a time of challenge and enormous potential for growth; it can also be a time of frustration and confusion both for the adolescents and for the adults—parents and catechists— who care for them.

Social Development

As young people move into adolescence, their interests begin to extend beyond family and school to wider horizons. As these new interests develop, relationships that had been of primary importance, especially those with family, sometimes seem to recede. Although there is still an essential need for the security and support of family and other adults, it is a time when old ties and the excitement of an enlarging world can conflict. The growing desire of the young people for greater freedom and their continuing need for support and security offer a real challenge to parents and catechists, who must find ways to facilitate this process of progressive emancipation. The sociability of the teenagers should be utilized and their energies channeled into common pursuits. It is the right age for such educational techniques as small-group projects or discussions, debates, panel presentations, retreat days, youth days, and service projects.

Intellectual Development

Young adolescents are increasingly capable of all the intellectual operations. There is specific growth in the ability to deal with abstract ideas and judgments in those young people who have matured beyond the egocentrism of an earlier stage. As they come more and more into contact with the judgments and opinions of others, they will need to be helped and challenged to think more accurately, perceptively, and critically. The broadening intellectual and social world of the young people stimulates a questioning and critical spirit. We can foster a *positive* questioning and critical attitude in the young people by challenging them to explore, probe, and reflect.

Also on a positive level, God's relationship with the young people is often expressed in a more "spiritual" way than before. Prayers become more other-oriented and less egocentric. The Church can be more readily understood as a community of believers, and worship is seen as a natural expression of belief and a way to become a better person.

The catechist should be aware that as real religious insights such as these occur, there can also be a tendency for negative attitudes to develop. This is often especially true for less mature young people, who, when faced with the struggle to move from an egocentric to a more mature religious belief, find it difficult to wrestle with the problems this involves and retreat into indifference or hostility. The challenge to the catechist is great. The first challenge is to recognize some very basic needs of adolescents.

Some Basic Needs

1. *Affirmation and Approval.* Young people must consistently be affirmed by their parents, catechists, and peers. Most have a precarious sense of self-esteem. They suffer anxiety about their physical appearance, their popularity, their skills and talents. They need to be told and shown that they are accepted, appreciated, and approved for who they are right now.

2. *Security and Success.* Because intellectual and other abilities vary so broadly among adolescents, they need multiple opportunities to succeed. An effective catechist discerns and draws out the particular skills of each young person. When a relationship of trust is nurtured between catechist and young person, the young person feels secure enough to do his or her best.

3. *Freedom and Structure.* Like fledgling pilots, adolescents love to fly but they depend heavily on the voice from the control tower. They want freedom to experiment and explore yet they require a reliable home base to return to as needed. Catechists who come to the group well-prepared, who require young people to abide by simple rules, and who consistently offer opportunities for choice and self-expression will do well with this age group. Giving clear directions and guiding young people step-by-step through a new process or ritual reinforces awareness of structure.

4. *Idealism and Self-Definition.* Youth have a great capacity for energetic idealism which can be effectively harnessed in the causes of justice, equality, and peace-making. When motivated and well directed, they will unselfishly participate in the works of mercy—particularly in one-on-one situations. However, if their idealism and altruism are not channeled by catechists and adult mentors, youth readily take refuge in cynicism and hostility. Their need for self-definition must be met through individual attention from adults and by enlisting their particular abilities in ways that serve others.

5. *Physical Activity and Social Interaction.* Driven by hormonal changes and uncontrollable growth spurts, adolescents literally "cannot sit still" for extended lectures. They need to move from place to place, activity to activity, individual to partnered or group pursuits. Their hunger for interaction with peers can be met in diverse ways (discussions, debates, art or craft projects, sharing food and music, games, dancing, human sculptures).

Thinking Skills for Discipleship

More and more often, a complex and technological society demands critical thinkers. Critical thinkers see beneath surface impressions to the root of an issue or event. They are able to discern causes rather than symptoms, and they are able to project consequences rather than to be satisfied with quick solutions. Above all, critical thinkers are capable of reflection—not only on issues outside themselves, but capable of their own responses and reactions as well. How can we help our young people develop critical thinking skills? And how can we encourage them to use these skills as disciples of Christ?

The ability to think critically can be developed in young adolescents through questions and activities that involve the following:

- solving problems
- making decisions
- imagining outcomes
- setting up criteria
- finding reasons
- reflecting/meditating
- choosing applications to life

"Who do you say I am?" Jesus asked his disciples. It was a question that demanded the disciples to go beneath surface impressions to the heart of the matter. Instead, the disciples responded by repeating what *others* had said— "Some say John the Baptist; others Elijah; still others responded Jeremiah or one of the prophets." Jesus refused to accept the superficial, unreflective answer. He probed further. "But who do you say that I am?"

This is the basic question of our faith. This is the question that we want our young disciples to answer with personal conviction, commitment, and hope.

"You are the Messiah, the Son of the living God" (Matthew 16:13–16).

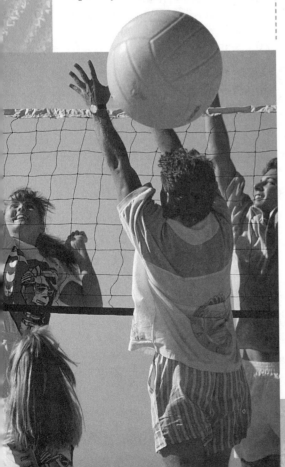

Prayer and the Young Person

A well-known youth minister was asked what advice he would give to religion catechists. "Be bold about the spiritual," he said. "These kids want and need religious experience. They need help with prayer."

Forms of Prayer

Many young people have experienced prayer as "talking to God" and reciting prayers. They are ready to explore new ways of expressing their relationship with God. In addition to liturgical prayer, the official prayer of the Church, they can enrich their prayer life by using prayer forms like the following:

- **The Breath Prayer**
  Seated with back straight and eyes closed, the person focuses on the flow of breath in and out of the body. As breath is exhaled, one can "breathe" a simple word or phrase like "Jesus" or "Here I am, Lord."

- **Prayer with Scripture**
  Herein lie unlimited riches. Try gospel meditations using imagination, i.e., "place yourself in the scene . . ."; read the psalms in choral fashion; learn personally chosen passages by heart; and practice proclaiming the word of God.

- **The Symbol Prayer**
  Potent symbols from the Bible and the liturgy (water, wind, oil, fire, light, incense) may speak more powerfully to meditating youth than would many words or explanations.

- **The Prayer of Music**
  This native tongue of youth speaks to them of God as they reflect on, participate in, and respond to music (religious, classical, contemporary).

- **The Prayer of Journaling**
  Prayers, Scripture responses, poems, dreams, doubts, questions, dialogues with Jesus and the saints are recorded in words and/or art in the young person's book of life. He or she comes to know God and self more intimately.

- **Traditional Vocal Prayer**
  Traditional prayers—prayers of the Catholic community—are the most used and taken-for-granted form of prayer. When they are prayed slowly and thoughtfully, instead of rattled off, they can be a source of comfort, rootedness, and connectedness for young people. One way to make traditional prayers take on new meaning is to pray them against a background of beautiful music or visual images.

Young people should be invited to help choose and prepare for these and other prayer experiences. Suggestions for these prayer experiences (about 10 minutes) are provided in the *Introduction* and *Conclusion* of each session. However, brief opening and closing prayers (a minute or two) may be used to frame the session itself as an extended prayer. Sources for these include: a line or two from traditional prayers, the Mass, the psalms, inspired songs, prayers of the saints, collections of prayers by teenagers, and the words of Jesus.

Do not assume that young people reject prayer. They are hungry for the spiritual, for relationship with God. Prayer is a way for them to touch the living God who is with them and in them.

Some resources that might be helpful:

Hokowski, Maryann. *Pathways to Praying with Jesus.* Winona, MN: Saint Mary's Press, 1993.

Koch, Carl, FSC. *More Dreams Alive: Prayers by Teenagers.* Winona, MN: Saint Mary's Press, 1995.

Bolton, Martha. *If the Pasta Wiggles, Don't Eat It. . . .* Ann Arbor, MI: Servant Publications, 1995.

Morris, Thomas H. *Prayer Celebrations for the Liturgical Year.* New York, NY: William H. Sadlier, 1998.

Questions That Matter

Questions have to be carefully prepared if they are to be truly effective. Part of preparation for teaching each lesson should be the formulation of questions that stimulate, challenge, and engender deeper thought. Besides simple recall, questions should motivate and stimulate emotion, evaluative thinking, imagination, and creative problem solving. Vary your techniques; allow time for responses (research shows that most teachers wait less than 4 seconds); above all, *listen* to the answers! Here are some sample questioning techniques.

Recall

- List the types of evidence for believing in God. Other "recall" words: name; define; outline; describe.

React

- Imagine a friend tells you that he no longer believes in God. List four questions you would ask your friend about his reasons for not believing.

Compare

- In what ways are the early Church (A.D. 33–300) and today's Church alike?

Contrast

- In what ways are they different?

Preference

- Which would you rather be—a stained glass window or a church bell?
- Which helps you to pray—silence or music?

Personification

- What questions would you like to ask Francis of Assisi (or Mary, or...)?
- What would Jesus think or say about this issue? How might he say it?

Creative Thinking

- What if there had been television in Jesus' time?
- What if you could trade places with Saint Paul (or Catherine of Siena...)?
- Suppose that Jesus had not come. What would the consequences be?

Application

- Give Luther a list of alternatives to leaving the Church.
- Ask several "when" questions about the Church.
- Ask five "why" questions about faith.

Research Skills

- Would it have been possible for Pope John Paul II to meet Hitler?
- Would it have been possible for Catherine of Siena to have dinner with Ignatius Loyola?

Synthesis

- What might be some of the moral consequences of violent or sexual content in some contemporary music?
- The answer is "life." What is the question?

Ways of Learning

In his book *Frames of Mind,* Dr. Howard Gardner identified seven types of intelligence of which educators need to be aware among their students.

Because young people vary so widely in their intellectual abilities, it is especially important that catechists recognize these multiple intelligences.

The following list describes seven intelligence types and suggests appropriate teaching strategies within the context of the FAITH AND WITNESS PROGRAM.

1. Linguistic Intelligence
Exhibits sensitivity to the meaning and order of words

- *Storytelling:* scriptural, traditional, contemporary and imaginary stories to be told, re-told, or written
- *Brainstorming:* unleashing a torrent of ideas on a specific issue or question, i.e., How would we describe Jesus to teen aliens who had never heard of him?
- *Speaking a New Language:* learning a prayer in Aramaic, Spanish, Latin, or American Sign Language
- *Publishing:* collecting and publishing a semester's worth of young people's reflections, prayers, responses

2. Logical-Mathematical Intelligence
Shows ability to discern patterns of reasoning and order; dexterity with numbers

- *Classification:* organizing information (on Church history, Creed, or New Testament) on attribute webs (listing attributes of a person, place or thing as spokes around the subject)
- *Devising Strategies:* for computer or board games on history or Scripture
- *Socratic Questioning:* catechist or leader questions young people's views to sharpen critical thinking skills (e.g., "Do you think human beings will eventually have the power to understand the mysteries of life?")

3. Spatial Intelligence
Demonstrates ability to grasp how things orient to each other in space

- *Making Maps and Architectural Models:* recreating scenes or places from Scripture and Church history
- *Making Timelines and Murals:* visualizing historical, liturgical and creedal developments

4. Bodily-Kinesthetic Intelligence
Using the body skillfully and handling objects with unusual aptitude

- *Drama and Dance:* role-playing moral decision-making; acting out stories from Scripture and history; ritual prayer in which dance or choreographed movement is integrated
- *Human Sculptures and Relays:* small groups form "sculptures" of faith concepts or objects (community, steeple, fishermen's boat) using only their bodies; teams perform physical "feats" and respond to faith questions on relay "batons."
- *Crafts:* using clay, pipe cleaners, papier-maché, looms, wood, beads to make faith-related objects (from Scripture, Church history, prayer traditions)

5. Musical Intelligence

Using sensitivity to sound, melody, instrumentation and musical mood

- *Rhythms, Songs, Chants, Raps:* employing these as aids to internalization and memorization (composing songs on moral issues or chants of favorite prayer lines)

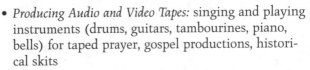

- *Producing Audio and Video Tapes:* singing and playing instruments (drums, guitars, tambourines, piano, bells) for taped prayer, gospel productions, historical skits
- *Collecting Disks:* resource of religious, classical and contemporary music to illustrate, amplify or embody content themes ("Godspell," "Messiah," "Tears In Heaven," plus nature recordings)

6. Interpersonal Intelligence

Showing relationship skills, understanding and empathy

- *Peer Sharing:* interacting with partners or small groups to explore content questions and personal responses; peer tutoring and mentoring by older youth or adults
- *Doing Simulations:* groups participate in "as-if" environments (e.g., "You have just heard Jesus' Sermon on the Mount and are now on the road home. What are you feeling, thinking, planning to do?")
- *Making Murals, Puzzles, Banners:* working cooperatively to produce an art project illustrating a faith theme
- *Peacemaking Strategies:* role-playing ways of reconciliation practiced by Jesus, saints, Gandhi, Martin Luther King, Jr., youth
- *Culture Sharing:* putting together prayer and worship experiences enriched by African-American, Hispanic, Asian, Native American and other cultural expressions within the Church

7. Intrapersonal Intelligence

Showing self-knowledge and self-discipline; awareness of one's inner life

- *Doing One-Minute Reflections:* taking "time out" in the midst of interactive learning for reflection or deep thinking (no talking; occasional background music)
- *Praying, Journaling, Retreats:* responding to youth's hunger for God and need for self-awareness
- *Offering Choices:* enhancing self-discipline and self-expression by offering choices on projects, methods, ways of responding to content
- *Expressing Feelings:* calling forth expressions of wonder, surprise, anger, joy, caring, humor, sadness in response to faith experiences (through stories, poems, videos, photos, music, personal witness, prayer)

The Learning / Teaching Process

Adolescents need to feel some ownership of the learning situation. They do not respond positively to being "talked at" or "talked down to." They need to participate as much as possible in the planning, presentation, and carrying out of the program. Above all, they need to be challenged to take responsibility for their learning.

The courses in SADLIER'S FAITH AND WITNESS PROGRAM are designed with these realities in mind. The process suggested is simple yet comprehensive. Each lesson consists of three steps:

1. Introduction

The lesson begins with an *opening prayer*—preferably led by one or more of the young people. (See page G21.)

- The opening prayer is followed by the *forum* (see page G20) in which the young people present their responses, reflections, or reactions to the assigned reading and activity.

2. Presentation

- The catechist clarifies the material the young people have read. This can be done through a variety of techniques including questions, activities, dialogue, highlighting, guest speakers, and so on.

3. Conclusion

- Young people and/or catechist give a brief summary of the work of the lesson.
- Catechist gives forum assignment for the next lesson.
- Session closes with a brief prayer or song.

This guide will suggest a variety of techniques, activities, questions to facilitate this process. The key with young people is to have a balance of consistency and variety so that every lesson is solid but not predictable.

Preparing a Lesson

If we truly believe that our catechetical work with young people is the most important teaching we can do, it is essential that we go to them prepared. Preparation for religion class is absolutely essential.

Here are a few suggestions for preparing to teach this course. The suggestions are especially intended for those who may be new—either to teaching religion or to teaching adolescents.

Remote Preparation

- Read the whole text carefully. This will give you an understanding of the scope of the whole course and the sequence of ideas throughout.

- As you read make marginal notes about any ideas you have regarding the material and how to present it.

- Look at the list of resources and try to familiarize yourself with at least one of them.

- Check the references given throughout to the *Catechism of the Catholic Church*. Read over the cited paragraphs and make them your own.

Immediate Preparation

- Read the chapter for the session.

- As you read highlight what you consider to be the main points of each lesson. The highlighted statements on the reduced pupil pages will help you.

- List these main points for yourself. It will help to clarify and to focus your objectives.

- Write out the questions you feel will help direct the group's understanding of the material. (See the suggestions for questioning on page G15.)

- Plan the activities you wish to use during the lesson. Make sure you know exactly what you wish the group to do. Assemble any materials you will need.

- Plan the *forum* assignment you will give the young people for the following lesson. Make the assignment clear and simple, but be creative.

- Immediately before the lesson begins, talk to those who are responsible for leading the opening prayer to make sure they have what they need.

- Take a minute for quiet reflection. Ask the Holy Spirit to be in your mind, heart, and mouth as you share the faith with your group.

Youth Interaction

Youth interaction is essential to the success of this program. Their participation in and ownership of the learning process provides stimulus, enthusiasm, and energy to the whole program.

The **Faith and Witness Program** is organized on the principle of youth involvement and responsibility. The two most important elements in the program are, therefore, the youth-directed prayer and the youth-led *Forum*.

Forum

The purpose of the *forum* is to involve the young people immediately and interactively in each session. We want them to become not simply passive receivers of information, but active partners and participants in the learning process.

It is essential, therefore, that the young people assume responsibility for the *forum* and for the preparation necessary to take part in it. If this is not done, the religion lesson will become a reading exercise or a lecture. These are not acceptable alternatives.

How Does the Forum Work?

◆ At the end of each lesson ask the young people to prepare for the next *forum* by doing two things:

• Read carefully the next chapter, and underline key ideas.

• Prepare a written or oral response to the question, reflection, or activity assigned.

◆ Following the opening prayer, each lesson begins with the *forum* in which the young people share both the results of their reading and their responses to the *forum* assignment.

The *forum* should take approximately 15 to 20% of the total class time. if the above process is not possible in your situation, see page G26.

Ideas for Forum Assignments

Each *forum* assignment should act as an interesting and creative "doorway" for the young people into the work of the lesson. Their responses and reactions at the outset of the lesson should provide an initial dialogue that helps them enter enthusiastically into the ideas and content of the lesson. Some ideas:

◆ Always the first part of the assignment is to read the pages of the lesson. Encourage the young people to underline in pencil sentences that they feel are key ideas on these pages.

◆ Some of the suggestions on *Questions That Matter* are excellent ideas for *forum* assignments—especially those under *Recall, React, Personification, Creative Thinking, Application, and Synthesis.* (See page G15.)

◆ *Journaling* could occasionally be the *forum* assignment. Be careful not to require a response that would be too personal or too revealing for a young person to share with the group.

◆ *Simple Research* to discover more information about an idea is helpful if the young people have access to computer on-line services.

Journaling

The young people keep a journal throughout the course. Journal suggestions appear in each chapter. There is a *Sadlier Journal* for *Creed, Morality, Liturgy and Worship,* and *New Testament.*

Purpose:
It provides an outlet for private, ungraded, uncensored expressions of the young people's thoughts, reflections, imaginations, feelings.

Outcomes:
• young people become more in touch with themselves, their feelings, their personal questions;

• young people become better writers;

• young people have something to look back on that will give them insights into their own change and growth.

Youth-Led Prayer

Purpose:

- provides immediate responsibility for and involvement by the young people in the spiritual dimensions of their learning;
- gives them the opportunity to express their own spiritual concerns and to lead others in prayer.

Outcomes:

- young people are enabled to be less self-conscious about their faith;
- they are given the freedom to express their relationship with God and their concerns in personal and creative ways;
- the experience can draw them deeper into their personal life of prayer with God.

Needs:

- especially in the beginning: the catechist's help, support, and suggestions;
- scriptural and other resources (see *Teaching Resources* chart for each chapter);
- partners! Sometimes it is easier with a friend.

How to:

- at the end of each session meet with the young people who will be leading prayer during the next session;
- if they request help, make resources available;
- encourage them—prayer does not have to be perfect; it only has to be sincere.

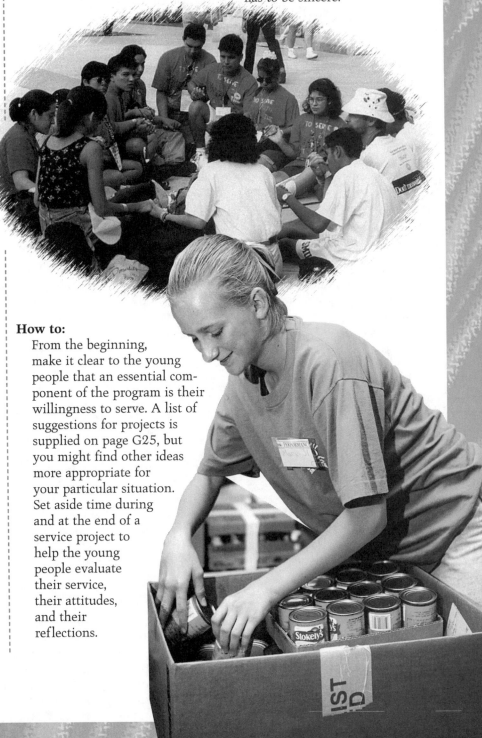

Faith in Action

*I*nvolvement in active service for others is an integral part of the FAITH AND WITNESS PROGRAM.

Purpose:

Young people have so much to give—energy, generosity, enthusiasm, idealism, compassion. It is essential that we help them find practical and immediate ways to share these gifts.

Outcomes:

They will find that they receive far more than they give—a humbling and joyful discovery. They will begin to develop and to live the values of God's kingdom in very real, practical, and sometimes demanding ways.

Needs:

Ideas and suggestions from the parish and communities concerning needs and opportunities the young people can address.

How to:

From the beginning, make it clear to the young people that an essential component of the program is their willingness to serve. A list of suggestions for projects is supplied on page G25, but you might find other ideas more appropriate for your particular situation. Set aside time during and at the end of a service project to help the young people evaluate their service, their attitudes, and their reflections.

FAITH AND WITNESS Program

Morality A Course on Catholic Living

We were made for happiness, a happiness that God alone can provide. Modeling our lives on Christ, we know that the only way to achieve happiness is by rejecting sin and freely choosing to do what is right. Through God's law and God's grace, we are called upon to form our consciences and make moral decisions as followers of Christ and members of the Church. The Church itself is the authentic teacher of the ways of Christ and the manner in which we are to live a moral life in the world.

Within this deeper framework of moral decision making, we explore the Ten Commandments in greater detail. Likewise, we concentrate on gospel formation (the Beatitudes) and what it means to live a life of virtue. This course will enable young people to navigate through challenging times with a clear and positive moral attitude that is essential for Catholics in the new millennium.

Liturgy and Worship A Course on Prayer and Sacraments

It is in the Church's liturgy, especially the seven sacraments, that Catholics celebrate all that God has done for us in Christ Jesus through the working of the Holy Spirit. Our salvation was made possible through the paschal mystery of Christ's passion, death, resurrection, and ascension. This mystery is made present to us in the sacred actions of the Church's liturgy.

As members of the Church, we are called upon to enter into this mystery of faith and truly be people of both word and sacrament. This is where our lives of faith are proclaimed, formed, and nourished. If young people are to be strong and faithful followers of Christ, they must make the liturgical life of the Church their own.

New Testament A Course on Jesus Christ and His Disciples

Young Catholics need to rub shoulders with the culture of Jesus and his times. Likewise, they need to know that in Scripture things are not always what they appear to be. Scripture presents so much more, and young people should never be afraid of the truth as presented in Scripture. This text will introduce them to questions people have asked over the ages: Were the Magi historical figures? Did Jesus really raise people

from the dead, or were they just asleep? Did Jesus really die, and did his body really come out of the tomb? By tackling such questions, this course will help young people to appreciate the contemporary Catholic understanding of Scripture and give them tools to avoid fundamentalistic leanings that distort real Catholic doctrine and Scripture itself.

Creed A Course on Catholic Belief in Two Parts

It is through divine revelation that we come to know God through the knowledge God has of himself. The gift of faith enables us to respond to this divine revelation.

Because our first parents rejected God's plan of original holiness and justice, the whole human race is born in the state of original sin. God promised us a savior and that promise was fulfilled through his only Son, who became flesh and took on our human nature. Jesus, the

Son of God and the son of Mary, is true God and true Man. He offered himself as the perfect sacrifice for us and for our salvation.

We are the Church, the people of God. Jesus promised that he would be with the Church until the end of time. He sent the Holy Spirit to guide the Church in all things. The course concludes with Mary and the saints and our belief in the communion of saints and life everlasting.

Church History A Course on the People of God

How important it is for young Catholics to be in touch with their roots, roots that took hold about two thousand years ago!

Beginning with the apostolic age and the age of persecution, young people will be introduced to the accomplishments of men and women of faith throughout the centuries. The successes and difficulties that the Church

has faced, both within and without, will be studied, but always with a view to help young Catholics of today face the challenges of their own time. As Catholics, we stand on the shoulders of giants. In helping others to know the story of this great Church community, we are preparing leaders for the new millennium.

Creed
Scope and Sequence for Part II

Chapter 1

THE GOOD NEWS OF JESUS CHRIST:
The paschal mystery—the passion, death, resurrection, and ascension of Christ; the truth of the gospels

Chapter 2

LIFE IN CHRIST:
The providence of God; sons and daughters of God; the kingdom of God; life in Christ

Chapter 3

THE LORD AND GIVER OF LIFE:
Third Person of the Blessed Trinity, the Holy Spirit; the Spirit in Scripture; life in the Spirit

Chapter 4

COME HOLY SPIRIT!
The Holy Spirit in the life of Jesus; Pentecost; the Paraclete, our Advocate; sanctifying grace; actual grace

Chapter 5

THE MYSTERY OF THE CHURCH:
images of the Church: people of God, body of Christ

Chapter 6

A COMMUNITY UNLIKE ANY OTHER:
The Church, human and divine; the family of God; essential features of the Church

Chapter 7

A STRONG FOUNDATION:
From apostle to bishop; teaching, governing, and sanctifying; the threefold ministry

Chapter 8

THE CHURCH OF JESUS CHRIST:
visible and invisible elements of the Church of Christ; beginning to build a definition

Chapter 9

CATHOLICISM: A WAY OF LIFE:
the mission of the laity; religious life in the Church; the contemplative and the active life; the evangelical counsels

Chapter 10

THE WHOLE CHURCH:
the ordained leadership of the Church, the clergy; the magisterium; a communion of Churches

Chapter 11

THE CHURCH ON ITS WAY:
a pilgrim Church; the second coming; the last judgment; heaven, hell; particular judgment, purgatory; the resurrection of the body

Chapter 12

DISCIPLES FOREVER:
Mary, the Morning Star; saints; canonization; the communion of saints; living as Catholics

Chapter 13

BRINGING THE WORLD TO CHRIST:
the call to evangelization beginning with oneself and one's family; living one's faith in daily practice

Chapter 14

BRINGING CHRIST TO THE WORLD:
evangelization of friends, the wider world; witnessing to the faith we profess

Why a Course on the Creed?

Imagine someone who never went to school applying for a teaching position. What would you think? Well, then, imagine a Catholic who has never studied the creed. That would be just as absurd. Knowing the creed and the mysteries of God's revelation as they are taught to us by the Church are essential to faith and give us our Catholic Identity.

In a course on the creed, we are exploring not just human knowledge. We are entering into the very knowledge God has of himself; we are probing the mysteries of the divine life to which God has called us. How awesome to get a glimpse of God and to be people of faith seeking such understanding! How critical it is for young people to get this firm foundation in their Catholic faith.

This is the second volume of a two-part study on the creed. In this book, *Creed: A Course on Catholic Belief* Part II, we begin with the questions of the Church and the Holy Spirit.

Objectives

- To invite the young people to open their hearts and minds to the truths of God's revelation so that, like the early Christians, their faith will burst forth in prayer and action; to develop persons of faith whose lives reflect the message and values of Christ.

- To encourage the young people to examine more closely the dynamic teachings of their Catholic faith by placing before them the truths of the faith in a clear and meaningful way.

- To help them explore as fully and richly as possible the depths of the gift of faith and the meaning of the gospel so as to become evangelizers of the word.

Faith in Action

Active, attentive, responsible service of others should be the hallmark of the Christian life of faith. Involve your group in individual or communal service projects to be carried out throughout this course. The young people should reflect on their commitment in their journals and give a report at the end of the course. (Note: All projects will need your support and coordinating efforts.) Some suggestions follow.

- The young people might ask a catechist from their parish catechetical programs if they could prepare to take over one lesson for a primary group. Then under the supervision of the regular catechist, they could teach it to the children.

In performing this service, the young people will not only be helping the catechist but also will gain an insight into how important it is to know the essentials of their religious faith. The teaching of a religion lesson will provide them with a small opportunity to share their knowledge of and love for their faith. Some of them might want to consider becoming a permanent catechist.

- Some young people may feel that belonging to the community of the Church is unimportant. Some may have had unpleasant experiences with organized religion. Others may not feel the need for religion at this time in their lives. Among their acquaintances, in or out of school, the young people may know someone like this who is turning a deaf ear to the message of Christ.

The young people might invite such a friend to accompany them to a parish liturgical celebration or to one of their parish functions for teens or even to a retreat weekend. They could simply speak with their friends about their feelings and sincerely attempt to express why they find meaning and value in their faith. In one of these ways they could possibly serve as catalysts in leading someone else to Christ.

Cross Curriculum Projects

- Young people who are interested in science, and history, and drama might do research on and then prepare their own "Scopes" trial in which they put forth and defend their beliefs about evolution and biblical faith.

- Those who have an interest in art and photography might put together a bulletin board display of photographs that "speak" of faith.

- If some young people are interested in music and dance, they might prepare a program for an assembly on one of these concepts: revelation, faith, life in the Spirit, for example.

HOW TO USE THIS GUIDE

Preparation

Well in advance:

◆ Read the entire text before meeting for the first time.

◆ Carefully prepare each session, using both text and guide.

Planning

◆ Go over *Teaching Resources.*

◆ Gather materials.

◆ Plan each *Forum* assignment.

◆ Estimate time you will allot for *Introduction, Presentation,* and *Conclusion* of the session. A place is provided to write your estimate beside each head on the guide.

◆ Prayer is an integral part of the catechetical process. It should be a priority in each session.

◆ At this age young people like to feel ownership and some control of the work of the session. If at all possible, encourage them to bring the text home so that they can become familiar with the theme, identify main ideas, and prepare for the *Forum.* (See page G20.)

◆ In order to become active partners and participants in the learning process, it is essential that the young people have time to prepare and that they be encouraged to assume responsibility for their learning. The *Forum* and the opening prayer especially require their preparation and interaction. All of this presumes that the young people can take their books home.

◆ Preview any videos or films to be used; listen to suggested music.

◆ Learn as much as possible about the young people with whom you will be meeting.

◆ Interaction and dialogue are key to the development of a deep and personal understanding of the ideas presented. We urge you to use the *Forum* activity to this end.

Other Options

If your situation does not allow for the books to be taken home, be creative. Find ways to help the group be ready to participate actively and fully in the work of the chapter. Here are some ideas:

◆ Have a small group prepare the chapter presentation and do the *Forum.* Select a different group each week.

◆ Provide reading and *Forum* preparation time at the beginning of each session. *This would work best with sessions of 90 minutes or longer.*

◆ Prepare and begin each session with a summary presentation of the key ideas of the chapter. *Invite and encourage discussion before moving on.*

Features

Adult Focus

helps you to focus on and be comfortable with the theme of the chapter.

Enrichment Activities

provide additional activities to enhance the sessions.

Teaching Resources

give an overview of the session including opening prayer suggestions and optional supplemental resources.

Journaling

Suggestions are provided for each session. A separate *Faith and Witness* Journal is available for each course. There is one journal for *Creed Part I* and *Creed Part II*.

Assessment

An optional assessment in standardized test format is provided as a blackline master. There is one at the end of each chapter in the guide. A blackline-master test book will be provided for use with the program.

Highlights for Home

This blackline master is provided as a communication to encourage family involvement.

The **Faith and Witness Program** provides a genuine opportunity for young people—with your guidance—to come to a powerful understanding of the faith through study, dialogue, and prayer. You, the catechist, have the challenging role of preparing them and calling them to be people of faith and witness.

The semester courses that together comprise Sadlier's **Faith and Witness Program** may be used for young people at the junior-high and high-school levels. You have the opportunity to develop the curriculum to suit your own needs.

Some considerations in choosing your semester course combination are:

- ◆ diocesan guidelines for specific grade levels
- ◆ maturity of students
- ◆ pre-Confirmation catechesis guidelines

Introduction

Opening Prayer: Ask the young people to look at the photo on page 7. Invite the group to reflect quietly as you read the following:

> In this second part of our study of Creed our focus is Jesus and his mission, which he left in the care of his Church enlightened and enlivened by the abiding presence of the Holy Spirit. Jesus is the full revelation of the Father. In Jesus we see what God is like. Jesus said, "I am in the Father and the Father is in me" (John 14:11).

We pray that you will truly encounter Jesus during the weeks ahead and that in this encounter you will find and share the life he offers.

Note: Encourage the young people to assume leadership roles in preparing and leading the opening-prayer activity for each session. There is a prayer activity described in the *Introduction* section of each session. The time allotted for this prayer should be about ten minutes. Also, if your opening-prayer time only allows for much shorter time, ideas are listed on the *Teaching Resources* chart at the beginning of each chapter. Let the volunteer prayer leader teams read these ideas and add or adapt them for your group's needs and circumstances. Encourage different young people to volunteer for each session and help them to prepare until they feel comfortable doing it themselves.

Presentation

◆ Invite the group to look at the photograph on page 7. Ask the young people to suggest descriptive words or feelings that come to mind as they view it. Then have them read page 6.

The Amazing Search Goes On

INTRODUCTION TO CREED PART II

We are about to continue an exciting exploration of our Catholic beliefs. Before we do, we should recall some of the important things we have already learned. Chief among these things is what we learned about faith. Faith is a gift and a grace. Faith enables us to begin to know God as God knows himself. That is why faith is a virtue. It gives us power. Faith gives us the power to go beyond our human understanding and beyond what we can see and feel and touch around us. We cannot do this on our own. Faith empowers us to see through the "eyes of God." It was because of faith that this book was written for you.

As people of faith, we look to all that God has revealed to us. God has opened himself to us and has let us know his deepest Self. Understanding divine revelation is essential to our whole life of faith. In fact it is the basis of everything Christians believe, and it helps to identify who we are as Catholics. The most important things we know about God come from one source: God himself. Through revelation God tells us not only about himself but also about ourselves.

Now we are ready to begin the second part of our exploration. We will continue our study of Jesus and his teachings. We will also look in depth at the Church and what it means to be a member of the Church. If we really understand all that is here, we will be informed Catholics, excited about the mysteries of God and ready to take on the challenge of bringing the world to Christ.

Let's begin.

6

◆ It is essential that the young people take an active part in every session. From the very beginning, they have an important role to play. Take a few minutes to explain the *forum*.

Forum is a Latin word for the place where the ideas and work of the community were explored and discussed. It was the center of public life in a Roman city. So important was this concept that the word *forum* today refers to an intense exchange of ideas, thoughts, and opinions.

7

Conclusion

✔ Read Chapter 1, pages 8–15. Underline in pencil six key ideas.

✔ On an index card write the name *Jesus*. Beneath that name write at least five thoughts that you have when you hear that name. As you write, say the name of Jesus slowly several times.

Remind the young people that along with the *Forum* the *Opening Prayer* in each session will be their responsibility to conduct. Choose volunteers for the *Opening Prayer* of Chapter 1. Provide the volunteers with the directions for the prayer on page 8–9 of this guide. Give any additional help they may need.

Closing Prayer: Take a moment to look again at the photograph on page 7. Then point out that our faith in God makes us people of great hope at the end of our pilgrimage. Our faith in Jesus Christ challenges us to make the present a time of grace, healing, and loving service of others. And so we pray:

> Your kingdom come.
> Your will be done on earth
> as it is in heaven.

Each group meeting will begin with this kind of exchange and dialogue. The *Forum Assignment* is prepared before the meeting. It has two steps.

1. The next lesson is read thoroughly. Key ideas are underlined in pencil.

2. The *forum* activity or question is prepared for discussion. Stress the importance of both preparation for and participation in the forum.

FOR CHAPTER 1

- preparation of opening-prayer volunteers
- Bibles, journals, and highlighters
- copies of handout *I Have Seen the Lord*, page 8C
- copies of *Chapter 1 Assessment*, page 15A (optional)
- copies of *Highlights for Home*, page 15B

THE GOOD NEWS OF JESUS CHRIST

Adult Focus

In the opening chapter of *Creed*: Part II, the young people learn that the gospel message is filled with mystery and surprise. It may be reassuring for them, who may occasionally be skeptical and questioning, to realize that the apostles gave their testimony about the death, resurrection, and ascension of Jesus not out of gullibility but out of firm conviction based on first-hand experience.

The presence of the risen Lord empowered the apostles to speak boldly, even when to do so was unpopular and dangerous. The young people with whom we work—often idealistic and attracted to challenges—may identify with the humble, yet courageous, apostles and disciples. Although they were without political or social power, these first followers of Jesus were entrusted with the gospel message and through its power helped to change the world.

Catechism Focus

The theme of this chapter corresponds with paragraphs 639–647 and 651–655 of the *Catechism*.

Enrichment Activity

Computer Connection

Have the young people think of special messages they would like to tell others regarding the good news of Jesus Christ. Encourage volunteers to share their messages. Then invite them to use a paint program, such as *Flying Colors*™, to design illustrated messages expressing the good news of Jesus.

If your group is using *Flying Colors*™, have the young people choose an appropriate background canvas, and then access the Text Tool, "T" on the side menu, to write their message on the canvas. Point out the alphabet that appears at the bottom of the screen and explain that letters can be clicked on and dragged to any position. Direct them to string together words and sentences to enter their "good news" messages. Then encourage them to use the paint tools and stamps to fill in their canvases.

Have the young people print their completed pictorials and present them to the entire group.

Teaching Resources

Overview

To discover that through his passion, death, resurrection, and ascension, Jesus Christ brought salvation to the whole world; to explore why the gospels and the rest of the New Testament were written.

Opening Prayer Ideas

Look at the photo on pages 8 and 9. Pray together Revelation 15:3.

or

Read together the account of Jesus' appearance to Mary Magdalene (John 20:11–18). Reflect quietly.

Materials

- Bibles, journals, and highlighters
- one copy for each person of words "Peace be with you" (Luke 24:36).
- box
- scrap paper for each person

REPRODUCIBLE MASTERS
- handout *I Have Seen the Lord*, page 8C
- *Chapter 1 Assessment*, page 15A (optional)
- *Highlights for Home*, page 15B

Creed Journal:
For Chapter 1, use page 36.

Supplemental Resources

VIDEO
Jesus' Suffering, Death, and Resurrection (*Children's Heroes of the Bible* series)

Ignatius Press
P.O. Box 1339
Fort Collins, CO 80522–1339

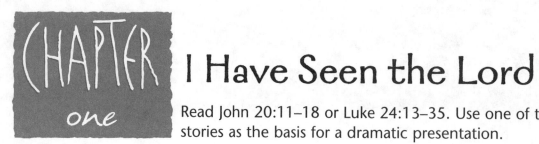

CHAPTER one

I Have Seen the Lord

Read John 20:11–18 or Luke 24:13–35. Use one of the stories as the basis for a dramatic presentation.

Narrator (sets the scene): _____

_____

_____

Jesus: _____

_____

_____ : _____

_____

Jesus: _____

_____

_____ : _____

_____

Jesus: _____

_____

_____ : _____

_____

Jesus: _____

_____

_____ :(to the other gathered disciples): _____

_____

(CHAPTER 1

THE GOOD NEWS OF JESUS CHRIST

Great and wonderful are your works,
Lord God almighty.
Revelation 15:3

Objectives: To discover that through his passion, death, resurrection, and ascension, Jesus Christ brought salvation to the whole world; to explore why the gospels and the rest of the New Testament were written.

Introduction ___min.

Opening Prayer: Before the session begins, prepare copies of Jesus' words to his disciples after the resurrection, "Peace be with you" (Luke 24:36). Make one copy for each person in your group. Place the copies on the prayer table, beside an open Bible.

At the beginning of the session, read together the account of Jesus' appearance to the two disciples on the road to Emmaus (Luke 24:13–35). Give the young people a few minutes to reflect quietly on the reading. Then ask the following questions and encourage the young people to share their responses:

• What closes our eyes and prevents us from recognizing Jesus in our midst?

• What makes us "slow of heart"?

• What helps us to open our eyes and lighten our hearts, enabling us to realize that Jesus walks with us on our journey of faith?

Ask the young people to list on scrap paper any fears, concerns, worries, or doubts that may weigh on their hearts and "close their eyes" to Jesus' presence. Then direct each person to crumple the list and carry it as if it were a heavy boulder. Finally, have the young people drop their crumpled list into a box on the prayer table and take a copy of Jesus' message from the pile you have provided.

After all have returned to their seats, invite the group to look at the photo on pages 8 and 9. Pray together Revelation 15:3.

Note: The Statue of Christ the Redeemer overlooks the city of Rio de Janeiro, in Brazil.

Forum: Have the young people form small groups to share their thoughts about the name *Jesus*.

Presentation ___ min.

◆ Have the young people quietly read pages 10 and 11. When you see that most are finished, invite them to play a reverse question-and-answer game. Write the following answers on the board, and ask the young people to suggest appropriate questions:

- the resurrection (*What brought to completion God's salvation of the world?*)
- mediator (*Which of Jesus' titles means he offers all our prayers to the Father?*)
- ascension (*What do we call Christ's return to his Father?*)
- paschal mystery (*What is the passion, death, resurrection, and ascension of Christ?*)

◆ Have the young people put themselves in the apostle Thomas's place. Then ask them these questions:

- When you heard others testify to Jesus' resurrection, what was your first reaction?
- How did you feel when Jesus appeared and asked you not to be unbelieving but to believe?

Note: Throughout the young people's text you will see the sunburst icon. The directives or questions featured here are meant to be *thought provoking*. They will help the young people to internalize the key concepts presented. Throughout the guide these directives and questions will be referred to as *thought provokers*.

◆ Point out the 🌟 **thought provoker** on page 11. Invite the young people to write their thoughts. Allow a minute or two; then have volunteers share what it means to be called "blessed."

WHAT difference does Jesus' resurrection from the dead make in people's lives? Is it really that important in your life?

The Paschal Mystery

If Jesus had not risen from the dead, we might never have heard of him, and Christianity would not exist. Jesus' life would have been a failure and would have ended in defeat. There would not be much good news to share, and no one would have wanted to write a New Testament.

But Jesus did rise from the dead. The testimony of his followers and of believers from the beginning has been absolutely clear. Soon after his death on the cross and his burial, they began to experience his presence in a whole new way. The gospels do not describe his resurrection but speak of finding

10

the empty tomb. According to Paul's account in 1 Corinthians 15:3–8, Jesus appeared to more than five hundred of his disciples.

Was it easy for all the followers of Jesus to believe that he had risen? Eyewitness accounts in the gospels relate that it was difficult for some. When the apostle Thomas, for example, heard the testimony of others to the resurrection, he did not believe it at first. When he heard that others had seen the Lord, Thomas said, "Unless I see the mark of the nails in his hands and put my finger into the nailmarks and put my hand into his side, I will not believe." Then a week later, when the risen Christ appeared to the disciples, he said to Thomas, "Put your finger here and see my hands, and bring your hand and put it into my side, and do not be unbelieving, but believe." Thomas's response was "My Lord and my God!" (John 20:25, 27–28). It took a lot to get Thomas to believe!

Jesus said to Thomas, "Have you come to believe because you have seen me? Blessed are those who have not seen and have believed" (John 20:29). At that moment Jesus was calling each of us who believe in him "blessed." What does that mean to you?

The resurrection of Jesus was a unique event, of course. Nothing like it had ever happened before. It astonished the followers of Jesus and challenged everything that they knew. In the resurrection of Jesus, God had brought to completion the salvation of the world and all that he wanted to accomplish in Christ. Jesus' crucifixion was not his final moment. It was in the resurrection that he was victorious over sin and death.

After a short time the appearances of the risen Christ came to an end, for Christ had to return to his Father. We call Christ's return to the Father his *ascension*. Jesus, risen from the dead, had entered into a whole new life, one that could not be limited to an earthly existence. That is why the gospel writer said that Jesus "parted from them and was taken up to heaven" (Luke 24:51).

With the ascension Jesus Christ was exalted in glory and enthroned at the right hand of the Father (Acts 2:33–35). There Jesus is our high priest, the one mediator between God and humanity (1 Timothy 2:5). This means that Jesus Christ offers all our prayers to the Father. This is why we pray at Mass, "Through him, with him, in him, in the unity of the Holy Spirit, all glory and honor is yours, almighty Father, for ever and ever. Amen."

11

◆ Take time now to go over the key ideas the young people have underlined in pencil in this chapter. Then have them highlight those ideas highlighted on the reduced pages.

Play some joyful music in the background (Handel's "Hallelujah Chorus" from *Messiah*, for example), while the young people do the journaling activity in the *Creed Journal*, page 34.

Note: During the course suggestions for journaling will be made. Sadlier publishes a journal that reflects the journaling activities suggested in this text or guide. However, the young people should be encouraged to express themselves in personal journals whenever and about whatever they wish.

◆ Discuss why we might consider each page of the gospels to be "filled with surprises." List specific surprises on the board as the group names them. You might include the following:

• Jesus was a poor, unknown Nazarene.

• The Savior of the world spent his time with sinners and society's outcasts.

• Jesus found time to be with people who were considered "unpowerful."

Presentation (cont'd)

◆ Write the words *paschal mystery* on the board. Ask, "What are the most important events in our redemption?" Have those who answer correctly write the words under paschal mystery: *passion, death, resurrection, ascension.*

Suggest that during the time before the next session the young people do the journal activity in the ☼ **thought provoker** on page 12. If they have the Sadlier *Creed Journal*, they can use page 39.

◆ Ask, "Why were the gospels and the other books of the New Testament written?" (*to celebrate the paschal mystery and to share the good news of Christ in the light of the resurrection*) Make sure the young people have highlighted the statement in the first paragraph of the right column on page 12 that answers the question.

Note: The following activity is optional.

◆ Form small groups to role-play a reunion of Jesus' disciples ten years after his death and resurrection. Direct each group to use pages 12 and 13 and Scripture to prepare a conversation in which the reunited disciples discuss:

• the day Jesus asked them to follow him

• the ways their individual characters and personalities blended or conflicted

• the fears they experienced when Jesus was condemned

• how their lives changed after the resurrection

Allow time for the groups to prepare, practice, and present their role plays.

For us the resurrection and ascension of Christ are not simply distant memories. We share in the new life of Christ right now. Just as we were once dead in sin, now we rise with Christ in Baptism to newness of life. This is our sharing in the death and resurrection of Jesus Christ, our paschal lamb, and the salvation he won for us.

Some people have spent a lifetime trying to summarize the wondrous events of Jesus' life, his teaching, and all that he did for us out of love. But we can summarize it all in one simple phrase: the paschal mystery. The *paschal mystery* refers to the passion, death, resurrection, and ascension of Christ. These are the most important events in our redemption. Through these events Jesus Christ brought salvation to the whole world.

In your journal write a letter to the risen Christ. Tell him what is happening in your life. Tell him what he means to you.

The Truth of the Gospels

Because of the resurrection Christians see the world in a whole new way. Just as a lamp lights up a dark room, so our belief in the resurrection enables us to see Jesus more clearly and to understand his message. This was the experience of Jesus' first followers and of the early Church community. That is why the gospels and the rest of the New Testament were written: to celebrate the paschal mystery and to share the good news of Christ in the light of the resurrection.

Some people, however, may have doubts about the truth of the gospels. They feel that the New Testament accounts are incredible, that they cannot be believed or trusted. They wonder how Jesus could have done the things that he did.

Even for nonbelievers there are certain things about the New Testament that cannot be denied. The first has to do with the closest followers of Jesus, the twelve apostles. As fishermen they had to be strong, rough, and ready. They were full of life and knew what hard work was. It would have been unlikely for such no-nonsense individuals to have been fooled easily. Only someone powerful in word and

12

deed could have attracted the apostles, convincing them to follow him and give up everything.

Jesus was just that type of individual. When he asked the apostles to follow him, they left everything and went everywhere with him. However, when Jesus was condemned to death by crucifixion, the apostles were afraid that they would suffer the same fate. All but one deserted Jesus for fear of their lives. They went and hid.

Only one thing transformed this fearful band: the resurrection. When they recognized the risen Lord and knew that he was still among them, they were filled with excitement. Transformed by the power of the Holy Spirit, they went out and boldly proclaimed the good news of Jesus. They did this with a unanimous voice. Remember that these were simple fishermen, not educated or used to public speaking. How could they have changed so quickly if the risen Christ were not with them?

Moreover the message that they shared was an unpopular one. Suddenly, after the resurrection, they as Jews were preaching a message that all Jews would find blasphemous: that a man should be worshiped as God. Their message was one that the rest of the world would say made no sense. Would anyone want to believe in a savior who had to die? Was it sensible to believe that a small-town carpenter from the middle of nowhere was now Lord of the universe? Yet this is exactly what the early Church preached.

How can we be sure that the gospel picture of Jesus is really true? What would you say?

Scripture UPDATE

Mary Magdalene is the only person to appear in all four gospel accounts as a primary witness to Christ's resurrection. Her testimony was crucial to the early Church. This is an amazing fact when we consider that at the time of Jesus a woman's testimony was not legally acceptable. It was accepted only when verified by the testimony of men. This acceptance of Mary Magdalene is another surprising turn of events in the gospels.

13

◆ Point out the **thought provoker** on page 13. Hold a court in which the witnesses present their evidence that the gospel picture of Jesus is true.

◆ Have prepared volunteers do a dramatic reading from the Gospel of John 20:11–18. After the reading, have another young person read the *Scripture Update* on page 13.

FYI

On the feast of the Ascension, we celebrate the day when Jesus Christ was exalted in glory and enthroned at the right hand of the Father (Acts 2:33–35). Historically, in distant kingdoms, being seated at the right hand of the king or other high authority meant sharing in that leader's power and authority. Still today, guests should consider it an honor to be seated to the immediate right of the host at a banquet or some other special gathering. In the future, when you celebrate the feast of the Ascension (forty days after Easter), remember you are celebrating Jesus' presence at the right hand of the Father, sharing in God's glory and power forever.

Presentation (cont'd)

◆ Invite the entire group to read aloud Philippians 3:8–9 on page 14. Then discuss the following:

• What did Paul lose? What did he gain?

• Would you give your life for something or someone you did not really believe in?

• Would you give your life for something or someone that meant more than all the world?

◆ Point out the ⁓ **thought provoker** on page 14. Allow a minute for reflection; then invite responses.

Conclusion ___ min.

◆ Form three groups. Assign each group one of the questions from *Things to Share* and *Things to Think About.* Allow about two minutes for preparation; then have the groups share together their responses.

◆ *On Line with the Parish,* which appears in each chapter, will suggest ways the young people can connect with, participate in and serve their parish. Take time to talk about these suggestions with the young people and find ways to facilitate their parish endeavors.

◆ Direct attention to *Words to Remember* on page 15. Have the young people write the definition of *paschal mystery.* It can be found on page 12.

Assessment: On page 15A of this guide, you will find a blackline master test for this chapter in standardized format. If you plan to administer *Chapter 1 Assessment,* allow about ten minutes for its completion.

Filled with Surprises

For people of the first century and for us, too, each page of the gospels is filled with surprises. Who would have imagined that the Son of God would appear on earth as a poor, unknown Nazarene, yet filled with love, gentleness, and the best of human qualities? Who would have thought that the Savior of the world would spend his time with sinners and lepers and all the outcasts of society? Who would have thought that the Messiah would criticize those in power and yet find time for those who had no power, especially women and children? No one could have thought up a religious leader like Jesus, least of all the apostles.

Not only that, but the first followers of Jesus were hated for their message. The early Church was even outlawed in the Roman Empire. At first it had to be an underground Church willing to suffer persecution and martyrdom. Belief in Jesus could send people to the Roman Coliseum, where they would be fed to lions.

The early Christians gained nothing of material importance because of their faith in the risen Christ. They did not become wealthy or powerful. Saint Paul said, "I even consider everything as a loss because of the supreme good of knowing Christ Jesus my Lord. For his sake I have accepted the loss of all things and I consider them so much rubbish, that I may gain Christ and be found in him" (Philippians 3:8–9). No one could say these words without being sure of the truth. People have trusted in the truth of the New Testament for almost two thousand years. It is the truth that we, too, can experience in the risen Christ.

Is there something about Jesus that surprises you? What is it?

14

Answers for Chapter 1 Assessment
1. c 2. c 3. a 4. b 5. a
6. c 7. d 8. a 9. a 10. Accept reasonable responses.

Things to SHARE

Why can we say the gospel message is believable? Give reasons that convince you.

Someone once said that there is a little bit of the apostle Thomas in each of us. How do you react to that statement?

OnLine WITH THE PARISH

Make a visit to your parish church. See how many signs or symbols you can find that tell you about the paschal mystery. Make a list, and share them with the group.

Things to Think About

How would you explain your belief in the resurrection to someone who does not know Christ?

WORDS to REMEMBER

Find and define:

paschal mystery

_____

_____

_____

YOU ARE MY WITNESSES

15

Conclusion (cont'd)

◆ Distribute copies of *Highlights for Home*. You will do this in each session. Encourage the young people to share these pages each week with their families.

FORUM Assignment

✔ Read Chapter 2, pages 16–23. Underline in pencil six key ideas.

✔ Complete the handout *I Have Seen the Lord*. You might want to work with a partner.

Closing Prayer: Invite the young people to look at the photo on pages 8 and 9 as they reflect on Isaiah 43:2–3. Remind them that Jesus is faithful. He goes before us and says to us: "Come, follow me."

Evaluation: Do the young people understand that Jesus Christ brought salvation to the whole world through his passion, death, resurrection, and ascension?

FOR CHAPTER 2

• preparation of volunteers for the opening prayer
• copies of handout *Who Cares?*, page 16C
• copies of *Chapter 2 Assessment*, page 28A (optional)
• copies of *Highlights for Home*, page 28B

Assessment

1 The gospels do not describe the moment of resurrection, but speak of finding
  a. an empty cross.
  b. an upper room.
  c. an empty tomb.
  d. Mary Magdalene.

2 The apostles of Jesus
  a. all found it easy to believe that Jesus had risen from the dead.
  b. were easily influenced.
  c. were transformed by the resurrection.
  d. were from the rich class.

3 One apostle would not believe that Jesus was risen unless he
  a. could see and touch him.
  b. could talk to him.
  c. could see a vision.
  d. all of the above

4 The gospels were written
  a. as Jewish holy books.
  b. to celebrate and share the paschal mystery.
  c. to tell everything Jesus did.
  d. to describe the miracles of Jesus.

5 The paschal mystery refers to the
  a. passion, death, resurrection, and ascension of Jesus.
  b. ministry of Jesus.
  c. raising of Lazarus from the dead.
  d. healing miracles of Jesus.

6 When we say that Jesus is the mediator, we mean that
  a. he died for us.
  b. he rose from the dead.
  c. he offers our prayers to the Father.
  d. he ascended to heaven.

7 Jesus was exalted at the right hand of the Father in glory at
  a. the Last Supper.
  b. the incarnation.
  c. the resurrection.
  d. the ascension.

8 Circle the *true* statement.
  a. All four gospel accounts name Mary Magdalene as the primary witness to the resurrection.
  b. The New Testament has too many incredible accounts.
  c. When Jesus was arrested, all the disciples deserted him.
  d. Jesus' crucifixion was his final moment.

9 _____ brought to completion the salvation of the world.
  a. The resurrection
  b. The crucifixion
  c. The incarnation
  d. The preaching

10 What does the resurrection of Jesus mean to you? Write your response on the reverse side of this page.

Highlights for Home

Focus on Faith

An understanding of the resurrection centers on an understanding of the complete story of Jesus, his growth and development, his words and teachings, his relationship to the Father and to his friends. While information about the historical Jesus is important, the impact and significance of the resurrection is the key to Christian life and faith. Jesus is alive and active in the world, and he calls us to share in his mission and to respond to the power of his Spirit. Just as the presence of the risen Lord empowered the apostles to spread the good news throughout the world, the risen Christ empowers us to live as people set free from sin and death.

Conversation Starters

. . . . a few ideas to talk about together . . . .

◆ How strong is my faith? Do I need physical proof of Jesus' presence in my life before I can say, "My Lord and my God"?

◆ Is Christ's new life for me? Do I share in it? How?

Feature Focus

The *Scripture Update* on page 13 refers us to the Gospel of John 20:11–18, which gives the account of Mary Magdalene's encounter with the risen Jesus. The account is beautiful but it is also remarkable that Jesus came first to a woman and sent her as his messenger to the apostles.

Reflection

Spend a few moments looking at the opening pages of this chapter. The famous statue of Christ the Redeemer towers over the city of Rio de Janeiro, in Brazil. But the arms of the risen Christ embrace the whole world. It is not hard to imagine yourself standing with Christ upon a mountaintop, sharing his vision of the kingdom of God in all its fullness.

The photo of the statue was taken from the back; thus, the face of Jesus cannot be seen. From this viewpoint, we might be reminded to look for the face of Jesus in the people we meet each day.

LIFE IN CHRIST

Adult Focus

Many people today are searching for the experience of unconditional love. In this chapter, the young people learn Jesus' message to us about God's overwhelming love and care for each person. Help them to hear in their hearts the words of Jesus about his Father's providence: "Do not be afraid. You are worth more than many sparrows" (Luke 12:7). The young people need to have that certainty that they will never be abandoned by God, that they can rely with complete trust on Jesus who said: "I will come back again and take you to myself, so that where I am you also may be" (John 14:3).

It is also important that the young people understand that faith is a growing thing. Getting to know Jesus is the work of a lifetime. And it is work. Help the young people commit themselves to this work with energy and generosity. Help them to realize that Jesus is with us always, "until the end of the age" (Matthew 28:20).

Catechism Focus

The theme of this chapter corresponds with paragraphs 305 and 541–545 of the *Catechism*.

Enrichment Activities

Faith Reminders

Some young people might like to make posters or banners presenting messages of faith. For example:

- "Do not let your hearts be troubled" (John 14:1).
- "You have faith in God; have faith also in me" (John 14:1).
- Jesus says, "I am with you always" (Matthew 28:20).

They may want to illustrate their posters or banners with symbols or photographs. If possible, display the finished work in your parish church.

Computer Connection

Perhaps the young people have already established a computer connection with a group of believers in another part of the country. Invite them to share via electronic mail their thoughts about God's providence and their faith in a personal God. They might use an online service such as *Prodigy*™.

Teaching Resources

Overview

To deepen understanding of the providence of God; to discover what Jesus meant by the kingdom of God.

Opening Prayer Ideas

Offer together spontaneous prayers of thanksgiving for all God has provided.

or

Look at the photo on pages 20 and 21. Read together Matthew 13:18–23 and 31–32. Reflect quietly.

Materials

- Bibles, journals, highlighters
- instrumental music

Creed Journal:
For Chapter 2, use pages 37–39.

REPRODUCIBLE MASTERS
- handout *Who Cares?* page 16C
- *Chapter 2 Assessment,* page 23A
- *Highlights for Home,* page 23B

Supplemental Resources

VIDEO
Jesus of Nazareth (segment on the resurrection)

Ignatius Press
P.O. Box 1339
Fort Collins, CO 80522–1339

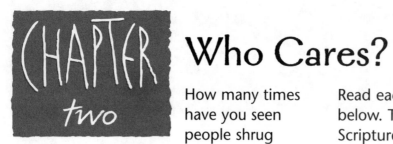

Who Cares?

How many times have you seen people shrug their shoulders and heard them ask, "Who cares?" Of course we know the definitive answer: God cares!

Read each of the Scripture passages listed below. Then draw a line from each Scripture citation to a description in the second column of someone who might find that passage of Scripture particularly meaningful.

Luke 2:49   someone suffering persecution

John 14:2–3   someone who feels unimportant

Matthew 5:45   someone worried about the future

Philippians 3:8–9   someone who needs forgiveness

Luke 12:6–7   someone facing death

Luke 15:11–32   someone who feels abandoned by God

Matthew 6:31–32   someone who has doubts about
                                   Jesus' divinity

Working for the Kingdom of God:

Identify other Scripture passages that would be particularly meaningful for people who need reassurance of God's providence. Explain who might find comfort in these words.

_____

_____

_____

_____

_____

_____

_____

_____

_____

_____

_____

LIFE IN CHRIST

Do not let your hearts be troubled.
You have faith in God; have faith also in me.
John 14:1

Objectives: To deepen understanding of the providence of God; to discover what Jesus meant by the kingdom of God.

Introduction ___min.

Opening Prayer: Gather the young people in a prayer circle and have them turn to pages 16 and 17. Ask them to imagine themselves in a small boat at sea. You may wish to use the following script to guide reflection:

> A storm comes up; the wind roars; the waves grow higher and higher. Suddenly you see land, and around the bend, a small cove. You manage to bring the boat into the cove and anchor it. The storm rages on but you are safe and secure, out of the surge of the sea.

> Life can often be stormy. We can be faced with winds of confusion and doubt; the waves of trouble and sorrow can often seem overwhelming.

What do we do? Jesus says: "Do not let your hearts be troubled. You have faith in God; have faith also in me (John 14:1)."

A Christian of the Middle Ages once wrote these words:

> Jesus, Deliverer, come thou to me.
> Soothe thou my voyaging over life's sea.
> When storms of doubt or grief, go roaring by
> Whisper, O Truth of truth, "Peace, it is I."

Allow a minute or two of silent reflection.

Forum: Appoint a "stage director" to direct the *forum* skits. Some young people who have worked with partners should be encouraged to present their skits to the whole group. Before closing the *forum*, the stage director should ask, "Why was it important for the disciples of Jesus to share the good news about Jesus' resurrection?"

Presentation ___ min.

◆ Ask a volunteer to read the opening story at the top of page 18. Invite responses to the final question. Then point out that in this session we are going to explore what it means to live fully the new life that Christ won for us in his paschal mystery.

◆ Ask, "Why is Jesus called 'the master teacher'?" Help the young people to understand that Jesus used what today's educators refer to as "the teachable moment." He used allusions to everyday things and activities to illustrate important truths about God the Father.

◆ Discuss responses to these questions:

• Do you think it is difficult to believe in God's providence in today's society?

• What would you tell someone who thought that God does not listen to and answer our prayers?

◆ Distribute copies of the handout *Who Cares?* The young people will need their Bibles. Read the directions together; then have the young people work independently to complete the handout. When most have finished, go over the responses.

• Luke 2:49 (someone who has doubts about Jesus' divinity)

• John 14:2–3 (someone facing death)

• Matthew 5:45 (someone who feels abandoned by God)

• Philippians 3:8–9 (someone suffering persecution)

• Luke 12:6–7 (someone who feels unimportant)

• Luke 15:11–32 (someone who needs forgiveness)

• Matthew 6:31–32 (someone worried about the future)

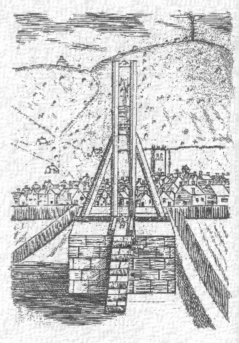

THE play *The Song of the Scaffold* is set in France during the French Revolution, a time when many priests and nuns were executed. A group of Carmelite nuns are ordered by the government to abandon their religious life. They refuse and are condemned to death. They remain firm in their faith and go up to the scaffold singing. As one after another is executed, the song becomes fainter and fainter until finally there is silence.

You would think the story would end here. Instead, it has just begun. It seems that one of the nuns had been afraid; she had gone into hiding. Now she must struggle all alone with her faith, her doubts, her fears. In the end she overcomes her terror and goes to the scaffold singing.

The point of the story is that this last nun is the bravest of all. Because the fear and doubt she had to overcome were so much greater, her courage was greater, too. Her song was the sweetest. Of all Christ's teachings, which one do you think might have been the one that gave her the courage to sing that final song?

The Providence of God

Knowing that Jesus had risen from the dead changed the apostles forever. The risen Christ was with them. Now they were certain that everything Jesus had taught them was true.

At the heart of Jesus' teaching was his concern for his Father and the fulfillment of the Father's will. Jesus' entire life centered on his Father. He wanted his disciples to know that God is personally concerned for each one of us. God loves us so much, in fact, that he sent his Son to redeem us. Jesus' first recorded words in Luke's Gospel tell us of his mission: He had to be about his Father's work (Luke 2:49).

Jesus used every moment to make his Father known. If a few sparrows settled near the place where Jesus was speaking, they could be used as an example in his teaching. One day he said, "Are not five sparrows sold for two small coins? Yet not one of them has escaped the notice of God. Even the hairs of your head have all been counted. Do not be afraid. You are worth more than many sparrows" (Luke 12:6–7). How wonderful to know that God cares for each one of us so much!

18

We use a special term to help us remember this overwhelming love and care of God; it is God's providence. *God's providence* is his personal concern for each of his creatures. And this was Jesus' message: Trust God because God cares. Jesus tells everyone of every age about the providence of God. "Do not worry and say, 'What are we to eat?' or 'What are we to drink?' or 'What are we to wear?' All these things the pagans seek. Your heavenly Father knows that you need them all" (Matthew 6:31–32).

Providence and Prayer

Does the providence of God mean that we get anything we want at any time we want it? Does it mean that God will answer every prayer exactly the way we want? It may be that what we ask for is not good for us. For example, we might ask God to help us pass every test we take with flying colors but without studying. This would be a foolish thing to ask, since it would hurt us in our future lives. God would never want to do that.

When we place our trust in God's providence, we know that everything will work out for the best. Each of our prayers, no matter how brief, receives God's personal and undivided attention. The answer to every prayer is yes—from God's point of view. But God may not answer us exactly as we expect. And this may be hard for us to understand. When we see God face to face, we will know all the reasons for God's providence.

Can you think of a time when you thought God's answer to your prayer was no, only to find out later that it was really yes?

Many Catholic homes display a crucifix, a symbol of God's providence in sending us his Son as our redeemer. Do you know what the letters INRI stand for on the crucifix? According to John's Gospel an inscription was placed on the cross that read in Latin *Iesus Nazarenus Rex Iudaeorum* (meaning "Jesus of Nazareth, King of the Jews"). So the INRI on a crucifix is made up of the first letter of each word in the Latin inscription.

Sons and Daughters of God

In Jesus' teaching on the Father, there is something for everyone. For a young person who feels unloved or abandoned, Jesus has a special message: The Father cares. Our heavenly Father makes the "sun rise on the bad and the good, and causes rain to fall on the just and the unjust" (Matthew 5:45). No one is forgotten by God; no one is ever abandoned for a single instant. God's offer of forgiveness extends always to each and every one of his children. This is why Jesus could tell the story of the prodigal son (Luke 15:11–32).

In his Father's plan, Jesus tells us, there is a special place for each one of us. It is like having our own room at home where things are familiar, warm, and secure. "In my Father's house there are many dwelling places. If there were not, would I have told you that I am going to prepare a place for you? And if I go and prepare a place for you, I will come back again and take you to myself, so that where I am you also may be" (John 14:2–3).

Sometimes a person may ask, "How does God see me? Am I just one of the crowd?" It is the individual person whom God loves. Because we are one with Christ, we are truly sons and daughters of this one Father of all. That is why we can pray both individually and as a community the words Jesus taught us.

Close your eyes and quietly pray the Our Father.

19

◆ Have the young people share the six key ideas they underlined in this chapter. Discuss their choices; then take time to have them highlight those highlighted on your reduced pages.

◆ Ask the group to reflect for a moment on the **thought provoker** at the bottom of the left column on page 19. Try to have a personal experience ready to share in order to stimulate the conversation.

◆ Ask a volunteer to summarize *Catholic ID* on page 19. If there is a crucifix in the room, have the young people look for the letters *INRI*.

◆ Direct attention to the second **thought provoker** on page 19. Have each person quietly pray, first "My Father" and then "Our Father," reflecting on the meaning of the words. Then pray the Lord's Prayer together.

Just in case...
some pronunciation helps

Jesus . . . . **Yea**-zus
Nazarenus . . . Nah-zah-**rey**-nus
Iudaeorum . . . You-day-**oh**-room

FYI Saint Francis de Sales (1567–1622) was appointed Bishop of Geneva, in 1602. He taught his people that God sees humankind as a wonderful but varied garden and that each person is beautiful in his or her way.

If your weakness troubles you, cast yourselves on God, and trust in him. The apostles were mostly unlearned fishermen, but God gave them learning enough for the work they had to do. Trust in him, depend on his providence, fear nothing.

Pass on Saint Francis's message about God's providence to someone asking "Who cares?"

Presentation (cont'd)

◆ Ask, "Why did some of the writers of the Old Testament refer to God as king?" List the responses on the board.

◆ Draw a large circle on the board; in the center write the phrase *kingdom of God*. Then ask the following questions about Jesus' teachings:

- What is the *kingdom of God*? (*God's rule and reign over people's lives*)

- Where can we find the kingdom of God? (*in Jesus—in his teaching, miracles, and healings*)

- What was one of the images Jesus used to teach about the kingdom? (*a seed planted in the ground*)

- How are we to be a part of the kingdom? (*by celebrating and proclaiming God's saving activity in the world*)

◆ Direct attention to *Catholic Teachings* on page 20. Ask a volunteer to summarize the paragraph. Point out that, as we pray in the Our Father, God's will must be done in order for his kingdom to come to fulfillment.

◆ Ask the group to suggest possible meanings for the silhouetted photograph on pages 20 and 21. Ask, "Are the hands waving? or reaching for something? or promising something?"

The Kingdom of God

The idea of God's providence can also be seen in Jesus' teaching about the kingdom of God. According to the Gospel of Mark, Jesus opened his public ministry by proclaiming, "The kingdom of God is at hand. Repent, and believe in the gospel" (Mark 1:15). What did Jesus mean by the phrase *kingdom of God*? He used it often in his preaching and teaching but never defined it.

To understand what that sense was, we turn to the Old Testament. There we find that God is frequently referred to as king. Why did the Old Testament writers choose this word? The king was supposed to be like the father of his nation. He was to care for his people, protect them from danger, and guarantee justice, especially for the weak and oppressed. God was, therefore, their king because he took care of them.

Jesus and the people of his time were familiar with this idea of God as a king. To be part of God's kingdom meant to be loved and protected by God. The *kingdom of God* was a symbol reminding everyone that God was the Lord of the universe, who would take care of his people and bring them salvation. Members of God's kingdom would return God's love and follow God's law. God would have a central place in their lives.

The kingdom of God was not a place; it was God's rule and reign over people's lives. Jesus wanted everyone to know that they would find the kingdom of God in him. Pointing to himself he said, "Behold, the kingdom of God is among you" (Luke 17:21). Jesus was saying that the kingdom had already burst upon the world in a marvelous way through his teaching, miracles, and healing ministry. God's kingdom is found in Jesus. What a wonderful way for God to care for his people and bring us salvation.

CATHOLIC TEACHINGS

About the Kingdom

All of us must work for the coming of God's kingdom, as we pray in the Lord's Prayer. To enter God's kingdom the Church teaches that we must turn toward God and do his will. And we remember that it is God's kingdom, not ours. The final completion of the kingdom will happen as God wants.

20

Jesus also taught that the kingdom of God was not yet complete. It had come in a dramatic way with Jesus, but as he said, it is like a seed that was planted (Matthew 13:18–23, 31–32). The kingdom still needs to grow and be nourished by us, Jesus' disciples. We must, therefore, look to the future as we celebrate and proclaim God's saving activity in the world. We are to take an active part in making that kingdom grow, a kingdom of justice and love. That is why we pray "thy kingdom come."

Jesus was so excited about the kingdom of God that he wanted all people to know about it. So he gathered around himself a community of disciples, the Church. He did this so that we could proclaim the good news of the kingdom and work for its completion. The Church and the kingdom of God are closely connected. Catholics believe that the Church is "on earth the seed and the beginning of that kingdom" (*Catechism*, 541).

Make a word collage that will help others understand the meaning of God's kingdom. What words come to your mind when you think of God at the center of our lives? Write them here.

◆ Invite the young people to respond to the ⟋⟍⟍ **thought provoker** on page 21. If they have trouble getting started, say, "A few words that come to my mind are *presence, loving care, direction.*" Ask, "What does God mean in your life?"

If time allows, the group might wish to make a poster collage of the words they have suggested. They might cut letters from construction paper, or use highlighters. Label the collage *Life in Christ* and display it in a prominent place.

21

FYI We can imitate the wholehearted but simple manner in which Saint Isidore the Farmer (1070–1130) helped the kingdom of God to grow. Isidore worked the land of a wealthy man's estate outside Madrid, Spain. He and his wife, Saint Maria de la Cabeza, dedicated their lives completely to God, especially after the death of their young son. Isidore went to early Mass every morning and then spent the rest of the day in prayer while planting and plowing. Though poor themselves, the couple shared their money, time, and spiritual comfort with those in need.

Saint Isidore is the patron saint of farmers. The Church celebrates his feast each year on May 15.

Presentation (cont'd)

◆ Have a volunteer read the first paragraph on page 22. Then ask, "What are the three truths Jesus stressed on the night before he died?"

Read aloud the thought provoker on page 22. If the young people have Sadlier's *Creed Journal*, encourage them to respond to the activity on page 38 of the journal.

Conclusion ___ min.

◆ Encourage the young people to work with partners to prepare responses to *Things to Share*. Take time to hear responses from several pairs.

◆ Direct attention to *Words to Remember*. Have the young people write the definition of *God's providence*. The definition is on page 19.

Assessment: If you are administering *Chapter 2 Assessment*, allow about ten minutes for its completion.

The Work of a Lifetime

If we want to know God, we look to Jesus. If we want to know what God asks of us, we listen to the message of Jesus. Only the risen Christ, living with us forever, can lead us to the love of God our Father. Jesus Christ is our teacher, and as he himself said, "My teaching is not my own but is from the one who sent me" (John 7:16).

On the night before he died, Jesus stressed three very important truths. He wanted to emphasize to the apostles the necessity of being united with him. These truths are:

• Only by a life united to Jesus will we ever reach the Father's house—heaven, our true home. Jesus said, "No one comes to the Father except through me" (John 14:6).

• Not only are we to be aware of our life in union with Christ, but we are also required to live it in a practical way. This we do by loving action and service on behalf of others every day. Jesus said, "This is my commandment: love one another as I love you" (John 15:12).

• Because we are united to Jesus in faith and Baptism, our lives are Christ-filled. Jesus said, "I am in my Father and you are in me and I in you" (John 14:20).

Getting to know Jesus is the work of a lifetime. We have only "scratched the surface." But that is all right. Jesus is patient. After all, he said to us, "I am with you always, until the end of the age" (Matthew 28:20).

"Getting to know Jesus is the work of a lifetime." Have you started this work? How do you plan to proceed?

22

Answers for Chapter 2 Assessment
1. c **2.** c **3.** b **4.** d **5.** c
6. a **7.** a **8.** b **9.** c **10.** See page 19.

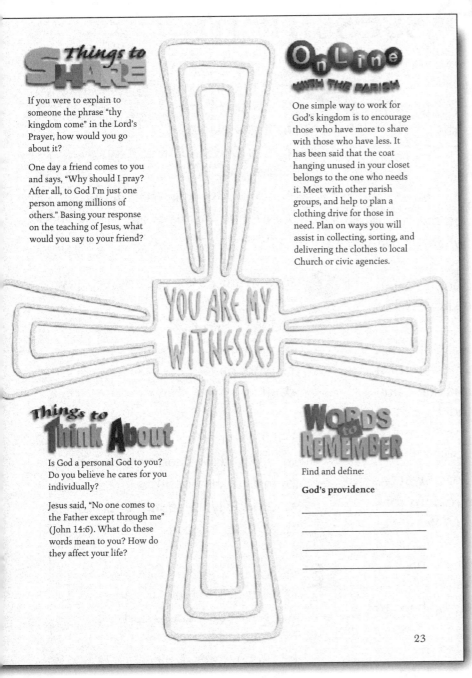

Things to SHARE

If you were to explain to someone the phrase "thy kingdom come" in the Lord's Prayer, how would you go about it?

One day a friend comes to you and says, "Why should I pray? After all, to God I'm just one person among millions of others." Basing your response on the teaching of Jesus, what would you say to your friend?

OnLine WITH THE PARISH

One simple way to work for God's kingdom is to encourage those who have more to share with those who have less. It has been said that the coat hanging unused in your closet belongs to the one who needs it. Meet with other parish groups, and help to plan a clothing drive for those in need. Plan on ways you will assist in collecting, sorting, and delivering the clothes to local Church or civic agencies.

Things to Think About

Is God a personal God to you? Do you believe he cares for you individually?

Jesus said, "No one comes to the Father except through me" (John 14:6). What do these words mean to you? How do they affect your life?

WORDS to REMEMBER

Find and define:

God's providence

_____

_____

_____

YOU ARE MY WITNESSES

23

Conclusion (cont'd)

FORUM Assignment

✔ Read Chapter 3, pages 24–31. Underline in pencil six key ideas.

✔ Complete the journaling activity on page 37 of Sadlier's *Creed Journal*. If this is not available, write a journal response to the two questions under *Things to Think About*, on page 23.

Closing Prayer: Ask the young people to look at the photo of the hand planting the tree sapling on page 22. Remind the group that getting to know Jesus and trying to do God's will is the work of a lifetime. Then read aloud the prayer in Ephesians 3:14–21.

Remind the young people that Jesus asked us to love and serve others. Suggest that the young people consider participating in a parish clothing drive to help others be aware of God's providence.

Evaluation: Have the young people understood the meaning of the providence of God? Have they shown a willingness to become vital members of the kingdom of God?

FOR CHAPTER 3

- preparation of opening prayer volunteers
- copies of handout *Sacred Temples*, page 24C
- *Chapter 3 Assessment*, page 31A (optional)
- *Highlights for Home*, page 31B

Assessment

1 The kingdom of God
- **a.** is a place where God reigns.
- **b.** is complete on earth.
- **c.** is found in Jesus.
- **d.** is in heaven alone.

2 The providence of God means that
- **a.** God will give us whatever we ask for.
- **b.** we need not ask God for anything because he knows what we need.
- **c.** God will make everything in our lives work out for the best.
- **d.** God cares for humankind but not for the individual.

3 Find the false statement.
- **a.** God answers all our prayers.
- **b.** We will know the reasons for God's answers when we are adults.
- **c.** God gives each prayer his personal attention.
- **d.** God's answers may be hard to understand.

4 At the heart of Jesus' teaching
- **a.** were his miracles.
- **b.** was his message of equality.
- **c.** was his preaching.
- **d.** was his fulfillment of his Father's will.

5 Catholics believe that the "seed" of the kingdom is
- **a.** Mary.
- **b.** the Apostles.
- **c.** the Church.
- **d.** the pope.

6 Find the *false* statement about God's kingdom.
- **a.** It is a place.
- **b.** It is God's rule and reign over people's lives.
- **c.** Jesus often preached about it.
- **d.** We find the kingdom of God in Jesus.

7 If we want to know God, we must first
- **a.** look to Jesus.
- **b.** read the Old Testament.
- **c.** work hard.
- **d.** none of the above

8 We are united to Jesus
- **a.** only in Holy Communion.
- **b.** in faith and Baptism.
- **c.** especially in Confirmation.
- **d.** all of the above

9 Which of these are *not* the words of Jesus in the New Testament?
- **a.** "Do not let your hearts be troubled."
- **b.** "Repent and believe in the gospel."
- **c.** "This is my beloved Son."
- **d.** "I am with you always."

10 Explain the statement: Each of our prayers, no matter how brief, receives God's personal and undivided attention. Write your response on the reverse side of this page.

Chapter 2: Life in Christ
Highlights for Home

Focus on Faith

One of the surprises contained in the gospel is that Jesus entrusted his message to humble people instead of to the rich and powerful. From Jesus' trust in his humble disciples, we learn that no one is small or insignificant to God and that each of us is tenderly loved by him. We can approach God in prayer with the certainty that in his providence he hears and answers us and will make everything work out for the best in our lives.

Jesus taught that God's kingdom had come into the world in him—through his teaching, miracles, and healing ministry. He taught that, even so, the kingdom is not yet complete. Catholics believe that the Church is "on earth the seed and the beginning of that kingdom" (*Catechism*, 541).

Conversation Starters

. . . . a few ideas to talk about together . . . .

◆ What does God's providence mean to you? Recall a time when you had to trust in God's providence.

◆ Recall a time when something turned out better than you had expected or when something good came out of a bad experience.

◆ What does it mean to say, "The answer to every prayer is *yes*"? How does that fit into your experiences of the providence of God?

Feature Focus

The *Catholic Teachings* feature on page 20 in this chapter directs our attention to the phrase *kingdom of God*. We pray for this kingdom in the Lord's Prayer: "Thy kingdom come, thy will be done on earth as it is in heaven." But for what exactly are we praying? We are praying for the rule and reign of God in our lives on this earth. Of course, at the same time, we are pledging our cooperation—pledging to do our part to help God's kingdom come through our acts of justice and love.

Reflection

"Behold, the kingdom of God is among you" (Luke 17:21). What is the kingdom of God for me? an idea? a place? a person?

The kingdom of God is among us in Jesus. If we want to know God, we look to Jesus. And only in a life united with his will we ever reach the Father. "No one comes to the Father except through me" (John 14:6).

THE LORD AND GIVER OF LIFE

Adult Focus

The focus of this chapter is on the Holy Spirit, who calls us, fills us, and empowers us. In this chapter, the young people will become better acquainted with the third Person of the Blessed Trinity. They will explore the relationship between the Holy Spirit and Jesus and will learn about the changes wrought by the Spirit in the lives of Jesus' disciples.

Saint Paul described Christians as temples of the Holy Spirit. (See 1 Corinthians 6:19.) Throughout this chapter the young people are challenged to understand what it means to be God's dwelling place and to discover how they can increase the recognition of the workings of the Holy Spirit in their lives. Remember that only by accepting the challenge ourselves can we effectively lead the young people to a deeper relationship with the Holy Spirit, who is sometimes called the "forgotten" member of the Blessed Trinity.

Catechism Focus

The theme of this chapter corresponds to paragraphs 687–693, 702–720, and 727–741 of the *Catechism*.

Enrichment Activities

Display

Reserve a bulletin board or other wall area for displaying the young people's art, poetry, and written reflections on the Holy Spirit. Have them add to the display each day so that by the end of the week they will have made a visual collage reminding them of the Holy Spirit.

Research

Provide hymnals or collections of songs and/or poems that celebrate the Holy Spirit. Give the young people time to look through the books and choose their favorite verses. Then gather for group sharing. The young people may want to copy and illustrate their selections for the Holy Spirit wall display.

Fine Art

The young people may enjoy looking through art books for visual representations of the Holy Spirit or of events involving the Holy Spirit. Suggest that they select their favorite such artwork and explain the reasons for their choice.

Teaching Resources

Overview

To know the Holy Spirit as the third Person of the Blessed Trinity and as Lord and Giver of Life; to explore the revelation of the Holy Spirit in Scripture.

Opening Prayer Ideas

Look together at the photo of volcanic fire on pages 24 and 25. Pray together: "Come, Holy Spirit" on page 121.

or

Pray together: "Lord, please pour out your Spirit upon us this day and always."

Materials

- Bibles, journals, and highlighters
- instrumental music

 Creed Journal:
For Chapter 3, use pages 40–41.

REPRODUCIBLE MASTERS
- *Sacred Temples*, page 24C
- *Chapter 3 Assessment*, page 31A (optional)
- *Highlights for Home*, page 31B

Supplemental Resources

VIDEO
What Catholics Believe About the Holy Spirit
Liguori Publications
Liguori, MO 63057–9999

CHAPTER three

Sacred Temples

Paul wrote to the Christians at Corinth:

> *Do you not know that your body is a temple of the holy Spirit within you, whom you have from God, and that you are not your own? For you have been purchased at a price. Therefore glorify God in your body.*
>
> 1 Corinthians 6:19–20

What does it mean to know that your body is the dwelling place of the Holy Spirit?

What are the implications for your physical self as well as for your spiritual life? What does this say about keeping yourself physically fit? about smoking cigarettes, drinking alcohol, or taking other drugs? about sexual immorality?

What does it say about the way you should treat other people?

Meditate on these ideas; then compose a prayer of commitment to the Holy Spirit.

CHAPTER 3

THE LORD AND GIVER OF LIFE

Come, Holy Spirit,
fill the hearts of your faithful.

25

Objectives: To know the Holy Spirit as the third Person of the Blessed Trinity and as Lord and Giver of Life; to explore the revelation of the Holy Spirit in Scripture.

Introduction ___ min.

Opening Prayer: Invite the young people to turn to pages 24 and 25 and react to the photograph. Ask, "Why would a photograph of a volcano be in a chapter on the Holy Spirit?" Use the following script to explain:

Volcanoes, which seem destructive, are truly sources of life. The great internal energy of the earth pushes to the surface, exploding in fire and lava. The molten rock pours down the sides of the crater covering everything in its path. And yet this same fiery liquid—when cooled and turned to volcanic ash—is affected by weather to form rich, fertile, life-sprouting soil. Such volcanic processes are believed to have caused the formation of the continents.

Invite the group to suggest words that come to mind as they look at the picture on these pages. List the words on the board. Make sure you list these key terms: *energy, strength, force, fire,* and *new life.*

As the young people look at the picture, read the following script:

The Holy Spirit is the fire, the energy, the strength of God—that which gives life to our souls. Every good deed ever done, every kindness ever offered, every moment of compassion, every hand held out in friendship, every act of justice, every work of peace is a visible sign of the Spirit in our world. Let us pray that the Spirit will work in us today.

All pray together, "Come, Holy Spirit," on page 121.

Chapter Warm-Up: Write the word *spirit* on the board. Invite the young people to name images that come to mind when they hear this word. Ask, "Do these images have anything to do with your understanding of the Holy Spirit?" Encourage the young people to explain their responses.

Forum: Gather the group in a circle. The leader begins the *Forum* by reading Matthew 6:31–32 quoted at the top of page 37 in the *Creed Journal*. The leader then goes around the circle asking, first of all, for the young people to mention daily worries. Then responses are solicited to the question about trusting God. Finally, the leader invites volunteers to share their endings to the prayer on page 37. If the *Creed Journal* is not available, the leader directs a discussion of the questions under *Things to Think About* on page 23 of the text.

Presentation ___ min.

◆ Have a volunteer read the opening questions at the top of page 26. Then point out that the Holy Spirit is often called the forgotten Person of the Blessed Trinity. Ask, "Why would the Holy Spirit be forgotten?" Point out that perhaps it is easier to talk to God the Father and to Jesus because we can visualize them.

Ask the young people to discuss in pairs responses to the following questions:

• Why do you think the image of a dove is used as a symbol of the Holy Spirit? (*A dove is also a symbol of peace, hope, and new life.*)

• What part does the Holy Spirit play in our prayer life? (*We pray to the Father, through the Son, and in the Holy Spirit.*)

Give the pairs time to prepare responses; then call on volunteers to share.

WHAT do you think of when you hear the word spirit? What image comes into your mind? Does this image have anything to do with your understanding of the Holy Spirit?

Holy Spirit window, St. Peter's Basilica, Rome

26

Third Person of the Trinity

Sometimes called the forgotten Person of the Blessed Trinity, the Holy Spirit is the Lord and Giver of Life. Why "forgotten"? Why "Lord"? Why "Giver of Life"?

Forgotten   When you think of God, how often do you think about the Holy Spirit? Perhaps not very often. Most people probably think about God the Father or God the Son when they think of God. Even in the celebration of the liturgy, we tend to think of our prayers as addressed to God the Father through Jesus Christ our Lord. But when we do this, we forget that there is another part to the prayers of the Church: We always pray to the Father, through the Son, in the Holy Spirit.

The Holy Spirit, the third Person of the Blessed Trinity, may also be forgotten for a simple reason. It may be easier for human beings to see the Father and the Son as divine Persons. Even traditional artworks may have contributed to the problem. How many times have we seen the Holy Spirit pictured as a dove? The dove is a wonderful symbol for the Holy Spirit, of course, because it comes from the Bible itself. Nevertheless it may make it harder for some to relate to the Holy Spirit as a divine Person.

Lord   One of the titles for God with which we are most familiar is "Lord." Just think how often the title is used in the Old Testament. Rather than referring to God as *Yahweh*, the sacred name of God that was given to Moses, the Old Testament writers often used *Lord*. This was done out of reverence for God's name.

Christians know the Lord God of the Old Testament as God the Father. And because Jesus is the only Son of God, he, too, is Lord. But do Catholics usually think of the Holy Spirit as the Lord? Perhaps not often enough. Remember, the Persons of the Blessed Trinity are distinct but equal. If the Father and the Son are both Lord, the Holy Spirit must be Lord, too. *Lord* is a title that refers to divinity. Each time we recite the Nicene Creed, we recall that the Holy Spirit "is worshiped and glorified" with the Father and the Son.

Giver of Life   The Holy Spirit is the only Person of the Blessed Trinity who is called the Giver of Life. This is true for a number of reasons. Probably the most important reason is that the Holy Spirit dwells in us through sanctifying grace. This means that we share in the divine life through the power of the Holy Spirit. Saint Paul explained this truth another way. In 1 Corinthians 6:19, he reminded the early Christians that they were temples of the Holy Spirit.

There is something else important to think about. Did you know that you cannot have faith unless the Holy Spirit gives it to you? We do not usually think of faith in this way, but this is one more reason why we call the Holy Spirit the Giver of Life. The Church teaches that without the Holy Spirit we cannot have faith, we cannot believe. This Catholic truth is stated dramatically in the New Testament. There we read, "No one can say, 'Jesus is Lord,' except by the holy Spirit" (1 Corinthians 12:3).

What does this mean for our lives? Actually a great deal. Our life of faith comes to us from the Holy Spirit. The Holy Spirit, therefore, is closer to us and more important to us than most of us realize. The Holy Spirit is the Lord and Giver of Life. Knowing all this, will you think differently about the Holy Spirit from now on? Don't let the Holy Spirit remain the forgotten Person of the Blessed Trinity for you.

How can you recognize the presence of the Holy Spirit in your life?

27

◆ Emphasize the following points about the Holy Spirit.

• The Holy Spirit dwells in us through sanctifying grace.

• Through the Holy Spirit we share in the life of God.

• Our faith itself comes from the Holy Spirit.

• The Holy Spirit is closer to us than most of us realize.

• In each sacrament the Church calls upon the Holy Spirit to make us holy and to build up the body of Christ.

◆ Remind the young people that we often use the word *Lord* to refer to God. Then ask:

• Why did the Old Testament writers often use the title *Lord* instead of God's name?

• Why do we also call Jesus "Lord?"

• Why do we call the Holy Spirit "Lord" as well?

◆ Now have the group read the thought provoker on page 27. Let the young people write their responses and keep them private if they wish.

◆ Ask the young people to share the key ideas they have underlined on pages 26 and 27. Discuss their choices. Then have them highlight the ones highlighted on your reduced pages.

FYI   The picture on page 26 is of the Holy Spirit window in Saint Peter's Basilica in Rome. It is set in the west wall behind the main altar. In the late afternoon the sun illumines the stained glass so that it shines like gold. It seems very fitting that the symbol of the third Person of the Blessed Trinity figures so prominently in the most important church in Christendom.

What other symbols of the Holy Spirit might be used for a stained-glass window?

Presentation (cont'd)

◆ Invite the young people to close their eyes and to take three deep breaths. Then tell them to continue breathing slowly and deeply as they remember that breath is essential to life. Point out examples from Scripture that illustrate this idea.

- The biblical writers associated the Spirit of God with breath, which gives and sustains life.
- In the creation story, God works in the wind "that swept over the waters" and breathes into Adam "the breath of life."
- In the New Testament, the coming of the Holy Spirit at Pentecost is described as a mighty rushing wind.

Suggest that the young people think of the biblical images of God associated with breath, strength, and wind as they fill their lungs with life-giving oxygen. As they meditate say:

Imagine that just as your body is cleansed and refreshed by deep breaths, your soul is nourished, empowered, and renewed by the Spirit of God who dwells in you. The Spirit is as essential for your life as breath itself. Now when you open your eyes, continue to be aware of God's Spirit as breath, wind, life, soul, mind, and power.

◆ Ask the young people to recall and name the Old Testament references to the Spirit of God. List these references on the board. Say, "What attributes of the Holy Spirit do these stories reveal?" (*The Holy Spirit is a gift which gives power, strength, vision, and life itself, even to the dead.*)

The Holy Spirit in Scripture

Have you ever heard anyone say, "Where there is life, there is breath"? Consider the simple act of taking a deep breath. At that moment our lungs are filled with life-giving oxygen. Without breathing, we would not stay alive very long. Breath is essential to life.

The biblical writers thought about the life of the world in much the same way. They said that the "breath," or Spirit, of Yahweh was present at creation and kept it in existence. The world would be lifeless without this Spirit of God. That is why the phrase *Spirit of Yahweh* is found frequently in the Old Testament.

What did the word *spirit* mean for the biblical writers? It had a variety of meanings: breath, wind, life, soul, mind, and power. At the beginning of the Old Testament, God's work is described as a wind that "swept over the waters" at creation (Genesis 1:2) and as "the breath of life" giving life to Adam (Genesis 2:7). God is seen as acting through his Spirit.

Later in the Old Testament, the Spirit of Yahweh gave the early leaders of Israel great power and strength. In helping to form God's people, they were able to do marvelous deeds only because God's Spirit was with them. Think about Samson, who rescued God's people from their Philistine enemies. One account about this legendary strongman explained the reason for his strength. As the story goes, one day Samson was attacked by a roaring lion. "But the spirit of the LORD came upon Samson, and although he had no weapons, he tore the lion in pieces" (Judges 14:6).

Finish this sentence: The breath of the Spirit is like . . . .

28

Alive in the Spirit

In one of the best-known passages of the Bible, the prophet Ezekiel writes about an unusual vision he had. In the vision the Spirit of Yahweh leads Ezekiel to the center of a plain filled with dried human bones. Suddenly the bones begin to rattle as they come together. After they are covered with flesh, the Spirit of God enters into them. Then they come alive and stand. By sharing this vision of the bones, Ezekiel is saying that the Spirit of Yahweh gives life—and can even give life to the dead (Ezekiel 37:1–14).

Another passage in the Bible, this one from the prophet Joel in the Old Testament, helps us to discover more about the Spirit of God for our own day. Joel speaks about the future and the time of the promised Messiah. Here the Spirit of God is described as God's gift to those who act on his behalf. In this famous passage God is saying,

> Then afterward I will pour out
>   my spirit upon all mankind.
> Your sons and daughters shall prophesy,
>   your old men shall dream dreams,
>   your young men shall see visions.
> Then everyone shall be rescued
>   who calls on the name of the LORD.
> Joel 3:1, 5

In every age God's Spirit is given to those who share in God's work.

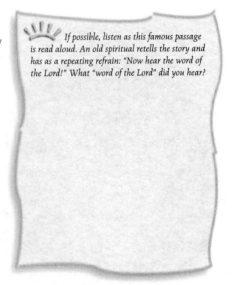

If possible, listen as this famous passage is read aloud. An old spiritual retells the story and has as a repeating refrain: "Now hear the word of the Lord!" What "word of the Lord" did you hear?

29

◆ Invite the young people to look at the photo on page 28 and respond to the caption. Then point out the photo on page 29. See how many can tell what that photo has to say about "breath" of God. Then ask, "If you were the illustrator of this book, what photos would you choose to convey the reality of the Holy Spirit?" Allow time for sharing.

◆ Point out the 👑 **thought provoker** on page 29. Have a volunteer (or volunteers) do a dramatic reading of Ezekiel 37:1–14. After the reading invite the young people to write the "word" that they heard. (*The "word" is that the Spirit of God gives life.*)

Have a volunteer read aloud Joel 3:1, 5 on page 29. Ask, "When did God fulfill this prophecy and pour out his Spirit?" (*at Pentecost*) Invite the young people to share how the words of the prophet make them feel alive or energized or hopeful.

◆ Take a few minutes to let the young people share the key ideas they underlined on pages 28 and 29. Invite discussion. Then have them highlight the two key points highlighted on your reduced pages.

Presentation (cont'd)

◆ Recall with the group the *Scripture Update* on page 30. Point out that the Temple was the place where God dwelt among his people in a special way. It was a sacred place.

Saint Paul's words in 1 Corinthians are very powerful. He tells the Corinthians (and us) that we are "temples of the Holy Spirit." God dwells in us. Ask the group to speculate on ways the world would be different if everyone realized and remembered that we are each a sacred dwelling place of the Spirit.

Have the young people respond to the ☼**thought provoker** on page 30. Then have them continue journaling by completing page 40 in the *Creed Journal.*

◆ Form three groups. Assign each group one of the following:

• *Item one* from *Things to Think About*
• *Item one* from *Things to Share*
• *Item two* from *Things to Share*

Allow the groups two minutes to prepare their responses and to choose a spokesperson. Then reassemble to share the thoughts of the groups.

Conclusion ___ min.

◆ Have the young people find and write the definition of *Holy Spirit* in *Words to Remember.* (See page 27.)

Assessment: If you plan to administer *Chapter 3 Assessment*, allow about ten minutes for its completion.

Christians know these words of Joel very well, for they appear again in the second chapter of the Acts of the Apostles. The apostle Peter quoted these words on the day of Pentecost. He tried to explain that the time of the Messiah had come, that God's work had now been brought to completion in Jesus Christ. Peter and the other disciples received the Holy Spirit because they were the followers of the risen Christ. Led by the Spirit, they would now share in Jesus' work on earth.

☼ *Do you think of yourself as someone on whom the Spirit of the Lord has been poured out? What does that mean to you? Write your thoughts in your journal.*

Scripture UPDATE

Saint Paul used a rich image to describe Christians In 1 Corinthians 6:19 he called each one of us a "temple" of the Holy Spirit. When he wrote this, Paul was thinking about the Temple of Jerusalem and how important it was in Jewish life.

Before the Temple was even built, the ark of the covenant, the symbol of God's presence with his people, was placed in a tent. A tent was used because the Israelites were nomads, wandering from place to place. Finally, after they had settled in the promised land, they constructed a permanent dwelling for the ark. This was the magnificent Temple of Jerusalem. There the ark of the covenant was placed in the holy of holies, the very heart of the Temple. This place was so sacred that the high priest alone could enter it.

The Temple was revered by all the people as the place where God dwelled among them in a special way. Knowing this, we can see what Saint Paul had in mind when he said that we are temples of the Holy Spirit. God's dwelling place is no longer to be regarded as being in one building. Now the Holy Spirit dwells in each of us. Can you imagine what the world would be like if all the followers of Jesus were to understand and appreciate what this means for their lives? It would change the world overnight!

30

Answers for Chapter 3 Assessment

1. a	2. d	3. b	4. a	5. a
6. b	7. b	8. d	9. c	10. Accept appropriate responses.

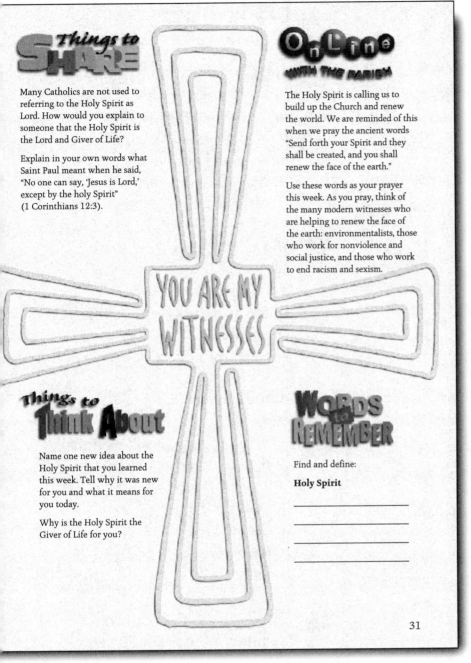

Things to SHARE

Many Catholics are not used to referring to the Holy Spirit as Lord. How would you explain to someone that the Holy Spirit is the Lord and Giver of Life?

Explain in your own words what Saint Paul meant when he said, "No one can say, 'Jesus is Lord,' except by the holy Spirit" (1 Corinthians 12:3).

OnLine WITH THE PARISH

The Holy Spirit is calling us to build up the Church and renew the world. We are reminded of this when we pray the ancient words "Send forth your Spirit and they shall be created, and you shall renew the face of the earth."

Use these words as your prayer this week. As you pray, think of the many modern witnesses who are helping to renew the face of the earth: environmentalists, those who work for nonviolence and social justice, and those who work to end racism and sexism.

YOU ARE MY WITNESSES

Things to Think About

Name one new idea about the Holy Spirit that you learned this week. Tell why it was new for you and what it means for you today.

Why is the Holy Spirit the Giver of Life for you?

WORDS to REMEMBER

Find and define:

Holy Spirit

_____

_____

_____

_____

31

Conclusion (cont'd)

FORUM Assignment

✔ Read Chapter 4, pages 32–39. Underline in pencil six key ideas.

✔ Complete the handout *Sacred Temples*. Be prepared to share the results.

Closing Prayer: Gather in a prayer circle. Have music playing softly. Invite a volunteer to read aloud *On Line with the Parish*, page 31. Then have the young people return to the opening photograph on pages 24 and 25. Pause for a moment to think of all those who are working to build a better world and of the poor who need a better world. Then say the prayer to the Holy Spirit together.

Evaluation: Have the young people deepened and expressed their understanding of God the Holy Spirit as Lord and Giver of Life?

FOR CHAPTER 4

- Bibles, journals, highlighters
- copies of handout *Like Sparks!*, page 32C
- copies of *Chapter 4 Assessment*, page 39A (optional)
- copies of *Highlights for Home*, page 39B

Assessment

1 In biblical writings *spirit* meant all of the following **except**
   a. temple.
   b. breath.
   c. wind.
   d. life.

2 Which of the following is **not** a name for the Holy Spirit?
   a. Lord
   b. Giver of Life
   c. third Person of the Blessed Trinity
   d. dove

3 Saint Paul tells us that the Holy Spirit dwells in
   a. the ark of the covenant.
   b. those who believe.
   c. the holy of holies.
   d. the Temple in Jerusalem.

4 The Holy Spirit is the only Person of the Blessed Trinity who is called
   a. Giver of Life.
   b. Father.
   c. Lord.
   d. Savior.

5 The Spirit of God
   a. was present at creation.
   b. was uninvolved in Jesus' life.
   c. is a lesser member of the Blessed Trinity.
   d. is not mentioned in the Old Testament.

6 The Church teaches that without the Holy Spirit
   a. there would be no churches.
   b. we could not have faith.
   c. we could not breathe.
   d. there would be natural disasters.

7 The Holy Spirit is sometimes called
   a. the ark of the covenant.
   b. the forgotten Person of the Trinity.
   c. the most important Person of the Trinity.
   d. the Father.

8 _____ prophesied that God would pour out his Spirit upon all mankind.
   a. Adam
   b. Ezekiel
   c. Peter
   d. Joel

9 _____ described us as "temples" of the Holy Spirit.
   a. Joel
   b. Ezekiel
   c. Saint Paul
   d. Saint Peter

10 Choose one description of the Holy Spirit and tell why it has meaning for you.

_____

_____

_____

_____

Highlights for Home

Focus on Faith

Saint Paul described Christians as temples of the Holy Spirit (1 Corinthians 6:19). Throughout this chapter, the young people were challenged to understand what it means to be God's dwelling place and to discover how they can increase the recognition of the workings of the Holy Spirit in their lives. They learned that without the Holy Spirit, we can not have faith.

In this chapter the young people were encouraged to deepen their understanding of the Holy Spirit—the "forgotten" Person of the Blessed Trinity. They learned that the Spirit of God dwells in us as Lord and Giver of Life, directing, guiding, loving, and energizing us.

Conversation Starters

. . . . a few ideas to talk about together . . . .

◆ My favorite symbol for the Holy Spirit is . . .

◆ I was most aware of the Holy Spirit as the Breath of Life when. . . .

Feature Focus

The *Scripture Update* in this chapter reminds us of the very mysterious and wonderful truth that each of us is a temple, a sanctuary, in which the Holy Spirit dwells. An understanding of this truth should make it impossible for anyone to have hatred for others. The awareness of the indwelling of the Holy Spirit should abolish bigotry and prejudice of any kind.

Reflection

Take a few minutes to reflect on Psalm 104:30:

When you send forth your breath, they are created,
and you renew the face of the earth.

Then pray for personal renewal with these words:

Holy Spirit, refresh and revitalize my spirit
that I may be used to help renew the face
of the earth.

COME HOLY SPIRIT!

Adult Focus

In this chapter the young people are encouraged to continue deepening their understanding of the Holy Spirit. They look at the Holy Spirit in the life of Jesus from the moment of his conception when the angel told Mary, "The Holy Spirit will come upon you, and the power of the Most High will overshadow you" (Luke 1:35). According to the gospel account, when John baptized Jesus, a dove was the sign of the Holy Spirit's presence. After his baptism, Jesus began his public life by reading Isaiah's prophecy, "The Spirit of the Lord is upon me" (Luke 4:18). On the night before he died, Jesus promised his apostles that he would ask the Father to send the "Advocate," the "Spirit of truth" to be with them always (John 14:16–17). After Jesus' ascension, the risen Christ shared his life with them—and with us—in the power of the Holy Spirit.

The Holy Spirit is still guiding Jesus' disciples. The source of all the activity in the Church, the Holy Spirit draws many people to the Church and strengthens its members with Christ as Head.

Catechism Focus

The theme of this chapter corresponds with paragraphs 702–720 of the *Catechism*.

Enrichment Activities

Computer Connection

Invite the young people to read the following passages and prepare a series of "Messages" about the presence of the Holy Spirit in our lives:

- Romans 8:1–4
- Galatians 3:1–5
- Ephesians 3:14–21
- 1 Timothy 4:1–7
- 1 Peter 1:10–12
- 1 John 5:5–12

They might use a computer paint program, such as *Flying Colors*™, to design illustrated messages gathered from Scripture about the Holy Spirit.

If they use *Flying Colors*™, they should select an appropriate background canvas, and then access the Text Tool, "T," on the side menu to write their message on the canvas. They use the alphabet that appears at the bottom of the screen; the letters are clicked on and dragged to any position. The young people string together the words to enter their messages about the Holy Spirit. They then use the paint tools and stamps to fill in their canvases.

Have them print their completed pictorials and present them to the group.

Teaching Resources

Overview

To deepen understanding of the Holy Spirit's presence in the life of Jesus; to grow in appreciation for the work of the Holy Spirit in the Church and in the world.

Opening Prayer Ideas

Pray together the words of the Irish prayer on page 33.

or

Pray the second verse of the same prayer:

Breathe on me, Breath of God,
Till I am wholly thine;
Until this earthly part of me
Glows with the fire divine.

Materials

- Bibles, journals, highlighters

Creed Journal:
For Chapter 4, use pages 41–43.

REPRODUCIBLE MASTERS
- handout *Like Sparks!* page 32C
- *Chapter 4 Assessment,* page 39A (optional)
- *Highlights for Home,* page 39B

Supplemental Resources

VIDEO
What Catholics Believe About the Holy Spirit
Liguori Publications
Liguori, MO 63057–9999

Like Sparks!

It is important to remember that the Holy Spirit is active in our lives through actual graces. These graces are like sparks that ignite a fire. The Holy Spirit gives them to us through other people and events in our lives. Complete the chart below by writing the ways people and events have brought you actual graces and helped you to deepen your Christian life.

Person or Event	Kindling the fire of God's love
My catechist	helped me to learn about God's great love for me
Parish food drive	helped me to experience being an instrument of God's providence

Come, Holy Spirit,
Kindle in us the fire of your love.

CHAPTER 4

COME HOLY SPIRIT!

Breathe on us, Breath of God,
Fill us with life anew
That we may love all that you love
And do what you would do.
Ancient Irish Prayer

Objectives: To deepen understanding of the Holy Spirit's presence in the life of Jesus; to grow in appreciation for the work of the Holy Spirit in the Church and in the world.

Introduction ___ min.

Opening Prayer: Gather in a prayer circle. Have music playing softly in the background. Encourage the young people to relax, to breathe deeply, slowly, and silently as they look at the photograph on pages 32 and 33. Invite them to try to imagine themselves on this open plain, looking at the clouds and listening to the gentle wind in the grasses. Pause briefly.

Have the young people concentrate on the breaths they are taking. Remind them that breath is the sign of life. The Holy Spirit is the Breath of God's life in us. Then say together the prayer on page 33.

Forum: All should have their handout *Sacred Temples*. Choose a "Saint Paul" to direct the *Forum*. He or she might begin by proclaiming to the group the words from 1 Corinthians 6:19–20 before inviting responses to the questions at the top of the handout. Invite volunteers to share their prayers.

Presentation ___ min.

◆ Have a volunteer read the first two paragraphs at the top of page 34. Then read the questions. Do not ask for answers. Tell the young people that we will go back to these questions later in the session.

◆ Discuss the photograph. Ask, "What are the emergency helpers trying to do? What happens if one's breathing stops?"

◆ Ask the young people to share the six key ideas they have underlined in this chapter. Discuss their choices. Then have them highlight those highlighted on your reduced pages.

◆ Draw a long horizontal line on the board to represent a timeline. Draw vertical lines to mark off six segments. Challenge the young people to place in order on the timeline the events in Jesus' life that specifically mention the involvement of the Holy Spirit.

The events and their order should be:

• the incarnation
• Jesus' baptism
• the temptation in the desert
• the beginning of Jesus' public life
• the promise of an Advocate
• Jesus' appearance to the apostles on Easter.

◆ Write the words *advocate* and *para-clete* on the board. Make sure that the young people understand that in the New Testament the two words are interchangeable. Have volunteers take turns giving descriptive definitions of the word *advocate*.

If someone has fainted, we are told, "Stand back. Give him air." A drowning person is resuscitated by someone breathing air into her lungs. Mountain climbers reach heights where the air is so thin that they are disoriented and lose consciousness. We simply cannot exist without pure air. It's a biological necessity.

In 1960 Pope John XXIII looked at the Church and said, "I want to open a window and let the air in." He was talking, of course, about the fresh air of the Holy Spirit. We cannot survive without that living breath of God.

What does the Spirit, the Breath of God, do for us? In what ways does the Holy Spirit affect our lives? make us more aware? awaken us to God's presence in our lives?

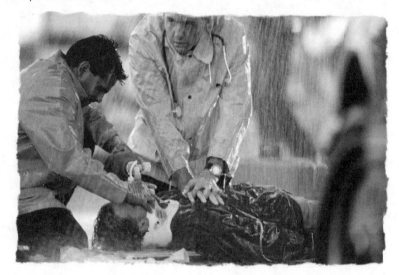

The Holy Spirit in Christ's Life

Modern Catholics may be surprised to find out how closely involved the Holy Spirit was in the life of Jesus. From the very beginning it was the Holy Spirit who came upon the Blessed Virgin Mary before Jesus' birth (Luke 1:35). Each time we recite the Nicene Creed, we profess our belief that at the incarnation the Son of God was born of the Virgin Mary "by the power of the Holy Spirit."

Later when John the Baptist baptized Jesus at the Jordan River, the Holy Spirit was present again. A dove was the sign of the Holy Spirit's presence. After Jesus' baptism the Holy Spirit drew him into the desert; there Jesus overcame the temptations of Satan. Then Jesus began his public life "in the power of the Spirit" (Luke 4:14). On returning to Nazareth, his hometown, Jesus announced the fulfillment of Isaiah's prophecy. Jesus said:

34

"The Spirit of the Lord is upon me,
because he has anointed me
to bring glad tidings to the poor.
He has sent me to proclaim liberty to captives
and recovery of sight to the blind,
    to let the oppressed go free,
and to proclaim a year acceptable to the Lord."
Luke 4:18–19

On the night before he died, Jesus promised his apostles that a new Helper would come to them. Jesus told them, "I will ask the Father, and he will give you another Advocate to be with you always, the Spirit of truth" (John 14:16–17).

To understand what Jesus is saying to us, we must know the meaning of the word *advocate*. In the New Testament the word *advocate*, or *paraclete*, has many meanings. It certainly can mean helper, but it means much more. An advocate is someone who speaks for others, who defends others and pleads for them. An advocate is also a comforter, a consoler, an intercessor, and a teacher. The Holy Spirit, then, is our intercessor, consoler, and teacher. He is the Advocate promised by the risen Lord to be with and for his disciples.

Think of the ways the Holy Spirit has been your advocate — your defender, comforter, consoler, intercessor, teacher. Write a prayer of petition or gratitude to the Holy Spirit.

The coming of the Holy Spirit was described in John's Gospel as taking place on Easter. After Jesus' death and resurrection, his apostles were afraid that they, too, would be killed. So they hid behind locked doors. John explains what happened next:

Jesus came and stood in their midst and said to them, "Peace be with you." When he had said this, he showed them his hands and his side. The disciples rejoiced when they saw the Lord. Jesus said to them again, "Peace be with you. As the Father has sent me, so I send you." And when he had said this, he breathed on them and said to them, "Receive the holy Spirit."
John 20:19–22

CATHOLIC TEACHINGS

About the Holy Spirit

How do we know the Holy Spirit, and how do we keep the Holy Spirit central in our lives? The *Catechism* (688) lists different ways. These include:

• Sacred Scripture, which was inspired by the Holy Spirit
• the tradition of the Church
• the teaching authority of the Church, which the Holy Spirit guides
• the sacraments and liturgy of the Church, in which we pray and worship together through the power of the Holy Spirit, who sanctifies us
• all our prayers, in which the Holy Spirit intercedes for us
• the lives of the saints and the ministries of the Church, in which the Holy Spirit brings us his holiness.

35

◆ Have a prepared volunteer do a dramatic reading from John 20:19–22. Then ask, "From whom did the power to forgive sins come to the apostles and to the Church?"

◆ Discuss the questions at the top of page 34. Then read *Catholic Teachings* on page 35. Go over each description of a way we can become more aware of the Holy Spirit in our lives. Have the young people identify the ways discussed. (*Scripture, tradition, teaching of the Church, the sacraments and prayer*)

Remind the young people that in each sacrament the Church calls upon the Holy Spirit to make us holy and to build up the body of Christ. (See Chapter 3 of *Liturgy and Worship* of the *Faith and Witness Program* for a presentation of epiclesis.)

Invite the young people to reflect quietly on the ideas at the top of page 41 of the *Creed Journal* and then do the journaling activity. If the *Creed Journal* is not available, they might reflect and write their thoughts about their need for the Holy Spirit at special times in their lives.

FYI You may want to have the young people learn the first stanza of the traditional hymn "Come, Holy Spirit." Explain that the hymn was written in Latin in the early ninth century but we now sing the following words for many liturgical celebrations:

Come, Holy Spirit, Creator blest,
And in our hearts take up thy rest;
Come with thy grace and heav'nly aid
To fill the hearts which thou hast made,
To fill the hearts which thou hast made.

Presentation (cont'd)

◆ Read aloud Acts 1:8. Ask the young people to contrast the way the disciples felt and acted before the coming of the Holy Spirit with the way they felt and acted after this event. Have a volunteer list the group's responses on the board under the headings *Before* and *After*.

Before

• did not know Jesus fully

• were frightened and without power

• could not bear the full revelation of truth.

After

• received power, courage, and strength to go throughout the world

• gave witness to Jesus with great courage and joy

• were ready to grasp all truth

• recalled all that Jesus had told them

• presented the teachings of Jesus for the Church throughout the ages.

◆ Remind the group that Jesus was a faithful Jew throughout his life. Therefore, it was in keeping with tradition that the Holy Spirit came upon his disciples on a Jewish feast day. Ask for the name and description of the feast. (*the Jewish harvest feast of Pentecost, the fiftieth day after Passover, when the Jews rejoice at God's rich blessings*)

◆ Have a volunteer read the *Catholic ID* aloud as the group looks again at the photograph on page 26.

Pentecost

Luke's account in the Acts of the Apostles describes the coming of the Holy Spirit in a different way, a description more familiar to most people. In Acts the Holy Spirit comes upon the community of Christians in Jerusalem on the Jewish harvest feast of Pentecost (Acts 2:1–11). It was the fiftieth day after Passover, a time for the Jews to rejoice at the rich blessings God had bestowed upon Israel.

With the coming of the Holy Spirit, Pentecost would now take on new meaning for Christians. Luke said that "suddenly there came from the sky a noise like a strong driving wind." Then he said that "tongues as of fire" came to rest on each of the disciples. "They were all filled with the holy Spirit" (Acts 2:2–4).

For the first Christians this day of Pentecost was the occasion for Jesus to pour out the Holy Spirit upon them, giving them an abundance of the gifts of the Spirit. The risen Christ was sharing his life with them—and with us—in the power of the Holy Spirit. Pentecost, therefore, was the completion of Christ's passover. The coming of the Holy Spirit is the completion of the paschal mystery—all that Jesus Christ did for us.

36

Have there been times in your life when you have felt the power of the Holy Spirit? Write about them here or in your journal.

One of the most recognizable stained-glass windows in the world is the window behind the main altar in Saint Peter's Basilica in the Vatican. In the window the Holy Spirit is symbolized as a dove. It reminds us of Jesus' baptism by John at the Jordan. Perhaps even more than this, it reminds us that at Baptism we are made a new creation through the power of the Holy Spirit. The biblical symbol of a dove goes all the way back to the Book of Genesis. In the story of the flood, Noah releases a dove to see whether or not the land has been renewed (Genesis 8:8–12). Thus the dove became a symbol of new life (see page 26).

Guided by the Spirit

Filled with the Holy Spirit, the early Christians went out with great excitement to bring Christ to others. These once-frightened disciples were given great power, courage, strength, and authority by the Holy Spirit. Jesus had told them, "You will receive power when the holy Spirit comes upon you, and you will be my witnesses in Jerusalem, throughout Judea and Samaria, and to the ends of the earth" (Acts 1:8).

Although the apostles had spent some of the best days of their lives with Jesus, they did not know him as fully as they thought. Jesus himself understood this. That is why Jesus said to them, "I have much more to tell you, but you cannot bear it now. But when he comes, the Spirit of truth, he will guide you to all truth" (John 16:12–13).

The coming of the Holy Spirit made a big difference in the lives of the apostles. Because Jesus sent the Holy Spirit to them, they were now ready to grasp all that he wanted them to know. Recall Jesus' words to the apostles, "The Advocate, the holy Spirit that the Father will send in my name—he will teach you everything and remind you of all that I told you" (John 14:26).

With memories refreshed and enlivened by the Holy Spirit, the apostles were able to give witness to the Jesus that they knew. The man they knew and with whom they walked was the Lord Jesus Christ, the God-Man—not dead, but alive! The Holy Spirit's coming enabled the apostles to recall and present the teachings that Jesus handed over to them for the Church throughout the ages. They now knew and understood their mission.

Today the Holy Spirit is still guiding Jesus' disciples. It is the Holy Spirit who guides the missionary activity of the Church. It is the Holy Spirit who draws so many people to the Church. It is the Holy Spirit who strengthens members of the Church to speak out against oppression, injustice, and poverty in our world.

Are you ever aware of the Holy Spirit working in the life of the Church? Give one example. Write it in your journal.

37

◆ Ask a volunteer to read Acts 2:1–4. Point out that the coming of the Holy Spirit was not for the apostles alone but for us also. It is the completion of the paschal mystery. Ask, "How do we keep the Holy Spirit central in our lives as Jesus did?" Remind the young people of the points made in *Catholic Teachings* on page 35.

◆ Have a volunteer read the last paragraph on page 37. Initiate a discussion on the signs of the Holy Spirit's presence in the Church and the world today. Encourage the young people to remember that, when the problems, trials, and sorrows of life seem to make the world a dark and depressing place, the Holy Spirit continues to guide, inspire, and energize people to work for justice and peace.

Invite the young people to do the journaling activity on page 43 of the *Creed Journal*. If this is not available, have them do a journal entry on the **thought provoker**, page 37.

Presentation (cont'd)

◆ Ask the young people to define *sanctifying grace* and *actual graces*. Then have them write the definition of *actual graces* under *Words to Remember* on page 39.

◆ Discuss actual graces; emphasize that we may experience them directly through urgings or promptings or indirectly through events and people in our lives. Ask the young people to identify some ways the Spirit gives us actual graces. Distribute the handout *Like Sparks!* Have a volunteer read the directions. Discuss the examples provided. Then explain that the *Forum Assignment* for the young people is to complete the chart. You may want to have them draw a decorative border around the chart.

Conclusion ___ min.

◆ Move into small groups to prepare responses to the four items under *Things to Think About* and *Things to Share.* Allow time for the groups to come together for general sharing.

◆ Have a volunteer read *On Line with the Parish* on page 39. List the young people's examples on the board.

Assessment: If you plan to administer *Chapter 4 Assessment,* allow about ten minutes for its completion.

The Life of Grace

We are temples of the Holy Spirit. Through Baptism we have been initiated into the life of sanctifying grace, a participation in the very life of God.

Our experience of the Holy Spirit, the sanctifier, does not end with sanctifying grace, however. The Church teaches us that the Holy Spirit is active in our lives through actual graces. *Actual graces* are interventions of God in our daily lives. These interventions are urgings or promptings from the Holy Spirit. Like sparks that can ignite a fire, these graces help us to deepen our Christian life and live the good news of Jesus as members of the Church.

There are many examples of actual graces. The Holy Spirit gives them to us either directly or indirectly through other people and events in our lives. These include the good example of others or the awareness to do good that we might gain from reading a book. Actual graces might also include the feelings that come spontaneously into our lives and that help lead us to holiness.

What would happen if the Holy Spirit were no longer present? Only then might we truly understand what he means to us. Like a world without water, we could not really live without the Holy Spirit. We sometimes forget how important water is until we do not have it. Without water, green fields dry up and become deserts. Without the Holy Spirit, our spiritual lives would be much the same; they would wither away and become desertlike. The Church reminds us of this truth when we pray these words:

> When you hide your face, they are lost.
> When you take away their breath, they perish
> and return to the dust from which they came.
> When you send forth your breath, they are
>   created,
> and you renew the face of the earth.
> Psalm 104:29–30

38

Answers for Chapter 4 Assessment
1. a   2. d   3. c   4. b   5. a
6. a   7. c   8. d   9. c   10. See page 35.

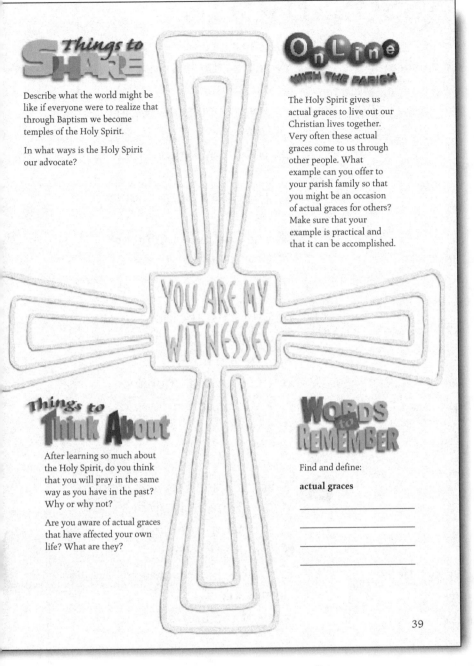

Things to SHARE

Describe what the world might be like if everyone were to realize that through Baptism we become temples of the Holy Spirit.

In what ways is the Holy Spirit our advocate?

OnLine WITH THE PARISH

The Holy Spirit gives us actual graces to live out our Christian lives together. Very often these actual graces come to us through other people. What example can you offer to your parish family so that you might be an occasion of actual graces for others? Make sure that your example is practical and that it can be accomplished.

Things to Think About

After learning so much about the Holy Spirit, do you think that you will pray in the same way as you have in the past? Why or why not?

Are you aware of actual graces that have affected your own life? What are they?

WORDS to REMEMBER

Find and define:

actual graces

_____

_____

_____

_____

39

Conclusion (cont'd)

FORUM Assignment

✔ Read Chapter 5, pages 40–47. Underline in pencil six key ideas.

✔ Complete the handout *Like Sparks!* Be prepared to share the results.

Closing Prayer: Use the following script to engage the young people in a one-minute meditation.

> Imagine you are in a desert. A hot sun burns you; you have no water. The sand stretches endlessly, and there is not a tree or stream in sight. How do you feel? What do you long for? Suddenly you stumble over a dune. Before you is a beautiful oasis where lush, leafy trees give cooling shade, and clear, cold water pours from a waterfall into a pool. You reach the oasis; you drink the water, and you swim and rest in the shade.

Point out that without the Holy Spirit our spiritual lives are like deserts without life, energy, or refreshment. With the presence of the Spirit, we are enlivened, refreshed, and renewed. Read together the excerpt from Psalm 104 on page 38.

Evaluation: Do the young people understand the ways that the Holy Spirit is our Advocate? Have they deepened their appreciation of the active presence of the Holy Spirit in the Church and in their lives?

FOR CHAPTER 5

- copies of handout *The Body of Christ*, page 40C
- copies of *Chapter 5 Assessment*, page 47A
- copies of *Highlights for Home*, page 47B

Assessment

 1 Circle the *false* answer. *Advocate* means

a. lawyer.

b. helper.

c. comforter.

d. teacher.

2 Pentecost was

a. a Jewish harvest feast.

b. the day the Holy Spirit came upon the apostles.

c. fifty days after Passover.

d. all of the above

 3 Pentecost is the completion of

a. the Triduum.

b. the work of the Spirit.

c. the paschal mystery.

d. the apostolic life of the Church.

 4 The image of the dove symbolizes

a. flight from this earth.

b. new life, new creation.

c. Peter's Basilica.

d. death.

 5 An example of an actual grace is

a. the impulse to do something kind.

b. the grace of Baptism.

c. the grace of the Eucharist.

d. none of the above

 6 Which of the following is *not* true of actual graces?

a. They are bestowed only at Baptism.

b. They may be the good example of others.

c. They may be spontaneous feelings.

d. They include urgings or promptings.

 7 At Pentecost the Holy Spirit came upon the disciples like

a. a gentle breath.

b. the sound of thunder.

c. a strong, driving wind.

d. a whisper.

 8 Which of the following events involved the Holy Spirit?

a. the baptism of Jesus

b. the incarnation

c. the beginning of Jesus' public ministry

d. all of the above

 9 *Paraclete* means

a. father.

b. captive.

c. helper.

d. son.

 10 List four ways you can keep the Holy Spirit central in your life. Write your responses on the reverse side of this page.

Highlights for Home

Focus on Faith

In this chapter the young people examined the presence of the Holy Spirit in the life of Jesus. They recalled that the Spirit's coming upon the disciples at Pentecost gave them great power, courage, strength, and authority. They discovered ways in which they are able to keep the Spirit central in their lives.

The young people learned that the Holy Spirit blesses and supports us through actual graces. Actual graces are interventions in our daily lives that help us to deepen our faith. They can take many forms. Sometimes they are spontaneous feelings or promptings. At other times they may come through the good example of others or through books, music, or good advice.

The Holy Spirit works in many ways, both direct and indirect, to lead us to holiness. We need to pray to be alert and attuned to the presence and work of the Spirit in our lives.

Conversation Starters

. . . . a few ideas to talk about together . . . .

◆ An actual grace that I am aware of in my life. . . .

◆ Some ways I think I can be more sensitive and responsive to the work of the Holy Spirit are. . . .

Feature Focus

The Holy Spirit is as essential to our lives as water is to the life of the world. According to Scripture, the Spirit can renew the face of the earth. We can participate in his work of renewal by working against poverty, injustice, violence, and oppression. *Catholic Teachings* on page 35 presents ways we can keep the Holy Spirit central in our lives. Take a minute to read this section.

Reflection

Daily prayer and frequent participation in the Mass deepens our awareness of our interior life—a spiritual universe as vast as the one outside of us. This spiritual life is where the Holy Spirit dwells in us.

How am I trying to develop my spiritual life? How can I be less materialistic?

What does it really mean to be a temple of the Holy Spirit?

THE MYSTERY OF THE CHURCH

Adult Focus

In this chapter the young people will learn about the great mystery that is the Church. They will examine the image of the Church as the people of God and as the body of Christ.

Both images help us to understand the connection between Jesus and his followers. Christ lives in us, and we live in him. The Spirit of the living God is present in us, the Church.

As the young people explore this wonderful mystery of the Church, help them deepen their vision of their membership in the body of Christ. Help them to explore what this membership in the Church means for them personally, and what it means for the world. Challenge them to take their place among the people of God. For we know, as the Old Testament psalmist expressed:

> How good it is, how pleasant,
>   where the people dwell as one! . . .
> There the LORD has lavished blessings,
>   life for evermore!

Psalm 133:1, 3

Catechism Focus

The theme of this chapter corresponds with paragraphs 760–762, 766–768, and 770–773.

Enrichment Activities

The Household

This is a group activity. Have the young people look at the photo on pages 40 and 41. Read together the Scripture passage on page 40.

On a large sheet of posterboard, have the young people draw an outline of a church. In the outline of the church, they place photos of themselves or others. The caption for the collage might be: "We are members of the household of God."

The Church Is Like . . .

Those who choose this activity should think of ways to complete this thought:

The Church is like. . . .

They might do this through a series of photographs, a photo collage, a poem, a song. They should use the images presented in this chapter to substantiate their project. The results should be presented to the whole group for discussion.

Teaching Resources

Overview

To deepen understanding of the mystery of the Church; to explore the meaning of the Church as "the people of God" and "the body of Christ."

Opening Prayer Ideas

Look at the photo on pages 40 and 41. Read together Ephesians 2:19–20.

or

Invite the group to pray aloud the antiphon: "We are one body, one body in Christ." Have a volunteer read aloud 1 Corinthians 12:12–31. Have the group repeat the antiphon.

Materials

• Bibles, journals, highlighters

Creed Journal:
For Chapter 5, use pages 44–45.

REPRODUCIBLE MASTERS

• copies of handout *The Body of Christ*, page 40C

• *Chapter 5 Assessment*, page 47A (optional)

• *Highlights for Home*, page 47B

Supplemental Resources

VIDEO
What Catholics Believe About the Church
Videos with Values
1944 Innerbelt Drive
St. Louis, MO 63114–5718

CHAPTER five

The Body of Christ

The first-century Christian community at Corinth had problems. Members were dividing themselves into factions according to their allegiances.

Paul, who had established the Church at Corinth on his second missionary journey, heard about the divisiveness and was saddened. He wrote the Christian Corinthians a letter, stressing their need for unity.

Read 1 Corinthians 12:12–31. With a small group, develop a skit that illustrates the Corinthians' point of view before and after they heard the message in Paul's letter.

THE MYSTERY OF THE CHURCH

You are fellow citizens with the holy ones and members of the household of God, built upon the foundation of the apostles and prophets.

Ephesians 2:19–20

Objectives: To deepen understanding of the mystery of the Church; to explore the meanings of the Church as "the people of God" and "the body of Christ."

Introduction ___ min.

Opening Prayer: Lead the young people in active prayer as outlined in the steps below.

- They make fists with both hands and look at their fists as you pray:

  God our Father,
  I clutch in my right fist all my selfish, unloving ways. I clutch in my left fist all my doubts and fears.

- They open their hands slowly as you continue to pray:

  You sent Jesus your Son to touch us, to heal us, to free us. We open our hands as a sign to you of our willingness to accept your love.

- All stand in a circle, shake hands with the person closest to them and pray:

  Jesus, accept our handshakes as a sign to you of our willingness to do as you ask—love our neighbors as ourselves.

- All in the circle join hands while you read Jesus' words in John 15:1–10.

- The young people form two rows such that each one is facing a partner. Partners join hands and raise them to form an arch representing a church steeple or grape arbor. You ask the group to imagine people of all generations passing beneath the arches. Then together sing a gathering song, such as "Gather Us In" by Marty Haugen or "We Gather Together," or read Psalm 100.

After the prayer activity, invite the young people to look at the photo on pages 40 and 41. Have a volunteer read Ephesians 2:19–20.

Forum: The forum leader invites people at random to share their charts on the handout *Like Sparks!* Some might wish to add or change their ideas.

Presentation ___ min.

◆ Have the group look at the photograph on page 42 as a volunteer reads the introductory paragraph on this page. Invite the young people to imagine themselves gathered with other parishioners to pray. Have them share what they are thinking and feeling and why they have come together to pray.

◆ Ask the young people why they think the first section on page 43 is called "More Than Meets the Eye." On the board write "What is the Church?" Elicit their responses and list them below the question.

◆ Discuss the reasons why it is sometimes easier to see ourselves as the people of God when we gather after a disaster than when we gather under ordinary circumstances each Sunday.

◆ Challenge the young people to look at and speak with parishioners they meet entering and leaving the Church at next Sunday's Mass. Explain that these friendly actions can help us to strengthen the bonds of Christian community.

◆ Emphasize that the writers of the New Testament saw the Church as part of the continuing story of God's dealings with his chosen people. Ask, "Why did Paul address the Galatians as the 'Israel of God'?" (*The early Christians looked to the time of Abraham and Moses as the beginning of God's people.*)

◆ Put the following diagram on the board and have the young people write specific names to fill in the sub-categories.

SATURDAY evening a tornado hit with such great fury that it devastated the small town. Even the Catholic church was destroyed. The next morning Mass was celebrated in the public school gym, one of the few buildings left standing. As the people of the parish gathered together, the pastor reminded them that even though their building was gone, they were still the Church.

42

The People of God

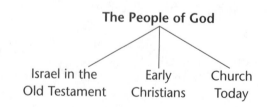

Israel in the Old Testament   Early Christians   Church Today

More Than Meets the Eye

Some people may be surprised at the pastor's words about being the Church. But he was right. The Church is more than buildings. It is really a great mystery, a mystery so deep that it is difficult to describe the Church in just a few words. That is why we are going to spend eight chapters exploring its meaning and depth.

The root meaning of the word *church* is "belonging to the Lord." In the Bible it means "a people called together." The Church is the assembly of those chosen by God in Jesus Christ, the assembly of God's people. Being the Church involves not only being the gathered community but also the process of gathering together. The Church, therefore, is not only an established group but also an event: people coming together, especially for the purpose of worshiping God and serving others. The Church is Christ's faithful people, the people of God.

The People of God

The idea of people of God goes back to Old Testament times. Israel became God's people because God chose it to be his own possession. God said, "I will take you as my own people, and you shall have me as your God" (Exodus 6:7). God's choice of this small nation to be his possession rather than other great nations took place solely from God's love. It was a grace.

Jesus, too, gathered a people to himself. The early Christian community was the new assembly of God's people. After the Pentecost experience in Jerusalem, the community gradually grew through the preaching of the apostles and their helpers. Wherever the people of God were found, they gathered together to hear God's word and to offer eucharistic worship for all that he had done for them.

Just as the choosing of Israel was the result of God's love, so, too, the Church came into being because of the love and grace of God. In fact the early Church taught that even before the creation of the world, God chose us in Christ (Ephesians 1:4) to be

"a chosen race, a royal priesthood, a holy nation, a people of his own" (1 Peter 2:9). We are a people because God dwells in us and moves among us. This means that we are a sign of God's presence in the world. God has chosen his people, and this is a mystery of divine grace.

There is also something more that we should recognize. Using the image of God's people, the writers of the New Testament saw the Church as part of the continuing story of God's dealings with his chosen people. By using the term *people of God*, they were pointing out the bond that existed between the Christian community and the people of Israel.

43

◆ Explain that on special feasts the Church prays together the *Te Deum*. This fourth-century Latin hymn has become the Church's song of thanksgiving. The English version of the hymn is known as "Holy God, We Praise Thy Name." Write on the board the first and third stanzas. The hymn will be used for *Closing Prayer*.

Holy God, we praise thy name!
Lord of all, we bow before thee;
All on earth thy scepter claim,
All in heav'n above adore thee;
Infinite thy vast domain,
Everlasting is thy reign.

Lo! the apostolic train
Join the sacred Name to hallow;
Prophets swell the loud refrain,
And the white-robed martyrs follow;
And from morn to set of sun,
Through the Church the song
    goes on.

◆ Take a few minutes to have the young people present the key ideas they have underlined in this chapter. Discuss their choices. Then have them highlight the ideas highlighted on your reduced pages.

Invite the young people to do the journaling activity on page 44 of the *Creed Journal*.

Just in case...
some pronunciation helps
Te Deum . . . . . . Tay-**Day**-um

Presentation (cont'd)

◆ Have the young people read aloud the words of Jesus in the second paragraph: "When I am lifted up from the earth, I will draw everyone to myself" (John 12:32).

Ask, "What do you think Jesus meant by these words? When was he 'lifted up'?" (*on the cross*) "How did he draw everyone to himself?" (*by redeeming us in his blood*)

◆ Invite three volunteers to go aside and prepare a dramatic reading of Acts 9:1–9. There are parts for a narrator, Jesus, and Paul. While they are preparing, ask the group:

• What difficulties did Paul run into when working with the early Christians?

• Were these difficulties particular to the Church of the first and second centuries?

◆ Remind the group that Paul often referred to the Church as the body of Christ. His conversion experience gave him the insight to recognize the Church as such. Invite the dramatic readers to present the story of Paul's conversion.

After the presentation say, "Paul was persecuting Christians. Why did Jesus say that Paul was persecuting him?" (*By persecuting Jesus' followers, Paul was persecuting Jesus himself!*)

All this means that the early Christians did not date or place the beginning of God's people from Jesus' birth or ministry. Rather, they looked to the times of Abraham and Moses. That is why among those names that belong to God's people and were adopted by the Church, one of the most meaningful was the name *Israel*. Paul himself addressed the Christian community this way when he wrote, "Peace and mercy be . . . to the Israel of God" (Galatians 6:16).

Jesus once said, "When I am lifted up from the earth, I will draw everyone to myself" (John 12:32). He still works to draw everyone to himself through his people. Just as God once chose and gathered his people by delivering them from Egypt, now he gathers his community, the Church, through the redeeming blood of his Son. Jesus has given himself for us in order to redeem us, "to cleanse for himself a people as his own" (Titus 2:14).

The Body of Christ

The Church is people, no one of whom is perfect. Paul himself knew this when he worked with the early Christians. When we read his letters in the New Testament, we can see that he ran into many difficulties. There were disagreements among the members of the Church. Some even formed into rival groups, claiming as their authority Peter, Paul, or one of the other leaders of the Church.

Disagreements, of course, are not unusual. They go on in the Church in every age. The Church is a visible organization; and in its human reality, it is often too human. Its human weaknesses offend many and, at times, turn them away. But is the Church only a human organization?

No. The Spirit of the living God is present in the Church. The Church is founded on Jesus Christ and guided by the Holy Spirit. This is why Paul frequently mentioned that Christians are united to Christ in one common life. He taught that the Church is the body of Christ, with the life-giving Holy Spirit flowing through that body. "For in one Spirit we were all baptized into one body, whether Jews or Greeks, slaves or free persons, and we were all given to drink of one Spirit" (1 Corinthians 12:13).

44

Paul gave us this understanding of the Church as the body of Christ. The experience of his own conversion gave him that wise insight. One day he was on his way to the city of Damascus with one purpose in mind: to destroy the followers of Jesus. Suddenly Christ appeared to him. Paul heard a voice saying to him, "Why are you persecuting me?" When Paul asked who it was he was persecuting, the voice replied, "I am Jesus, whom you are persecuting" (Acts 9:4–5).

Paul got the message! During the rest of his lifetime, he saw more and more the connection between Jesus and his followers. Jesus Christ lives in us and we in him. Paul taught that we are one body; that is, we belong to Christ's body. Each Christian has a special role to play. Each is uniquely related to Christ. "As a body is one though it has many parts, and all the parts of the body, though many, are one body, so also Christ" (1 Corinthians 12:12).

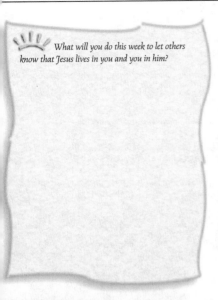

What will you do this week to let others know that Jesus lives in you and you in him?

A Unique Image

The individual parts of a human body share a common life and cannot live apart from one another. In the same way we share the life of Christ, the head of the body that is his Church. "Now you are Christ's body, and individually parts of it" (1 Corinthians 12:27). Individually and together we are the fullness of Christ, the whole Christ. If others want to meet Christ now in our time, they meet him in us! What a wonderful way to think of Jesus Christ and his Church.

Paul was not alone in his thinking. His image of the Church as the body of Christ is similar to other New Testament images, such as the image of the vine and branches (John 15:1–8). These comparisons try to express the close connection between Jesus Christ and his people. They also bring out the closeness that Church members must have with one another. After all, we are members of the same body. The Church in the New Testament, then, is most appropriately called the body of Christ. But the image does not replace that of the people of God—it deepens it. The Church is the people of God as the body of Christ.

It is clear, then, that *body of Christ* is a unique image. It expresses a relation between Christ and the Church that is as close as can be imagined. It reminds us that Christ and the Church are so close that no one can come to Christ without the Church. Our personal union with Christ, therefore, also involves our belonging to the Church. This means that no one can be an isolated follower of Jesus Christ; one must be a member of the Church.

The chart on the following page lists some familiar images of the Church. Study them and discuss their meaning for your life.

◆ Read aloud the **thought provoker** at the top of page 45. Stress that in order to fill in the blank they have to examine how they are treating others. Allow a few minutes for the young people to write a response. Do not ask the young people to share their responses because this activity has the quality of a journal entry.

◆ Distribute copies of the handout *The Body of Christ*. Form small playwriting groups. Have a volunteer read the directions aloud. Have each group begin by reading 1 Corinthians 12:12–31 and then develop its skit. Point out that the short lines at the left of the page are for the names of the characters who are speaking.

Allow about ten minutes. Then bring the groups together to share their skits.

45

Presentation (cont'd)

◆ Give the young people a minute to look over the chart on page 46. If time allows, have four volunteers look up and read aloud the Scripture reference for each image.

◆ Have a volunteer read the *Scripture Update* on page 46. Point out that the term *body of Christ* can be used in different ways.

• Jesus had a human *body* like ours.

• The sacrament of Eucharist is the Body of Christ.

• The image of the Church as the body of Christ is used to describe the closeness of the union between Christ and the Church.

◆ Direct attention to *Words to Remember* on page 47. Have the young people find and define the term *body of Christ* as it is used in this chapter. (See page 45.)

Conclusion ___ min.

◆ Use the *Sharing Circle* format to discuss the young people's responses to *Things to Think About* and *Things to Share* on page 47.

Assessment: If you plan to administer *Chapter 5 Assessment,* allow about ten minutes for its completion.

Other New Testament Images of the Church

Image	Biblical Source	Meaning
ark of salvation	1 Peter 3:19–22	The Church is compared to Noah's ark. As a means of salvation through water, the ark reminds us of Baptism and our initiation into the Church.
bride of Christ	1 Corinthians 11:2	The union of Christ and his members is one of intimate, mutual, and permanent interdependence.
building on a rock	Matthew 16:18–19	*Rock* is a title of God in the Old Testament. The Church teaches and guides us with God's authority.
mother	Revelation 12:17	Through the sacraments the Church brings us into and nourishes us in the divine life.

*Scripture*UPDATE

In the New Testament and in Catholic writings, the term *body of Christ* is used in three different ways. It can refer to:

• the human body of the historical Jesus

• the sacramental presence of Christ in the Eucharist

• the Church.

Answers for Chapter 5 Assessment

1. a   **2.** d   **3.** b   **4.** c   **5.** a

6. d   **7.** d   **8.** d   **9.** c   **10.** Accept appropriate responses.

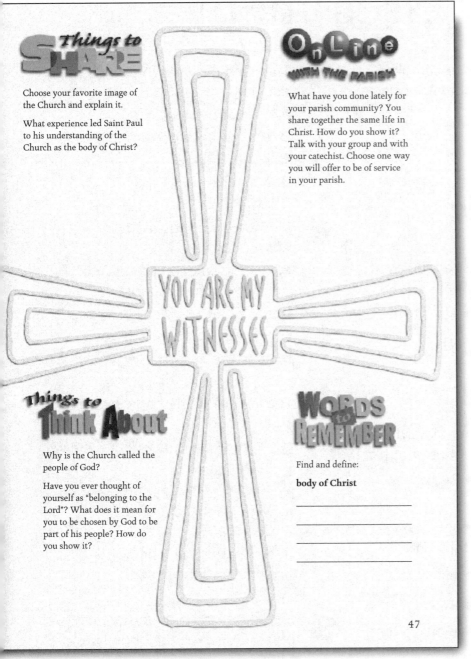

Things to SHARE

Choose your favorite image of the Church and explain it.

What experience led Saint Paul to his understanding of the Church as the body of Christ?

OnLine WITH THE PARISH

What have you done lately for your parish community? You share together the same life in Christ. How do you show it? Talk with your group and with your catechist. Choose one way you will offer to be of service in your parish.

Things to Think About

Why is the Church called the people of God?

Have you ever thought of yourself as "belonging to the Lord"? What does it mean for you to be chosen by God to be part of his people? How do you show it?

Words to REMEMBER

Find and define:

body of Christ

_____

_____

_____

_____

47

Conclusion (cont'd)

FORUM Assignment

✔ Read Chapter 6, pages 48–55. Underline in pencil eight key ideas.

✔ Think about the images of the Church you have explored. Choose one and draw a symbol that expresses its meaning for you. Be prepared to share the results.

Closing Prayer: Have the young people turn back to pages 40 and 41. Invite the young people to raise their arms prayerfully as they sing or pray the words of "Holy God, We Praise Thy Name." As they pray, have them imagine that they are joining their voices to those of our ancestors in faith singing in praise and thanksgiving.

Evaluation: Do the young people understand that the Church is founded on Jesus Christ and guided by the Holy Spirit? Have they explored the image of the Church as the body of Christ?

FOR CHAPTER 6

- copies of handout *The Vine and the Branches*, page 48C
- copies of *Chapter 6 Assessment*, page 55A (optional)
- copies of *Highlights for Home*, page 55B
- branch of a tree in a pot
- strips of paper, materials for symbols
- a stone for each person

Assessment

Choose the correct letter to complete the statement that describes a specific image of the Church.

- **a.** People of God
- **b.** Bride of Christ
- **c.** Mother
- **d.** The ark of salvation

1 _____ emphasizes our bond with the people of Israel.

2 _____ reminds us of our Baptism.

3 _____ expresses the union of mutual and permanent interdependence between Christ and his Church.

4 _____ is the image that best reflects spiritual nourishment.

5 Circle the *false* statement.
- **a.** There were no divisions in the early Church.
- **b.** Paul was once a great persecutor of Christians.
- **c.** All baptized persons are part of the body of Christ.
- **d.** It is not possible to be an isolated follower of Jesus.

6 That God has chosen us to be his people is
- **a.** a great mystery.
- **b.** only to be expected.
- **c.** just an image.
- **d.** a miracle.

7 In Church writings the *body of Christ* refers to
- **a.** the sacramental presence of Christ in the Eucharist.
- **b.** the Church.
- **c.** the human body of Jesus.
- **d.** all of the above

8 The images of the body of Christ and the bride of Christ
- **a.** are poetic words with little real meaning.
- **b.** are not from Scripture.
- **c.** were first used at Vatican Council II.
- **d.** emphasize the intimacy of Christ and the Church.

9 ____ gave us the understanding of the Church as the body of Christ.
- **a.** John
- **b.** Jesus
- **c.** Paul
- **d.** Matthew

10 What does it mean to you to be part of the body of Christ? Write your response on the reverse side of this page.

Highlights for Home

Focus on Faith

When you hear the word *church*, what image comes to your mind? Do you think of the building in which we worship, the people of the parish, the popes and bishops? The Church is all of these, of course, and much more.

In this chapter, "The Mystery of the Church," your son or daughter learned that the Church is much more than meets the eye. The young people examined several images of the Church, including the Church as the ark of salvation, the bride of Christ, and the body of Christ.

This last image deepens the meaning of all the others. It expresses a relationship between Christ and his Church that is as close as can be imagined. It means that no one can come close to Christ without the Church. We cannot be isolated from the Church and still be a follower of Christ.

Conversation Starters

. . . . a few ideas to talk about together . . . .

◆ What comes to mind when you think of the *Church*? Trade answers back and forth to see how many different people, places, and events come to mind.

◆ Do you ever think of yourself as "belonging to the Lord"? What do these words mean to you?

Feature Focus

The *Scripture Update* on page 46 summarizes the three ways that the term *body of Christ* is used in the New Testament and in Catholic writings. In these works, the term refers to the human body of Jesus, the sacramental presence of Christ in the Eucharist, and the Church.

Reflection

Take some time to look at the photo on the opening pages of this chapter. What does it seem to say to you about the meaning of the Church?

Let us start with the obvious: hands. The strength or weakness of a hand depends on how well connected it is to the source of its life. How do you stay close to the life-giving Spirit of Jesus?

In our mission as the body of Christ, we accept the invitation to put our hands to the plow. We take heart in recalling the words of Jesus: "My yoke is easy, and my burden light" (Matthew 11:30). Jesus was no doubt expecting many hands to join together for the good of the kingdom.

A Community Unlike Any Other

Adult Focus

In this chapter the young people look at the Church as "a community unlike any other"— a community that combines what is human and what is divine, what is earthly and what is heavenly.

Every Sunday at Mass, we affirm that we believe in a Church that is one, holy, catholic, and apostolic. Without these characteristics the Church would not be the Church that Jesus founded. In this chapter, we look carefully at these four essential features to deepen our understanding of the Church and of our place in it. We look at the members of the Church, our "family of God," and see that we are all different, that we all have different roles to play.

We are, indeed, "living stones" who come together in Christ to be built into a "spiritual house" (1 Peter 2:4, 5). Together we complete one another and, united to Christ, we are the Church.

Catechism Focus

The theme of this chapter corresponds to paragraphs 770–773 and 781–785 of the *Catechism*.

Enrichment Activities

Imagine you are a first-century Christian with a flair for the communication arts. The community has asked that you devise brief messages, slogans, or symbols to illustrate the following truths about the Church:

• We are the living stones; Christ is the cornerstone.

• The Church is both human and divine.

• We are unlike any other community because. . . .

• The essential features of the Church are one, holy, catholic, apostolic.

How do you make these statements into slogans that will catch the eye or ear of first-century pagans?

Computer Connection

Have the young people use a program such as *HyperStudio®* to make a multimedia presentation in which they identify and discuss the four essential features of the Church. Pose the question, "What does it mean when we say the Church is one, holy, catholic, and apostolic?"

Those using *HyperStudio®* can arrange their presentation as a single stack of cards with customized buttons to manipulate the stack. They should first design an Introduction Card that includes one button for each feature. Then guide them to use text and graphic tools, as well as scanned-in pictures, imported sounds, and clip art, to make cards for each individual feature. Each of these should include a button to return to the Intro-duction Card.

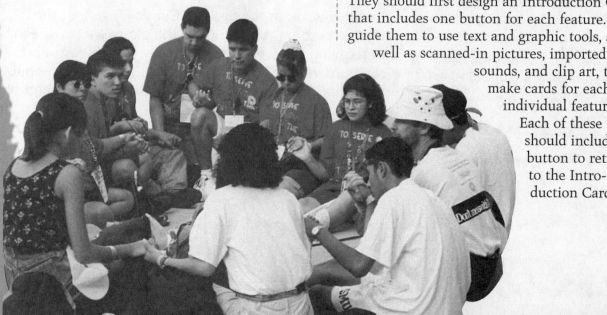

Teaching Resources

Overview

To explore the human and divine dimensions of the Church; to appreciate that the Church is the family of God; to examine the essential features of the Church.

Opening Prayer Ideas

Pray together the Apostles' Creed. See page 121.

or

Gather in a prayer circle. Offer spontaneous prayers of thanksgiving for the Church.

Materials

- Bibles, journals, and highlighters
- branch of a tree in a pot
- strips of paper; materials for symbols
- a stone for each person

REPRODUCIBLE MASTERS

- handout *The Vine and The Branches*, page 48C
- *Chapter 6 Assessment*, page 55A
- *Highlights for Home*, page 55B

 Creed Journal:
For Chapter 6, use pages 46–47.

Supplemental Resources

VIDEO
The Splendor of the Church
Ignatius Press
P.O. Box 1339
Fort Collins, CO 80522

The Vine and the Branches

"I am the vine, you are the branches.
Whoever remains in me and I in him will bear much fruit."

John 15:5

Read and reflect on the words of Jesus. Look at the photo on this page. Picture a vine with a strong stem and many branches and leaves as you complete the following activity.

Who is the "vine"—the source and support of all the "branches"? Write the name in large letters on the name card.

What does it mean for you to be a "branch" on this vine? How connected are you to the source?

Picture yourself as a branch close to the vine. Write your name in large letters on the name card.

Picture the people who help you to flourish, to be more connected to Christ as other branches on the vine. Write their names on the name card.

Read the words of Jesus again. Cut out the name card. Write a prayer to Jesus on the reverse side of the card. Tell of the ways you will try to "remain" in him. Pray for those who help you to flourish.

A COMMUNITY UNLIKE ANY OTHER

Come to him, a living stone,.... and, like living stones, let yourselves be built into a spiritual house.
1 Peter 2:4, 5

Objectives: To explore the human and divine dimensions of the Church; to appreciate the Church as the family of God; to examine the essential characteristics of the Church.

Introduction ___ min.

Opening Prayer: Gather the young people in a prayer circle. Give each one a stone or a small rock to hold. Ask the prayer leader to move to the center of the circle and proclaim 1 Peter 2:1–10. Have the group respond: "Thanks be to God." Then ask the prayer-leadership team to read the following petitions. Invite the group to respond to each petition:

We come to you, Jesus, as living stones.
Build us into a spiritual house.

• Rid us of all malice and all deceit, Lord.

• Keep us from insincerity and envy.

• Help us to live as a chosen race, a royal priesthood, a holy nation.

• Build us to be people of your own, Lord, so that we may announce your praises—you who have called us out of darkness into your wonderful light.

Play as background music, or have the group sing, a hymn such as *Earthen Vessels* or *The Church's One Foundation*. (See *Glory and Praise*.)

Invite the young people to carry their stones to the prayer table and place them on the open Bible as symbols of their desire to be "living stones."

Forum: Have a volunteer list on the board the images of the Church discussed previously. Ask the forum director to call on as many as possible to share the symbol the young people have devised for one of the images. Invite each person to explain the symbol, respond to any questions from the group, and display it for all to see.

Presentation ___ min.

◆ Have a volunteer read aloud the opening paragraphs at the top of page 50 and invite responses to the questions. Then ask, "How do you think we go about becoming "living stones"? (*We participate in the life of the Church, Mass and the sacraments, social-justice activities, prayer, and service.*)

◆ Discuss with the young people the key ideas they have underlined in this chapter. Discuss their choices. Then have them highlight those highlighted on your reduced pages.

◆ Write the words *human* and *divine* on the board. Invite the young people to find the statements on page 50 that explain that the Church is both human and divine.

• The Church is the body of Christ.

• It is presided over by human beings whose authority comes from God.

• It proclaims God's word in human language by the power of the Holy Spirit.

• When members worship together, they are not an ordinary group of people; they are united to Christ.

• When members sin and repent, mere human words spoken by a priest give divine forgiveness.

◆ Discuss what Saint Peter meant when he referred to the Church as "the household of God." (*We can think of the Church as our family, the family of God.*)

LIKE living stones....

Isn't it interesting that the practical, down-to-earth fisherman would choose such a poetic image to tell us about the Church? We must come to Christ the cornerstone, Peter tells us, and like living stones be built on him into a "spiritual house."

Do you feel that you are a "living" part of the Church? Or do you see yourself out on the rock pile — unused, unwilling, and unavailable for service?

Human and Divine

It is clear that the Church is an organized community unlike any other. As the people of God, it is a union of people guided by the Holy Spirit and under the direction of its leaders. Like any other group of people, it is both shaped by and shapes history. It rejoices in the goodness of its members but suffers from their weaknesses, too.

As the body of Christ, the Church is made up of both human and divine dimensions. It is presided over by human beings, yet they act with the authority they have received from God (Matthew 18:18). When the Church proclaims God's word in human language, it relies, not on human wisdom, but on the power of the Holy Spirit (1 Corinthians 2:13).

Whenever the members of the Church worship together, they are more than an ordinary group of people; they are a people intimately united with their Lord (1 Corinthians 11:27). When they have sinned and they repent, mere human words spoken by a priest become the bearers of divine forgiveness (John 20:23).

We can say that the Church combines what is human and divine, what is earthly and heavenly, and what is found in time and in eternity. Like the moon reflecting the light of the sun, the Church brings the light of Christ to the world. It is clear, then, that the Church is a mystery, a truth of faith that we know only because God revealed it to us.

50

In what way is the Church a mystery? How is it unlike any other community?

The Family of God

The Church is a mystery and the union of what is human and divine. We probably do not think of it that way each day, but we should. We can also think of the Church as our family, the family of God. This idea goes back to the earliest times when the Church was spoken of as "the household of God," another way of saying God's family (1 Peter 4:17). We enter this family through Baptism, the sacrament by which we become children of God.

It is in the parish, the basic unit of the Church, that most Catholics live out their membership in the family of God. All the members begin to share a common, or family, life through the sacraments of Baptism, Confirmation, and Eucharist. And these sacraments of initiation, as well as the other sacraments, are celebrated in the parish.

The members of the Church, like the members of any family, are all different. Each has his or her own gifts and talents and graces. Each fills a different role. Some are ordained deacons. Others are ordained priests. Still others are ordained bishops, who share the fullness of the priesthood. Bishops, priests, and deacons are called the clergy. The *clergy* are the members of the Church who have received the sacrament of Holy Orders. Most members of the Church, however,

are the laity. The *laity* are the baptized members of the Church. This includes everyone who is not in Holy Orders or who is not a vowed *religious*, a member of a religious order or community. No less than the clergy and religious, the laity have an important part in the whole life of the family of God.

Clergy, religious, and laity depend on one another in the parish family and must work as a team. Paul wrote about the different activities of various members of the Church family. He explained that the smooth functioning of the body depends on the cooperation of all its parts. You may wish to read what he has to say about this in 1 Corinthians 12:18–26.

Among laity, religious, and clergy there must be a deep bond. Each works to bring the risen Christ into the world. Each is able to do this in ways that the other cannot. Each is able to do for people what the other cannot do. Together they complete one another in the sense of being united in Christ for the common good of everyone they meet.

One way the laity are actively involved in the life of a parish is through the parish council. A *parish council* is a group of parishioners who are elected or appointed to help the pastor in the administration of the parish. The pastor presides over the council, and council members work closely with him. They advise him about the needs of the parish, including parish finances, education, liturgy, and social justice.

From your experience as a member of a parish, complete the chart on the following page by describing the different functions of parish members.

51

◆ Point out the ⛭ **thought provoker** at the top of page 51. Give the young people a minute or two to jot down their ideas before inviting them to share.

◆ Remind the group that the members of the Church, like the members of any family, have different roles and different gifts. Write on the board the words *clergy*, *laity*, and *religious*. Ask volunteers to define them. Then discuss the roles within parish communities of each of these members of the Church family. Emphasize the deep bond that should exist among these groups.

◆ Have a volunteer read the *Catholic ID* aloud. Point out that in many parishes this is a vibrant and faith-filled activity provided by the laity.

◆ Remind the young people that each member of the Church has his or her own gifts, talents, and graces. However, as Saint Paul tells us, simply having these gifts is nothing; we need to use them to strengthen our family bonds, the bonds of Christ's love.

✎ Read together 1 Corinthians 13:1–7. Have the young people list in their journals their particular gifts, talents, and graces and then write their reflections on the reading. Use page 47 in the *Creed Journal*.

FYI Today we still read the poetry of Gerard Manley Hopkins (1844–1889). His powerful lyrics were linked to his ministry as an ordained priest serving in various Jesuit parishes. After reading the following excerpt from, "As Kingfishers Catch Fire," think of the people who reflect Christ's light and love to others.

> For Christ plays in ten thousand
>   places,
> Lovely in limbs, and lovely in
>   eyes not his
> To the Father through the
>   features of men's faces.

Presentation (cont'd)

◆ Direct attention to the ☀ thought provoker on page 51. Discuss the different roles listed on the chart. Explain that in some parishes one person may have more than one role.

Have the young people complete the chart. Then invite them to discuss ways their present roles as students and participators in the celebration of the sacraments can help them prepare for some of the roles listed on the chart.

◆ On the board, write the word *unique*. Discuss the features or characteristics that make every person unique. Then ask the young people to name the four essential features that make the Church "the Church that Jesus founded."

Have the young people form four groups, and assign each group a different one of the four features of the Church. Ask each group to develop a presentation of its assigned feature. Allow about fifteen minutes for the groups to work together. Circulate among them to check for any misunderstanding of the assigned characteristics. Then invite the groups to teach their lessons. Suggest that the "teachers" include discussion of those statements they underlined for the *Forum Assignment*.

Who's Who in the Parish

Name	Your Description
pastor	
other priests	
deacons	
pastoral ministers	
eucharistic ministers	
lectors	
altar servers	
ushers	
director of religious education	
Catholic school principal	
religious sisters	
religious brothers	
catechists	
teachers	
director of music	
members of parish organizations	

Essential Features

What makes you the person you are? Is it the color of your hair or the fact that you wear glasses? Of course not. Things like these are only superficial, only on the surface. Each of us is so much more. Each of us is unique and has a set of unique characteristics. Without your own unique characteristics, you would not be who you are.

The same is true of the Church. The Church also has certain characteristics, or essential features. Without them the Church would not be the Church that Jesus founded. Four essential features of the Church are that it is one, holy, catholic, and apostolic. These characteristics are so important for Catholics that we profess our belief about them each week at Mass. Let's look at them more closely.

Unity: A Gift Never to Be Lost When we say that the Church is *one*, we are talking about the unity of the Church. And this unity of the Church comes from its source, the Blessed Trinity. This means that God the Father calls us into the one body of Christ, to whom we belong. The Holy Spirit gives life to that body.

From the earliest times this wonderful unity of the Church has been expressed in its one profession of faith handed on to each generation from the time of the apostles. The unity of the Church is also expressed in the celebration of divine worship, especially the sacraments. We are united in one Baptism and gather as one around the table of the Lord in the Eucharist. Through the sacrament of

52

Holy Orders, the Church can trace its unity back to the time of the apostles. Paul described this unity when he wrote, "Because the loaf of bread is one, we, though many, are one body, for we all partake of the one loaf" (1 Corinthians 10:17). We are one in the Lord and constantly striving for greater unity.

A Work of Grace The Church is *holy* because our sins are forgiven, and we are sanctified, or made holy, by our union with Christ. Through our Baptism in Christ's death and resurrection, we enter into the life of grace, which is God's own life. God alone is holy, and we participate in that holiness through the Church, especially the sacraments.

Christ so loved the Church that he sent us the Holy Spirit. The Holy Spirit fills and guides the Church for all time. The Church teaches us that as members of the Church we are temples of the Holy Spirit. Through Jesus Christ the whole structure of the Church is held together and "grows into a temple sacred in the Lord"; in Christ we also "are being built together into a dwelling place of God in the Spirit" (Ephesians 2:21–22).

As members of the Church, we are also bearers of the fruits of the Holy Spirit: love, joy, peace, patience, kindness, generosity, faithfulness, gentleness, self-control (Galatians 5:22). As baptized members of the Church, we are a holy people and constantly striving for greater holiness.

At Home Around the World The Church is *catholic* because it is universal and missionary. It is meant for the whole world and has a message for the whole world. The Church can never be narrow or associate itself with only one place or time. Jesus never placed any limits on the Church, where it was to go or thrive. Rather, the Church must gather to itself all who are called by God.

The Church, therefore, is not called catholic because it does missionary work. Rather, the Church engages in missionary activity precisely because it is catholic and has a message for all. That is why Jesus says, "Go, therefore, and make disciples of all nations" (Matthew 28:19). The Church is catholic and must never rest from bringing Christ to the world. The task is not over until the end of time.

> *Because you belong to a Church that is catholic, you must be open to all. What impact does this have on any prejudices you might have?*

Group of teens praying together during World Youth Day

53

◆ Distribute strips of paper and have each young person write one way of holiness on a strip.

Present a previously prepared tree branch secured in a large pot. Invite the group to turn it into a "Family of God" tree by decorating it with symbolic cutouts. Offer these suggestions:

• house for "household of God"

• moon to represent Church reflecting Christ's light

• ark for image of the Church as ark of salvation

Have the young people glue their "act of holiness" strips to the back of their ornaments. Then direct them to attach a piece of yarn or string to the top of each ornament and hang it on the tree branch.

Place the "Family of God" tree in your prayer space for use during the *Closing Prayer*.

◆ Discuss the Church as catholic with a small "c" and its missionary call to bring Christ to the world. Then have the young people read and respond to the **thought provoker** on page 53. Stress that one cannot be a faithful follower of Christ and be bigoted or prejudiced in any way. Invite the young people to discuss the bigotry or prejudice they encounter in themselves or others. How can it be overcome?

FYI Saint Peter Claver (1580–1654), a Jesuit novice, requested to be sent from his native Spain to be a missionary in the "New World." In 1610, his request was answered; his order sent him to the Colombian port city of Cartagena in South America. There, Peter was ordained in 1616. At this time Cartagena was a major center of the slave trade. Here, Peter provided food, clothing, and encouragement to the thousands of slaves who passed through the port. The missionary priest instructed the slaves in the Catholic faith, and it is said that he baptized 300,000. Saint Peter Claver is just one example of someone who truly became a "living stone."

Presentation (cont'd)

◆ Invite a volunteer to read aloud Jesus' commission of Peter as the "rock" on which the Church would be built (Matthew 16:13–19).

Then write the word *apostolic* on the board and ask for explanations of this feature of the Church.

◆ Have someone summarize *Catholic Teachings* on page 54. Then discuss the choice of photographs on pages 53 and 54. In what ways do they illustrate the essential features of the Church?

Direct attention to *Things to Think About* on page 55. Have the young people write in their journals their responses to the first question.

◆ Form groups to discuss the remaining questions in *Things to Think About* and *Things to Share*.

Conclusion ___ min.

◆ Direct attention to *On Line with the Parish*. Challenge the group to brainstorm different ways young people can be active parishioners. List their ideas on the board. Pause briefly and ask the young people to read the list quietly. Suggest that they give themselves a deadline and plan a strategy for getting involved.

Assessment: If you plan to administer *Chapter 6 Assessment*, allow about ten minutes for its completion.

The True Foundation The Church is *apostolic* because it was founded on Christ and the apostles. Jesus chose the apostles to lead the early Church in his name. They were sent by Christ himself—by him and by no other—to be his witnesses "to the ends of the earth" (Acts 1:8). Guided by the Holy Spirit, the apostles handed on the teachings of Christ. That is why the Church always looks back to the apostolic foundation of Peter and the other apostles when it looks for the deposit of faith. This apostolic foundation can never be replaced.

Until Christ comes again at the end of time, the Church will continue in the apostolic tradition under the leadership of the pope and bishops, the successors to the apostles. They teach, sanctify, and govern the Church in the name of Christ. The Church is apostolic and must always strive to stay in tune with its true apostolic foundation.

CATHOLIC TEACHINGS

About the Church's Essential Features

It is Christ, through the Holy Spirit, who makes the Church one, holy, catholic, and apostolic. And it is Christ who calls the Church "to realize each of these qualities" (*Catechism*, 811).

Missionary priest, Brothers and Sisters of the Cross, Lebanon

Pope John Paul II in Ghana, Africa

Answers for Chapter 6 Assessment
1. d   2. c   3. b   4. c   5. b
6. d   7. c   8. d   9. b   10. See page 54.

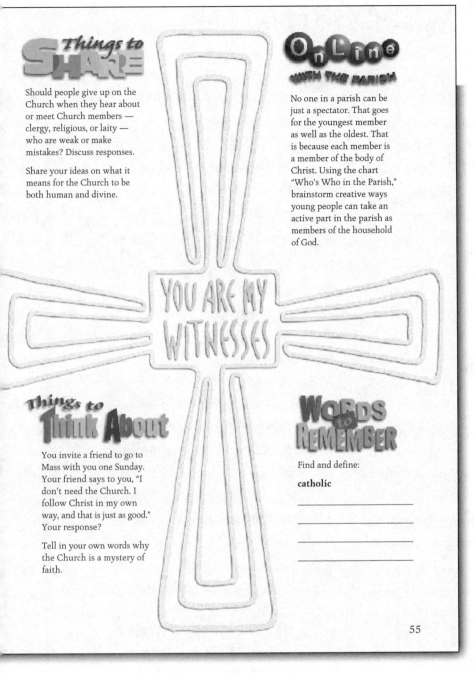

Things to SHARE

Should people give up on the Church when they hear about or meet Church members — clergy, religious, or laity — who are weak or make mistakes? Discuss responses.

Share your ideas on what it means for the Church to be both human and divine.

OnLine WITH THE PARISH

No one in a parish can be just a spectator. That goes for the youngest member as well as the oldest. That is because each member is a member of the body of Christ. Using the chart "Who's Who in the Parish," brainstorm creative ways young people can take an active part in the parish as members of the household of God.

Things to Think About

You invite a friend to go to Mass with you one Sunday. Your friend says to you, "I don't need the Church. I follow Christ in my own way, and that is just as good." Your response?

Tell in your own words why the Church is a mystery of faith.

WORDS to REMEMBER

Find and define:

catholic

_____

_____

_____

_____

55

Conclusion (cont'd)

◆ Direct attention to *Words to Remember*. Have the young people write the definition of *catholic*. This can be found on page 53.

◆ Distribute copies of the handout *The Vine and The Branches* for the *Forum Assignment*.

FORUM Assignment

✔ Read Chapter 7, pages 56–63. Underline in pencil six key ideas.

✔ Complete the handout *The Vine and The Branches*. Be prepared to discuss the results.

Closing Prayer: Invite the young people to gather near the "Family of God" tree. Have them remove one ornament (not their own) from the tree. Ask them to read the ways of holiness written on the slip of paper on the back of the ornaments and make a resolution to try and practice this way during the coming week.

Evaluation: Do the young people understand that the Church is both human and divine? Have they explored the meaning of the Church's four essential features?

FOR CHAPTER 7

- preparation of opening-prayer volunteers
- copies of handout *In Appreciation*, page 56C
- *Chapter 7 Assessment*, page 63A
- *Mid-semester Assessment*, page 124
- *Highlights for Home*, page 63B
- photos of buildings destroyed by natural disasters

Assessment

1 The Church is
a. an Old Testament term.
b. divine only.
c. a building.
d. both human and divine.

2 The Church is called *catholic* because
a. it does missionary work.
b. it is founded on Christ.
c. it has a universal message.
d. it is faithful.

3 Select the *false* statement.
a. The Church is a mystery.
b. The Church is only like most.
c. The Church is the family of God.
d. The Church is a truth of faith.

4 Members of the Church who have received Holy Orders are called
a. religious.
b. popes.
c. clergy.
d. Catholics.

5 Members of the Church who are not religious or clergy are called
a. unbaptized.
b. laity.
c. parish council.
d. converts.

6 Those who have made vows in religious communities are called
a. cardinals.
b. apostles.
c. Christian workers.
d. religious.

7 The Church is _____ because our sins are forgiven and we are sanctified by our union with Christ.
a. apostolic.
b. catholic.
c. holy.
d. one.

8 The basic unit of the Church is
a. a religious community.
b. the rectory.
c. the diocesan cathedral.
d. the parish.

9 A parish council
a. is made up of priests from different parishes.
b. helps in the administration of the parish.
c. is presided over by the bishop.
d. usually has nothing to do with parish finances.

10 What is significant about the fact that Jesus changed Simon's name to *Peter*, a word that means "rock"?

_____

_____

Highlights for Home

Focus on Faith

We say the Church is a community "unlike any other" because it is the body of Christ. It is, like Christ, both human and divine. The Church combines what is earthly and heavenly, and what is found in time and in eternity. The Church is a mystery of faith, a truth we know only because God has revealed it to us.

Every Sunday at Mass we affirm that we believe in a Church that is one, holy, catholic, and apostolic. These are the four essential features of the Church. In this chapter your son or daughter has looked more closely at these features so that they can proclaim more faithfully the words of Creed:

We believe in one holy catholic and apostolic Church.

Conversation Starters

. . . .a few ideas to talk about together. . . .

◆ If Jesus would change my name to express my membership in his Church, what might he call me?

◆ What am I more aware of in the Church—its humanity or its divinity? How can I begin to see a balance?

Feature Focus

Catholic Teachings on page 54 reiterates the essential features of the Church stressing that it is Christ, through the Spirit, who makes them possible. It is the Church who is called by Christ to make them real in the world.

Reflection

From the very beginning, Christ called his Church to be one. We are not made to live alone. At the end of his life, Jesus gave us his own Body and Blood in the Eucharist to be the sign of unity among his followers. He prayed that we all "might be one."

The early Christians, beset by perils and persecutions, found strength, hope, and encouragement in the fellowship of the community and in the "breaking of the bread" of the Eucharist.

How do I convey the strength, hope, and encouragement I receive in the Eucharist to others? How do I contribute to the unity Christ so desires in his Church?

A STRONG FOUNDATION

Adult Focus

In this chapter, the young people learn that the roots of Church leadership extend back to Jesus and the apostles. Jesus handpicked a group that we know as the Twelve. Jesus shared his mission and authority with them. They were to be the pillars upon which he would build his Church.

The ministry of the apostles was continued and assured in the ministry of the local bishops. These bishops were the vital link to the apostles and thus to Christ himself. By A.D. 110 Ignatius of Antioch could speak of the threefold ministry of bishop, presbyter (priest), and deacon as "established in the farthest parts of the earth." Through the laying on of hands, we have the same threefold ministry today.

Bishops succeed the apostles in their office of teaching, governing, and sanctifying in the name of Christ. As links to the apostles, the bishops are charged with the sacred duty of passing on the complete and authentic teaching of Jesus and the apostolic Church. The bishop of each diocese coordinates its work, helping it to keep focused on its true mission of building God's kingdom. With the priests whom he ordains, he sanctifies the Church through prayer and the ministry of both word and sacrament, especially the Eucharist.

Catechism Focus

The theme of this chapter corresponds to paragraphs 813–822 and 857–862 of the *Catechism*.

Enrichment Activities

Diocesan News

For the next several sessions, provide a few diocesan weekly newspapers (available in most church vestibules) for the group to read. Ask them to pay particular attention to the bishop's messages and to report about his activities among the parishes throughout the diocese.

Computer Connection

Invite the young people to use a crossword software program, such as *Word Cross*®, to make crossword puzzles that feature terms presented in this chapter or the previous six chapters.

Have the young people work in small groups. Direct each group to confer among themselves to make up a list of words and corresponding clues. If necessary, allow the young people to refer to the text. When all are ready, direct the groups to enter their words and clues into the computer to be processed into crossword puzzles. Then have the groups print and exchange puzzles. Allow ample time for the young people to solve one another's puzzles. Then challenge them to use other words from the text to make more crossword puzzles to share.

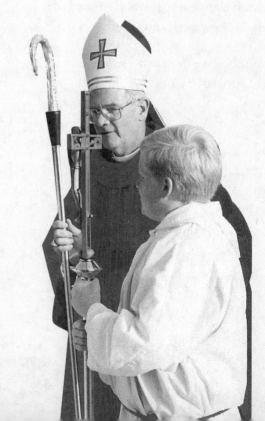

Teaching Resources

Overview

To trace the roots of Church leadership to Jesus and the apostles; to explore the ways the bishops succeed the apostles in their office of teaching, governing, and sanctifying in the name of Christ.

Opening Prayer Ideas

Reflect on and discuss the Scripture reading about Saint Peter and Jesus from Matthew 16:18–19.

or

Pray together Psalm 23:1–4.

Materials

- Bibles, journals, and highlighters
- photos of buildings destroyed by natural disasters
- sheets of paper

REPRODUCIBLE MASTERS
- handout *In Appreciation*, page 56C
- *Chapter 7 Assessment*, page 63A (optional)
- *Midsemester Assessment*, page 124 (optional)
- *Highlights for Home*, page 63B

Creed Journal:
For Chapter 7, use pages 48–49.

Supplemental Resources

VIDEO
Peter and Paul
Ignatius Press
P.O. Box 1339
Ft. Collins, CO 80522

In Appreciation

Write a note to the bishop of your diocese, thanking him for his ministry. You may also want to share with him some of the things you have learned about the Church. The following are salutations you should use:

◆ To a bishop — Dear Bishop (last name),

◆ To a cardinal — Dear Cardinal (last name),

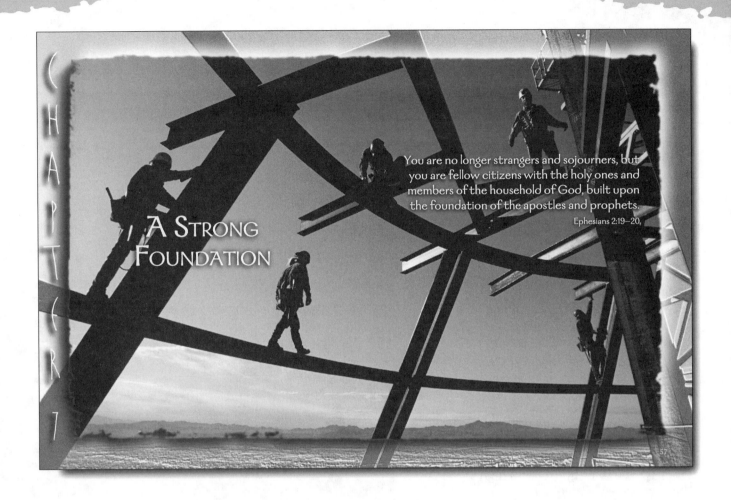

A STRONG FOUNDATION

You are no longer strangers and sojourners, but you are fellow citizens with the holy ones and members of the household of God, built upon the foundation of the apostles and prophets.

Ephesians 2:19–20,

Objectives: To trace the roots of Church leadership to Jesus and the apostles; to explore the ways the bishops succeed the apostles in their office of teaching, governing, and sanctifying in the name of Christ.

Introduction ___ min.

Opening Prayer: Display pictures of houses being destroyed by floods, hurricanes, or earthquakes. Allow the young people to examine them, and discuss briefly the need to build away from the edge of water and to use earthquake engineering techniques. Write on the board:

Without a strong foundation, nothing can stand.

Now have the group look at pages 56 and 57. Ask a prepared volunteer to slowly and clearly read Luke 6:47–49.

You might want to have the section read a second time for emphasis. Then read the following script:

We are the Church, the people of God. We come to God, listen to his words, and act on them. Our Church is built on him, our strong foundation.

Have another volunteer read Ephesians 2:19–20. Then invite the young people to read the passage together. Have them replace the pronoun *you* with *me*.

Chapter Warm-up: Distribute blank sheets of paper, one sheet to each person. Direct the young people to fold the sheet in half vertically. Explain that they are to make a "passport" attesting to the fact that they are "fellow citizens . . . of the household of God." Some suggestions:

• On the cover, devise a seal that indicates who has issued your passport.

• On the inside, tell who you are: your name, date of birth, date of Baptism.

• Describe the community, the "country" of God to which you belong.

• Sign your "passport" as a mark of your citizenship.

Share the "passports" and discuss some of the information they contain.

Forum: An appointed reader begins by reading John 15:1–5. Then the leader selects young people at random to share the prayers they have written on the name card for the handout *The Vine and the Branches.* After as many as possible have responded, the leader invites all to read verse 5 from John's Gospel at the top of the handout.

Presentation ___ min.

◆ Have the group look at the photograph on page 58 while someone reads the opening copy. Invite responses to the questions. Stress that the most logical place to look for leadership was to those whom the apostles had ordained and appointed as their successors.

◆ Have a volunteer read the second and third paragraphs on page 59. Ask, "Why do you think Jesus gave Simon the new name of Peter? Why not a name that meant 'love' or 'sacrifice' or 'leader'?" (*Because Jesus was naming Peter to be the visible foundation of his Church on earth.*)

◆ Ask the young people to share the six key ideas they have underlined in this chapter. Discuss their choices; then take a minute to have them highlight those highlighted on your reduced pages.

◆ Ask the young people to react to the photograph on page 58. What might it symbolize about the Church after the death of the apostles? (*The ministry of the apostles was continued by the bishops who "walked in their footsteps" and led the Church to the farthest parts of the earth.*)

Invite the group to suggest other images that might convey this idea.

If the Church is founded on Christ and the apostles, what happened after the apostles died? Where did the people of God turn for leadership? What do you think?

58

From Apostle to Bishop

The roots of Church leadership extend back to Jesus and the apostles. Jesus handpicked a group we know as the Twelve and gathered them around himself. These were the apostles. From their close contact with Jesus, they were privileged to know "the mysteries of the kingdom of heaven" (Matthew 13:11). Jesus shared his mission and authority with them. They were to be the pillars upon which he would build his Church.

While Jesus was speaking to the Twelve one day, he asked them what people were saying about him and who he was. It was Simon Peter who finally spoke up and said, "You are the Messiah, the Son of the living God" (Matthew 16:16). Simon was speaking for the other apostles as well when he said that Jesus was the promised Messiah.

Jesus answered this expression of faith in him by changing Simon's name to Peter, meaning "rock." Jesus said, "I say to you, you are Peter, and upon this rock I will build my church, and the gates of the netherworld shall not prevail against it. I will give you the keys to the kingdom of heaven" (Matthew 16:18–19).

Jesus' special recognition of Peter gave him a place of authority above the others but not apart from them. The work of teaching, governing, and sanctifying people in Jesus' name was not to be his alone. It was to be shared by all the apostles with Peter. The Twelve formed a single body, or college; they received their mission together. Although the keys to the kingdom were given to Peter's care, he and the other apostles were the foundation of that Church in which Christ is the cornerstone.

After the ascension of Jesus and Pentecost, the apostles traveled to every part of the world that they knew. With great courage they followed the promptings of the Holy Spirit and established local Churches wherever they went. They did not stay in any one place, however, because they were leaders of the whole Church.

A Wider Ministry The twelve apostles shared their work with others in the wider ministry of founding and organizing Churches. Sometimes these others, like Paul, were also called "apostles" even though they were not part of the original Twelve. But other names, such as "prophet" and "evangelist," were also used to describe these apostolic leaders. The reason is that official titles had not yet been determined by the Church.

A Local Ministry Once a local Church became established, the apostolic leaders moved on. But they chose and left behind local Church officers, whom they had ordained by the laying on of hands. These men, too, were called by a number of different titles: "pastor" or "teacher" or "presbyter" (priest, elder) or "bishop" (overseer). The words seemed to have been used interchangeably. Assisted by deacons, these local Church officers presided over their Churches under the authority of the apostles, prophets, and evangelists. But their official titles, like those of the apostolic leaders, had not yet been determined.

The Threefold Ministry After the Church began to spread around the world, the general traveling ministry of the apostolic leaders became less necessary. It gradually died out as the apostolic leaders passed away. Some of them may have settled in local Churches, as we know James had done in Jerusalem and Timothy in Ephesus. In any event the title of bishop became reserved only for the successors of the apostolic leaders and the title of presbyter (priest) for the other local officers. The title of deacon remained unchanged.

The ministry of the apostles, therefore, was continued and assured in the ministry of the local bishops. These bishops were the vital link to the apostles and thus to Christ himself. By A.D. 110 Ignatius of Antioch could speak of the threefold ministry of bishop, presbyter (priest), and deacon as "established in the farthest parts of the earth." Through the laying on of hands, we have the same threefold ministry today.

59

◆ Form two teams. Let each team choose a name and appoint a "Responder" for their team. Before responding to a question, they may confer with one another before the "Responder" gives the team's answer to the whole group. Appoint an "Emcee" who asks the following questions of the teams in turn. If a team fails to give an appropriate answer, the other team may respond. Appoint a scorekeeper, and you be the judge!

• How far into the past do the roots of Church leadership extend? (*to Jesus and the apostles*)

• Who were the apostles? (*the Twelve, who were handpicked by Jesus*)

• What did Jesus share with the apostles? (*his mission and his authority*)

• In what works were the apostles to engage? (*teaching, governing, and sanctifying*)

• What did the apostles do after Pentecost? (*They traveled to every part of the world that they knew and established local Churches.*)

• What names were used to describe the Church's apostolic leaders? (*apostles and evangelists*)

• How did the apostolic leaders provide for leadership in the local churches? (*The apostles chose and ordained by the laying on of hands local Church officers. These men were called by a number of different titles: pastor, teacher, presbyter, bishop.*)

• What happened after the apostolic leaders died? (*The ministry of the apostles was continued and assured in the ministry of the local bishops.*)

• What was the threefold ministry that Ignatius of Antioch referred to as being "established in the farthest parts of the earth"? (*bishop, presbyter [priest], and deacon*)

Presentation (cont'd)

◆ Ask the young people to take a minute to respond to the 👑 **thought provoker** on page 60. Listen to their questions and invite the group to suggest possible responses the apostles might give.

◆ Have a previously prepared "visitor" join the group. Introduce him as Saint Ignatius of Antioch. Ignatius tells the group that he wants to share with them a letter he has just finished writing to the Christians in Smyrna reminding them to be strong in faith and to know what is important. Ignatius then reads the excerpt from his letter on page 60.

◆ Ask the young people to delineate the clear picture of the Church presented by Saint Ignatius (see paragraph one, right column, page 60). Then ask a volunteer to summarize the importance of the bishop in the Church. The summary should include the following three points:

• Without the bishop there would be no priests or deacons because they must be ordained by the bishop.

• There would be no celebration of the Eucharist and/or of most of the other sacraments.

• The link to Christ through the apostles would be missing.

◆ Direct attention to the photos on these pages. Discuss how each tells about the work of a bishop.

👑 *If you could ask a question of an early Church leader who knew Jesus, what would the question be?*

Acting in the Name of Christ

Imagine that you are a member of the early Church and that it is a time of persecution. During the Eucharist one Sunday, a letter is read to the assembled community. The letter is from the bishop of a neighboring Church. His name is Ignatius, the bishop of Antioch, and not many days ago he was led away in chains. Knowing that you and other Christians might be afraid, Ignatius wants you to be strong in your faith and to know what is important. This is what he writes:

> All of you must follow your bishop, as Jesus followed the Father, and follow the presbyters as you would the apostles; and to the deacons pay respect, as to God's law. Let no one carry on the work of the Church apart from the bishop. There is only one true Eucharist: the one over which the bishop or one of his delegates presides. Wherever the bishop is, that is where the people should be; even as where Jesus is, there is the Universal Church.
> *Letter to the Smyrnaeans, 8*

60

What a clear picture Ignatius presents of the Church. The people of God are assembled at the altar, with the bishop or one of his presbyters presiding over the celebration of the Eucharist. The bishop stands at the center of the community. Assisted by the presbyters and deacons, he leads the Church with the authority of the apostles and in the name of Jesus. In fact he is the vital link to them in the life of the Church.

How important is the bishop? Very important! Without him there would be no presbyters (priests) or deacons because they are ordained by the bishop. This means that there could be no Eucharist and that most of the other sacraments could not be celebrated. Without the bishop the link to Christ through the apostles would be missing. That is why Cyprian, a third-century Father of the Church, could say, "The bishop is in the Church and the Church in the bishop."

CATHOLIC ID — What is the relationship between the bishop of a diocese and the pope? The pope, the bishop of Rome, is the successor of Saint Peter. He holds the first place in the college of bishops as Peter held the first place in the college of apostles. Therefore the pope and the other bishops must always work together. One bishop does not work independently of the others.

Teaching, Governing, Sanctifying

Jesus wanted all his disciples to be servants of one another, not masters. He said, "Let the greatest among you be as the youngest, and the leader as the servant," and "I am among you as the one who serves" (Luke 22:26, 27). This does not mean, however, that no one was to have authority in the Church. Every human organization must have some authority to help it identify itself, to help bring unity, and to resolve any conflicts or problems. The Church is no different.

Jesus is the source of all authority and ministry in the Church. Knowing how important this authority would be, he shared it with the apostles and those who were to succeed them. That is why bishops succeed the apostles in their office of teaching, governing, and sanctifying in the name of Christ.

Teaching The bishops are the chief teachers of the Church. As the chief teachers, they succeed to the office of the apostles and prophets. As links to the apostles, the bishops are charged with the sacred duty of passing on the complete and authentic teaching of Jesus and the apostolic Church. Guided by the Holy Spirit, they are to transmit and make clear what has been revealed to us by God; they are entrusted by God to safeguard the great deposit of faith that belongs to the Church.

What do these pictures tell us about the work of a bishop?

◆ Ask, "What do we mean when we say the bishops are the chief teachers of the Church?" (*As successors of the apostles, they have the sacred duty of passing on the complete and authentic teaching of Jesus and the apostolic Church.*)

◆ Ask a volunteer to summarize *Catholic ID*. Have the young people identify the diocese in which they live and its bishop. Explain that if it is a large diocese with many Church members, the bishop may be an archbishop or cardinal; he may be helped by a few auxiliary bishops.

FYI Saint Charles Borromeo (1538–1584) acted in the name of Christ. He was ordained a priest in 1563 and appointed Bishop of Milan in Italy shortly after. Charles is remembered for his concern for the poor and for establishing the Confraternity of Christian Doctrine for the religious education of children. In 1576 when a plague struck Milan, Charles ministered to the sick and dying until the plague subsided two years later. Charles had little concern for wealth and possessions. Although he suffered from a speech defect, he and his message of the gospels were heard and accepted by many.

Presentation (cont'd)

◆ Ask the young people to describe the bishop's role in *governing* the Church. (*The bishop directs the life of the Church in his diocese; he keeps it focused on the mission of building God's kingdom; he cares for the weak.*) Then have them describe the bishop's role of *sanctifying*. (*He sanctifies through prayer, word and sacrament, especially the Eucharist.*)

◆ Point out the ☼ **thought provoker** on page 62. Invite a discussion of these ideas. If the young people do not mention it, point out the words of Jesus on page 61.

◆ Have a volunteer read *On Line with the Parish*. Encourage the young people to pray for their bishop at Mass this week.

Assessment: This chapter marks the midpoint of the semester. If you wish to use the *Mid-Semester Assessment*, see pages 124 and 125. Allow about twenty minutes for its completion.

If you plan to administer *Chapter 7 Assessment*, allow about ten minutes for its completion.

Conclusion ___ min.

◆ Direct attention to *Words to Remember*. Have the young people find the definition and write it in the space provided. The word *presbyter* is defined on page 59.

This work of the bishops is done as a service to the other members of the Church so that our faith may rest secure on a strong foundation.

Governing   The bishops are the chief authorities and pastors (shepherds) in the Church. Each bishop exercises authority in his diocese. He also shares a worldwide authority with the pope and the other bishops. In the diocese the bishop directs the life of the Church. He is the visible sign of its unity. He coordinates its work, he helps it to keep focused on its true mission of building God's kingdom, and he brings people of different backgrounds together in harmony. Like Christ the Good Shepherd, the bishop is to watch over all those under his care, especially the weak.

Sanctifying   The bishop has the fullness of the sacrament of Holy Orders. He is the chief priest of the diocese and shares this priesthood with the presbyters, whom he ordains. With these coworkers he sanctifies the Church through prayer and the ministry of both word and sacrament, especially the Eucharist. Through the bishop we are reminded that the Eucharist is the center of the life of the Church.

☼ *Do you think the person who has the most authority should be the one who serves others? Why or why not? What did Jesus think?*

62

Answers for Chapter 7 Assessment
1. c 2. a 3. d 4. a 5. d
6. b 7. c 8. b 9. — 10. Accept correct responses. (See page 61)

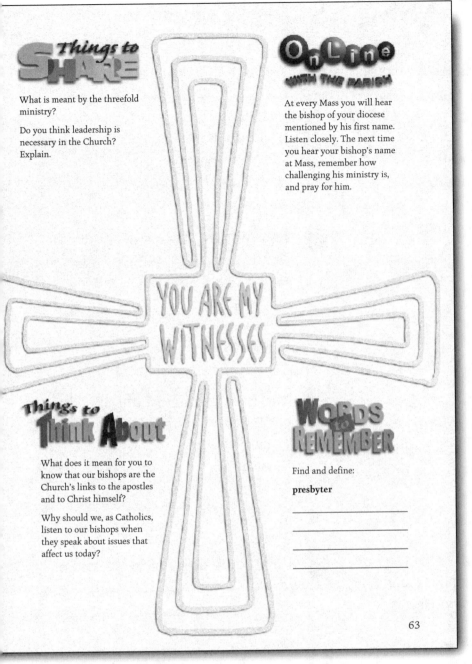

Things to SHARE

What is meant by the threefold ministry?

Do you think leadership is necessary in the Church? Explain.

OnLine WITH THE PARISH

At every Mass you will hear the bishop of your diocese mentioned by his first name. Listen closely. The next time you hear your bishop's name at Mass, remember how challenging his ministry is, and pray for him.

Things to Think About

What does it mean for you to know that our bishops are the Church's links to the apostles and to Christ himself?

Why should we, as Catholics, listen to our bishops when they speak about issues that affect us today?

WORDS to REMEMBER

Find and define:

presbyter

_____

_____

_____

63

Conclusion (cont'd)

◆ Form four groups. Assign each group one of the issues from *Things to Share* and *Things to Think About*. Allow a few minutes of preparation; then have a general sharing of ideas.

FORUM Assignment

✔ Read Chapter 8, pages 64–71. Underline in pencil six key ideas.

✔ Complete the handout *In Appreciation*, a letter to the bishop of your diocese.

Closing Prayer: Pause for a few seconds to establish a quiet, prayerful atmosphere. Play music softly in the background.

Ask the young people to read thoughtfully the journaling suggestion on page 51 of the *Creed Journal*. After their reflection, allow time for them to write their thoughts. If the *Creed Journal* is not available, have them write in their own journals their thoughts and feelings about belonging to the Catholic Church.

Evaluation: Do the young people understand that the bishops succeed the apostles in their office of teaching, governing, and sanctifying in the name of Christ?

FOR CHAPTER 8

- preparation of opening-prayer volunteers
- copies of handout, page 64C
- copies of *Chapter 8 Assessment*, page 71A (optional)
- copies of *Highlights for Home*, page 71B

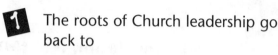Assessment

1 The roots of Church leadership go back to

a. Moses.

b. Adam and Eve.

c. Jesus and the apostles.

d. Jesus and John the Baptist.

2 The twelve leaders chosen by Jesus were called

a. the apostles.

b. the early Church.

c. the disciples.

d. bishops.

3 The work of the bishop is

a. whatever he is most interested in accomplishing.

b. to be the pastor of a parish.

c. not necessary to the life of the Church.

d. to teach, govern, and sanctify.

4 The threefold ministry refers to

a. bishops, priests, and deacons.

b. the Father, Son, and Holy Spirit.

c. the presbyter, priest, and pastor.

d. the overseer, bishop, and episcopacy.

5 What title was not used in the early Church for men ordained by apostolic leaders?

a. teacher

b. pastor

c. bishop

d. cardinal

6 Priests and deacons are ordained by

a. the pope.

b. a bishop.

c. other priests.

d. none of the above

7 Jesus wanted those in authority to be the _____ of others.

a. masters

b. disciples

c. servants

d. friends

8 The chief teachers of the Church are the

a. cardinals.

b. bishops.

c. priests.

d. presbyters.

9 What is the name of the bishop of your diocese? _____

_____

10 Name two ways the bishop exercises authority in his diocese.

_____

_____

_____

_____

_____

_____

_____

Chapter 7: A Strong Foundation

Highlights for Home

Focus on Faith

In this chapter the young people learn that the roots of Church leadership extend back to Jesus and the apostles. Jesus handpicked a group that we know as the Twelve. Jesus shared his mission and authority with them. They were to be the pillars upon which he would build his Church.

Through the laying on of hands, the bishops succeed the apostles in their office of teaching, governing, and sanctifying in the name of Christ. As links to the apostles, the bishops are charged with the sacred duty of passing on the complete and authentic teaching of Jesus and the apostolic Church. The bishop of each diocese coordinates its work, helping it to keep focused on its true mission of building God's kingdom. With the priests whom he ordains, he sanctifies the Church through prayer and the ministry of both word and sacrament, especially the Eucharist.

Conversation Starters

. . . . a few ideas to talk about together . . . .

◆ Do I ever think of praying for the bishop of my diocese? What should I ask for him?

◆ If one of the apostles showed up in my parish this week, what might surprise him?

◆ Why does the Church compare the role of a bishop to that of a shepherd?

Feature Focus

In *Catholic ID* on page 60, the young people learned about the relationship between the bishop of a diocese and the pope. They learned that the pope, the bishop of Rome, is the successor of Saint Peter. The pope and the bishops of all dioceses throughout the world always work together. No one bishop works independently.

Reflection

Look at the photograph of the building framework on pages 56 and 57. Draw one like it on a piece of paper. On each beam, write one of the leadership qualities the apostles and their successors needed to teach, govern, and sanctify in Jesus' name.

Now draw another framework. Write on each beam a leadership quality you have or would like to develop. Ask the Holy Spirit to strengthen these qualities within you so that you may serve others in Jesus' name.

THE CHURCH OF JESUS CHRIST

Adult Focus

Studying and discussing this chapter will help the young people to broaden their understanding of the Church as they learn about its visible and invisible elements. Together all of these elements make up the Church of Christ, which can be found in its essential completeness in the Catholic Church.

The Catholic Church is the community of those who profess faith in Jesus Christ, Son of God and risen Lord, and publicly affirm this faith through Baptism. Members of the Church celebrate that faith through the Eucharist and other sacraments, and accept the teachings of Christ passed down from the apostles. They carry out the sacramental life and mission of the Church under the leadership of those ordained in apostolic succession, that is, the pope and other bishops, together with their priests and deacons.

Although we Catholics accept all Christians as brothers and sisters in Christ, we also recognize that the Catholic Church is different from other Churches in belief, practice, and organization. We pray that someday separations will be healed and Christ's followers will believe as one.

Catechism Focus

The themes of this chapter correspond to paragraphs 877–896 of the *Catechism*.

Enrichment Activities

Doing an Interfaith Project

Arrange a meeting between representatives from your group and members of a Protestant youth group. Plan these interfaith events, such as the following:

◆ a "fun and food" event

◆ a small group exchange on personal faith experience and mutual faith questions

◆ a prayer service to pray for those in your local community who are in need

◆ a prayer service of remembrance for faith ancestors who suffered from and worked to end intolerance.

Charting the Elements

Form small groups. Give each group a sheet of posterboard, and direct the groups to make a chart outlining the visible and invisible elements of the Church. Ask the groups to design a visual symbol for each element.

Teaching Resources

Overview

To explore the elements of the Church; to develop a clear description of the Catholic Church; to engender appreciation for the gift of membership in the Church.

Opening Prayer Ideas

The leader calls the group to prayer: "Let us listen to the ways our ancestors in the Church lived their faith." Then read together Acts 2:42–47. Pause in silence.

or

Look at the photo on pages 64 and 65. Pray together the words on page 65.

Materials

- Bibles, journals, and highlighters

Creed Journal:
For Chapter 8, use page 49.

REPRODUCIBLE MASTERS
- handout *I Believe*, page 64C
- *Chapter 8 Assessment*, page 71A
- *Highlights for Home*, page 71B

Supplemental Resources

VIDEO
What Catholics Believe About the Church
Videos with Values
1944 Innerbelt Center Drive
St. Louis, MO 63114–5718

CHAPTER eight

I Believe

You have learned a great deal about the Church in these last few sessions. Think over what you have learned. Ask yourself: Are these just *facts* I have learned or are they *deep beliefs*? Then write some things that you really believe about the Church.

I believe

I believe

I believe

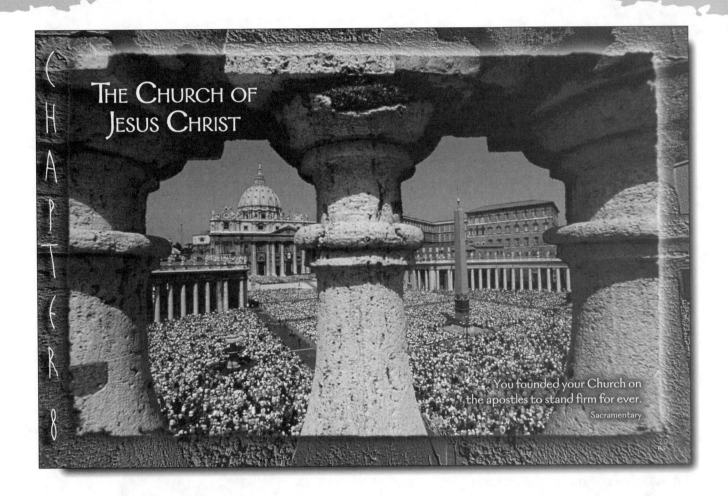

THE CHURCH OF JESUS CHRIST

You founded your Church on the apostles to stand firm for ever.
Sacramentary

Objectives: To explore the elements of the Church; to develop a clear description of the Catholic Church; to engender appreciation for the gift of membership in the Church.

Introduction ___ min.

Opening Prayer: Have the young people form small groups for shared Scripture reflection. Assign each group one of the following Scripture passages:

• Walking on the Water (Matthew 14:22–33)
• Peter's Confession about Jesus (Mark 8:27–30)
• The Transfiguration of Jesus (Mark 9:2–8)
• Peter's Denial of Jesus (Mark 14:66–72)
• Jesus Appears to the Disciples (John 21:1–14)

Allow the young people about five minutes to reflect on and discuss what their reading says about Peter's relationship with Jesus. Then ask a representative from each group to share the group's reflections.

After the sharing, read together Jesus' discussion with Peter (John 21:15–17). Ask, "Why do you think Jesus used the image of shepherding?" "Why did Jesus ask Peter to lead the Church?"

Chapter Warm-up: Invite the young people to look at the photo of Saint Peter's Square on pages 64 and 65. Explain that thousands gather in the square each Sunday to hear the pope, the successor of Saint Peter, address them. In A.D. 324 Constantine began the building of a basilica on the spot where it was thought Saint Peter was buried. The basilica was finished during the reign of his son Constantius. Work to replace Constantine's basilica, which was leveled in war, began on April 18, 1506, when Pope Julius II laid the cornerstone. Between 1657 and 1663 the sets of colonnades designed by the architect Bernini were erected. They include 284 columns over which stand 140 statues of martyrs and confessors.

If possible have several views of St. Peter's available to show the group.

Forum: Have the young people form small groups. There should be a leader for each group who invites the members to share their letters to the bishop. After hearing the letters, each group should decide on the letter they think is best. The director invites each group to share its chosen letter; then the whole group should choose one letter to be prepared and sent to the bishop. You may want to invite all the young people to sign their names.

Presentation ___ min.

◆ Have a volunteer read the opening experience on the top of page 66 while the group looks again at the photograph on pages 64 and 65. Invite the young people to share any experiences like this that they might have had. Then ask them to reflect quietly on the final question before responding. A "secretary" might list their ideas on the board.

◆ Ask, "What did the Second Vatican Council teach about the meaning of the Church?" (*that the Church, founded upon Christ and the apostles, is made up of a number of different elements, visible and invisible*) Then review the marks of the Church: the Church is one, holy, catholic, and apostolic.

◆ Invite the young people to share the six key ideas they have underlined. Discuss their choices briefly. Then have them highlight those highlighted on your reduced pages.

◆ Ask volunteers to name the visible elements of the Church. (*Scripture, Baptism, episcopacy, Eucharist, doctrines of faith, and devotion to Mary*)

RECENTLY some young Americans found themselves in St. Peter's square in Rome. They joined thousands who had gathered for a Mass with the Holy Father.

"It was like swimming in a sea of people from all over the world, speaking every language imaginable!" one of them remarked later.

"Then Mass began," said another. "It was amazing. Suddenly nationalities and languages didn't seem to matter. We were all one. I'll never forget it."

Have you ever had an experience like this? What does it really mean to belong to the people of God?

The Church of Christ

A correct understanding of the Church is so important for Catholics that it was one of the major topics of the Second Vatican Council. After long reflection and discussion, the bishops, who had gathered from every part of the world, gave us a deep insight into the meaning of the Church. They taught that the Church of Christ, the Church founded upon Christ and the apostles, is made up of a number of "elements." Without these basic elements there would be no Church.

First and foremost the Church is one, holy, catholic, and apostolic. These characteristics

are essential features of the Church. But there are other elements that are essential to the Church, too. These include both visible and invisible elements.

The *visible elements*, as the name suggests, are those that make the Church a recognizable body in the world. After all, the Church is an organization of people with leaders, beliefs, laws, and practices. This organization can be readily seen and recognized by all. Among the vital elements of the Church that make it visible, the council bishops mentioned the following:

66

- Scripture, which is the Church's written record of God's revelation. Scripture cannot be changed or ignored because it is a permanent document.
- Baptism, along with the other sacraments of the Church. Remember that no one can become a member of the Church without first having been baptized.
- Episcopacy, which is the office of bishop. This includes the pope, the bishop of Rome. Episcopacy links the Church through the apostles to Christ himself.
- Eucharist, which is the source and high point of the Church's life.
- Doctrines of faith, which are the teachings that come down to us from the time of the apostles.
- Devotion to Mary, the Mother of God. Her spiritual motherhood extends to all the members of the Church.

Second Vatican Council, 1962–1965

The *invisible elements* have to do with the Church's inner life. As the name suggests, the elements cannot be seen except in their results. The members of the Church show these elements by the way they live. Among the vital elements of the Church that cannot be seen, the council bishops mentioned the following:

- The life of grace, which is a participation in the very life of God.
- The theological virtues of faith, hope, and love, which are gifts from God. They are powers enabling us to act as children of God.
- The gifts of the Holy Spirit, who is continually sanctifying the Church.

CATHOLIC TEACHINGS

About the Gifts of the Holy Spirit

The Church teaches that there are seven gifts of the Holy Spirit and that these are part of the invisible elements of the Church. These gifts are wisdom, understanding, right judgment, courage, knowledge, reverence, and wonder and awe. Through these gifts we become open to the promptings of the Holy Spirit in our lives.

67

◆ You may want to share with the group the following imaging exercise as a mnemonic device to help the young people remember the visible elements of the Church.

Close your eyes and visualize your parish church building. Over the door of the church is a large sign bearing the letters **SBEED**. These are the first letters of the Church's visible elements: "S" for Scripture; "B" for Baptism; "E" for. . . .

◆ Direct attention to *Catholic Teachings* on page 67. List the gifts of the Spirit on the board and explain each one as follows:

- *Wisdom* helps us to know the right things to do.
- *Understanding* helps us to explain and live our faith as informed Catholics.
- *Right judgment* helps us to make good decisions.
- *Courage* helps us to do God's will without fear.
- *Knowledge* helps us to learn our faith from Scripture and Catholic tradition.
- *Reverence* helps us to show our love for God and to pray for ourselves and others.
- *The gift of wonder and awe* helps us to show respect for God, for others, and for God's gifts of creation.

Point out that we all share in these gifts of the Holy Spirit but we have to be more aware of how the Holy Spirit is "prompting" us to use them.

FYI New Testament writers used the Greek word *ekklesia* for Church. This was a translation of a Hebrew word that meant "an assembly called by God to hear his word, offer worship, and form a covenant community with him and each other." Now that's a powerful word! The Greek word *ekklesia* became *ecclesia* in Latin, then *chiesa* in Italian, *iglesia* in Spanish, and *église* in French. In German it became *kirche* and finally *church* in English.

Presentation (cont'd)

◆ Discuss the Second Vatican Council's teaching that the Church of Christ "subsists" in the Catholic Church. Ask the young people to highlight the sentence on page 68 that explains the meaning of *subsists*.

◆ Ask the young people to work in pairs to write clear descriptions of the Catholic Church. The descriptions should reflect all of the points listed on page 68.

Have the young people share and discuss their descriptions. Invite them to share the significance of the photos on pages 68 and 69. Ask, "How do these describe the mystery of the Church?"

Conclude the discussion by emphasizing that the Catholic Church is something special and that we are privileged to be members of it.

◆ Ask, "What is our relationship to other Christians?" (*We accept all other Christians as our brothers and sisters in Christ.*)

The Catholic Church

Look again at the elements of the Church. Each must be present in Christ's Church. And where do we find that Church of Christ? The bishops of the council gave a clear answer. They said that the Church of Christ can be found in its essential fullness in the Catholic Church. This is what they taught:

> This is the unique Church of Christ which in the Creed we avow as one, holy, catholic, and apostolic. . . . This Church, constituted and organized in the world as a society, subsists in the Catholic Church, which is governed by the successor of Peter and by the bishops in union with that successor, although many elements of sanctification and of truth can be found outside her visible structure.
> *Church*, 8

The council teaching is that the Church of Christ "subsists" in the Catholic Church. This means that the Church of Christ is truly present in its essential completeness in the Catholic Church. However, as the bishops pointed out, some of the elements of the Church are present in other Christian Churches and communities. For example, all Christians accept and revere Scripture. All Christians are received into the body of Christ through Baptism and enjoy the life of sanctifying grace. Not all Christians, however, continue fully in the apostolic life of the Church under the leadership of the pope and bishops, the successors of the apostles. Nor do all of them have the seven sacraments.

What does this council teaching about the Catholic Church have to do with our daily lives? Everything! That is why we will spend the rest of this chapter trying to understand its importance.

Something Special

If somebody asked you to give the best definition of a precious jewel, such as an emerald, it would not be an easy task. That is because there would be so much to say about the luster and beauty of the gem, its many sides and reflective powers. So it is with the Catholic Church. It, too, has so many aspects that it is difficult to capture all of them in just a few words. However, based on what we have already studied, we can begin to build a helpful definition of the Catholic Church.

We can say that the *Catholic Church* is the community of those who follow Jesus Christ, the community that:

• professes belief in Jesus Christ, the Son of God and risen Lord

• publicly affirms its belief in Christ through Baptism

• celebrates that faith through the Eucharist and other sacraments

• accepts the teachings of Christ that have come down from the time of the apostles

• carries out the sacramental life and mission of the Church under the leadership of those ordained in apostolic succession, that is, the pope and other bishops, together with their priests and deacons.

This definition of the Catholic Church summarizes the key elements of the Church of Christ, both visible and invisible. This is the Church that we experience in our local parish and diocese. This is the Church that we experience when we gather together around the Lord's table to celebrate the Eucharist. This is the Church that exists all over the world. This is also the Church that receives from Christ our Savior "the fullness of the means of salvation" (*Catechism*, 830).

Can there be any doubt, then, that the Catholic Church is something special and that we are privileged to be members of it?

Practical Matters

Knowing how special it is to be a Catholic, we need to ask an important question: What is our relationship to other Christians? Catholics should make no mistake about it. We accept all other Christians as our brothers and sisters in Christ. The Second Vatican Council taught that the Catholic Church accepts other Christians "with respect and affection" (*Ecumenism*, 3).

Nevertheless we do not believe that the Catholic Church and other Christian Churches are all the same. There are differences in belief, practice, and Church organization that separate us. We do not share unity now, but it is our hope that one day all of Christ's followers will be united as one. This is the hard work of ecumenism. *Ecumenism* refers to the effort on the part of Catholics and other Christians to work toward full unity among all baptized people around the world.

A nonbeliever asks you, "What makes the Catholic Church special?" What would your answer be?

◆ Ask the young people what their response would be to young people of other Christian denominations who say to them, "The only difference between our Churches is that you have to go to Mass every Sunday."

Then ask, "Are the Catholic Church and other Christian churches the same?" Help the young people understand that Christian unity is not yet a reality and that important differences in belief, practice, and Church organization remain.

◆ Write *ecumenism* on the board. Have a volunteer define the word. Make sure the young people have highlighted the definition on page 69.

Invite the young people to reflect on what it means to be a member of the Church. Then ask them to do the journaling activity on page 49 of the *Creed Journal*. If possible, allow about eight minutes for journaling.

Presentation (cont'd)

◆ Discuss the reasons why the Church advises any Catholic planning to marry a non-Catholic to spend time in serious thought and preparation. Ask, "What does the Church ask the Catholic to do?"

◆ Have a volunteer read aloud the *Scripture Update* on page 70. Then quietly read John 21:15–17 to the group. Ask, "What did Jesus mean by 'feed my sheep'?" "What authority and responsibility was Jesus giving to Peter as head of the apostles?" (*to teach, govern, and sanctify the Church*)

◆ Have the young people find a definition of *visible elements of the Church* and write it under *Words to Remember*.

Conclusion ___ min.

◆ Discuss the two questions of *Things to Share* and those posed in *On Line with the Parish*.

◆ Challenge the young people to do the second item for *Things to Think About*. When the definition is complete, encourage the group to learn it by heart.

Assessment: If you plan to administer *Chapter 8 Assessment*, allow about ten minutes for its completion.

To achieve unity, we try to pray and work together with other Christians. But true unity can never be attained if we ignore the real differences that separate us. Take the Eucharist, for example. Unlike some other Christians, Catholics believe that Christ is truly present in the Eucharist and that the Eucharist is a sign of unity. That is why those who do not share our faith are not invited to receive Communion when they visit and attend our celebrations of the Mass. The reception of Holy Communion is a sign of the unity we have in faith, life, and worship within our Catholic community. To share Communion with those not united with us would deny what is really true—that we are not yet one in faith.

In the same way Catholics may not receive communion in Churches that do not share with us our belief in the real presence and that do not have the sacrament of Holy Orders or the apostolic succession of bishops. Without these vital elements we cannot accept their communion as a valid sacrament. To do so would be to deny our belief in the sacramental system of the Church.

There are other occasions as well when we will need to look carefully at the special nature of our Catholic life and faith. Take, for example, marriage between Catholics and non-Catholics. The Church asks the couple planning such a marriage to spend serious time in thought and preparation before taking this important step. The Church, while respecting the faith of the non-Catholic party, asks the Catholic to reaffirm his or her faith. In addition the Catholic is asked to do all in his or her power to see that the children of this marriage are brought up as Catholics. This makes sense, of course. If being a member of the Catholic Church is so important, then all Catholics will want to share their faith with their children.

Think of some ways that you can grow in a deeper appreciation of your Catholic faith.

*Scripture*UPDATE

If anything is clear in the gospels, it is the close relationship Christ had with his apostles. They were the foundation upon which he built his Church. Our link to Christ and his mission is through the bishops, the successors to the apostles. This apostolic succession of the bishops is an important part of the apostolic succession of the whole Church.

70

Answers for Chapter 8 Assessment

1. c	**2.** d	**3.** d	**4.** c	**5.** a
6. c	**7.** b	**8.** b	**9.** c	**10.** See page 67.

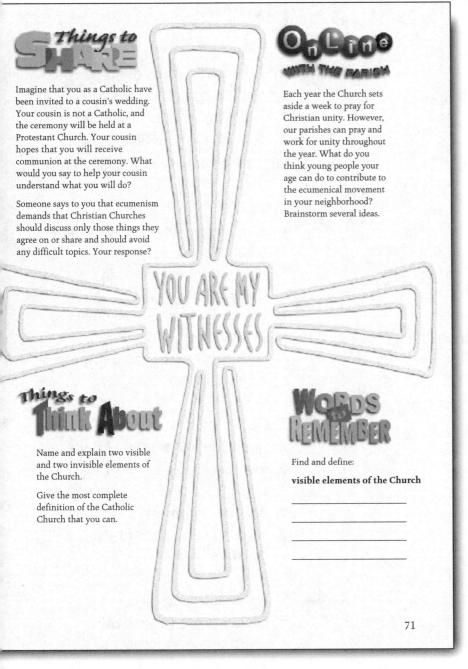

Things to SHARE

Imagine that you as a Catholic have been invited to a cousin's wedding. Your cousin is not a Catholic, and the ceremony will be held at a Protestant Church. Your cousin hopes that you will receive communion at the ceremony. What would you say to help your cousin understand what you will do?

Someone says to you that ecumenism demands that Christian Churches should discuss only those things they agree on or share and should avoid any difficult topics. Your response?

OnLine WITH THE PARISH

Each year the Church sets aside a week to pray for Christian unity. However, our parishes can pray and work for unity throughout the year. What do you think young people your age can do to contribute to the ecumenical movement in your neighborhood? Brainstorm several ideas.

Things to Think About

Name and explain two visible and two invisible elements of the Church.

Give the most complete definition of the Catholic Church that you can.

Words to REMEMBER

Find and define:

visible elements of the Church

_____

_____

_____

_____

YOU ARE MY WITNESSES

71

Conclusion (cont'd)

FORUM Assignment

✔ Read Chapter 9, pages 72–79. Underline in pencil six key ideas.

✔ Complete the handout *I Believe.* Prepare your response to the ⚡ **thought provoker** on page 69.

Closing Prayer: Invite the young people to look at the photograph on page 70. Explain that this photo shows an ancient form of "praying hands"—they are open, cupped, as if offering something or waiting to receive something. Invite the young people to hold their hands in this way, to close their eyes, and to think of all Christ has given them in the Church.

Then have the young people in turn mention one way they will try to grow in appreciation of their Catholic faith.

Evaluation: Do the young people demonstrate an understanding of the elements of the Catholic Church? Have they expressed appreciation for the gift of their Catholic faith?

FOR CHAPTER 9

- copies of handout *Whatever!* page 80C
- copies of *Chapter 10 Assessment,* page 87A
- copies of *Highlights for Home,* page 87B

Assessment

 1 The theological virtues are
  a. faith, respect, and love.
  b. poverty, chastity, and obedience.
  c. faith, hope, and love.
  d. faith, reverence, and love.

 2 The gifts of the Holy Spirit are
  a. visible elements of the Church.
  b. present in ordained persons only.
  c. theological virtues.
  d. invisible elements of the Church.

3 An invisible element of the Church is
  a. Scripture.
  b. devotion to Mary.
  c. episcopacy.
  d. our life of grace.

4 *Grace* means
  a. "receiving the good news."
  b. "the mission of the Christ."
  c. "participation in the life of God."
  d. "being linked to the apostles."

5 Without _____ , one cannot become a member of the Church.
  a. Baptism
  b. receiving Eucharist
  c. being an adult
  d. a long preparation period

 6 The term *episcopacy* refers to
  a. the theological virtues.
  b. working for Christian unity.
  c. the office of the bishop.
  d. the universality of the Church.

 7 The Church of Christ
  a. is found equally in all Christian Churches.
  b. is found in its fullness in the Catholic Church.
  c. has changed drastically over the centuries.
  d. no longer exists as it did in the early Christian Churches.

 8 The ecumenical movement
  a. has achieved its goal of unity.
  b. involves Christians working for unity.
  c. encourages rivalry.
  d. is based on argument over doctrine.

 9 Find the *false* statement.
  a. Catholics are to treat other Christians with respect and affection.
  b. All Christians are our brothers and sisters.
  c. All Christian Churches are the same.
  d. We hope one day to be united.

 10 Name and explain three visible elements of the Church. Write your response on the reverse side of this page.

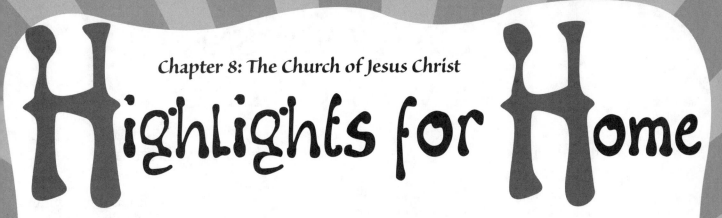

Chapter 8: The Church of Jesus Christ

Highlights for Home

Focus on Faith

In this chapter, the young people took a deep look at the Church. As we profess in the Creed each Sunday, the Church is one, holy, catholic, and apostolic. These characteristics are essential features of the Church. But other elements, both visible and invisible, are also essential to the Church. The Second Vatican Council mentioned the following visible elements, which make Christ's Church a visible organization in the world: Scripture; Baptism and the other sacraments; the office of bishop, which links the Church through the apostles to Christ; Eucharist; doctrines of faith that come to us from the time of the apostles; and devotion to Mary.

The Council mentioned the following invisible elements: the life of grace; faith, hope, and love; and the gifts of the Holy Spirit.

Conversation Starters

. . . . a few ideas to talk about together . . . .

◆ Why am I proud to be a Catholic?

◆ In what ways can I help in the Church's ecumenical work?

Feature Focus

Catholic Teachings on page 67 reminds us of the Holy Spirit's work in us and in the Church. It is interesting to note how each of the gifts of the Spirit is in vibrant opposition to those basic sinful attitudes that weigh human beings down: pride, anger, greed, lust, envy, excess, and spiritual laziness. We should call on the Holy Spirit to help us overcome these tendencies to sin.

Reflection

Think about the invisible elements of the Church as you read the following words of Saint Augustine:

All you who are reborn in Christ, hear me.
Sing to the Lord a new song! . . .
Sing with your voice
   but also with your heart and deeds . . .
Be what you sing;
   Be the praise of God by living in God!

CATHOLICISM: A WAY OF LIFE

Adult Focus

Mother Teresa wrote, "The young are the builders of tomorrow. Youth today is in search of selflessness and, when it finds it, is prepared to embrace it." In this chapter the young people are asked to embrace their Catholic faith as a way of life.

As you present this chapter's key ideas, keep in mind that the young people sitting before you are future directors of religious education, lectors, sacristans, parish council members, and parents. They are the Church.

With the help of the Holy Spirit, you are preparing them to take their place in tomorrow's Catholic Church. It is important to share with them your appreciation and love for the Church in its rich diversity and beauty and to provide them with opportunities to examine the possible ways they may live their baptismal promises as adult members of the laity, religious communities, or the clergy.

Remember to pray often with the young people to "ask the master of the harvest to send out laborers [from among their generation] for his harvest" (Luke 10:2).

Let us pray with Mother Teresa that we will "let Christ work in us, and through us, with all His power, all His desire and all His love."

Catechism Focus

The themes of this chapter correspond to paragraphs 871–873, and 914–916 of the *Catechism*.

Enrichment Activities

Guest Speakers

Invite members of active religious communities to speak with the young people about the ways religious combine a life of prayer with a life of service. Have the young people prepare questions for them and, after the meeting, discuss what interested them the most.

Powerhouses of Prayer

Have the young people write letters to contemplative religious thanking them for their prayers for the Church and asking for prayers for their special intentions. You can find addresses for these communities in a diocesan directory.

Teaching Resources

Overview

To discover the dignity and importance of laity and religious in the Church; to understand religious community life and the evangelical counsels.

Opening Prayer Ideas

Have three young people do a dramatic reading of the parable of the rich fool (Luke 12:16–21). Pause briefly for reflection; then pray together:

> Jesus, help us to be rich in all that matters to you.

or

Read together and reflect on Luke 10:2.

Materials

- Bibles, journals, highlighters
- hymnals or copies of words of hymns from *Glory and Praise*
- pictures of religious in various ministries (optional)

REPRODUCIBLE MASTERS
- handout *The Good Life*, page 72C
- *Chapter 9 Assessment*, page 79A (optional)
- *Highlights for Home*, page 79B

Creed Journal:
For Chapter 9, use pages 52–53.

Supplemental Resources

VIDEOS
- *Seeking God: The Way of the Monk*
- *Monsieur Vincent*
- *Mother Teresa*

Ignatius Press
P.O. Box 1339
Ft. Collins, CO 80522

The Good Life

Imagine that you are a reporter for a Catholic youth magazine. You have been asked to do a report on life in religious communities. You decide to title your article "The Good Life" to communicate that though the religious life is challenging, it is rewarding and full of joy. Think of five questions for your interview. Write them in the space below.

1. _____
_____
_____

2. _____
_____
_____

3. _____
_____
_____

4. _____
_____
_____

5. _____
_____
_____

If you have the opportunity in the future, ask your questions of a religious.

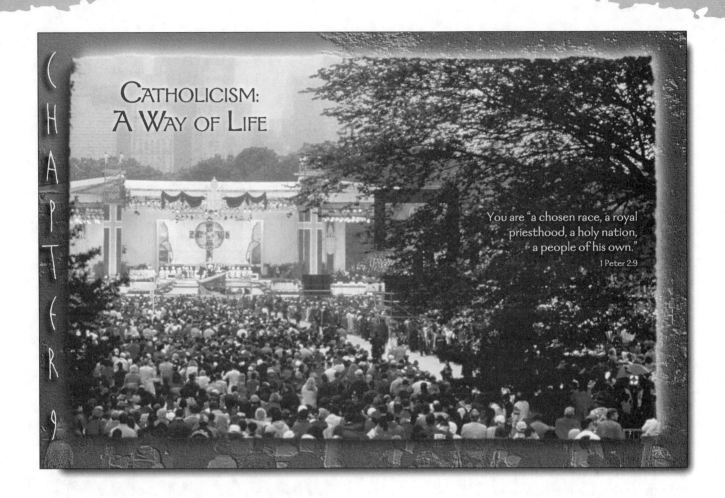

CATHOLICISM:
A WAY OF LIFE

You are "a chosen race, a royal priesthood, a holy nation, a people of his own."
1 Peter 2:9

Objectives: To discover the dignity and importance of laity and religious in the Church; to understand religious community life and the evangelical counsels.

Introduction ___ min.

Opening Prayer: Invite the young people to listen carefully to the following meditation written by Jonathan Huth when he was a student at St. John High School in Gulfport, Mississippi. Have them close their eyes and imagine they hear God speaking to them.

I call you: I'm a voice in nature, a silent whisper of faith. Sometimes you run from my open hands. I call you in service, I am present in the wind and warmth of the sun. I'm calling you to a life of peace. My voice is in the hills, the mountains, and lakes. It is in the face of a mother struggling to conquer hunger. It is the warmth of a father's

hands, striving to keep his family warm in their little thatched hut. I call you within the deserts of Mexico and in the kindness of oppressed people.

I call you from this material world to a world of true happiness, one that gratifies the soul and mind. My voice is calling you to be a servant for Christ, a messenger, a guide, and a life-lover. I'm calling you to reach out and be concerned for the world. Love all people, and never let go of my voice. It may start as a whisper but become a yell. Answer it. Come to me. Live out your true destiny. Become one with yourself, God, and society. Never reject my voice. You can learn so much about yourself and others from such a small whisper inside this troubled world.

Then ask the young people to look at the photo on pages 72 and 73. Have a volunteer read 1 Peter 2:9. Then gather together and pray Come, Holy Spirit on page 121.

Forum: Native Americans have a design called a "dream catcher." It is intended to catch dreams before they drift away from us. The leader of today's *forum* is a "belief catcher." The belief catcher's task today is to "catch" the belief statements the young people have formulated. The "belief catcher" calls on people at random to share the beliefs they have written on the hand-out sheet.

Presentation ___ min.

◆ Ask the three questions on page 74. Urge the young people to reflect before they respond. Encourage thoughtful, honest responses. Emphasize each one's importance in the Church.

◆ Take a minute to have the young people share the six key ideas they have underlined in this chapter. Discuss their choices. Then have them high-light those that are highlighted on your reduced pages.

◆ Have two volunteers do a dramatic reading of Jeremiah 1:4–7. Then explain, "Something wonderful happens when we are baptized. What is it?" (*We become new creations in Christ, share in God's own life, and are called to a new way of life—to join in the mission of Christ to the world.*)

Then have a volunteer write on the board the three ways Catholics live this new life. (*as members of religious communities, as ordained ministers, or as laypeople*)

ARE you an important member of the Church? Does what you do really make a difference? What do you think?

74

The Laity

Something wonderful happens when people are baptized and become members of the Church. From that very moment they are changed forever. At Baptism we become not only new creations in Christ and share in God's own life, but we are called to a new way of life. We are called to join in the mission of Christ to the world.

How do Catholics live this new way of life? Basically in one of three ways: Some people become members of religious orders and communities. Others are called to live as ordained ministers. But most of the baptized live their Catholic lives as members of the laity—that is, as laypeople.

As laypeople our way of life begins in and revolves around the parish. There we receive the sacraments of initiation: Baptism, Confirmation, and Eucharist. There we celebrate the sacrament of Reconciliation for the first time. In the parish we continue our instruction in faith that was begun by our parents. We learn more about Jesus, his Church, and what it means to be a Catholic in today's challenging world.

Years later we may celebrate the sacrament of Matrimony in our parish church and begin to journey down a new path in life. It is in the parish as well that we say farewell for the last time to those we love at the celebration of a Christian funeral. Truly the parish is our home in the Catholic Church from the first moment of our lives until the last.

The sacramental life and religious instruction are truly important, but parish life doesn't end there. A parish offers many opportunities for the laity to serve Christ. That is why the first thing that Catholics do when they move into a neighborhood is to register in, or join, the local parish. By adding their names and addresses to the list of parishioners, they become part of the local Catholic family.

It is in the parish that Catholics discover many opportunities to serve others. All their talents can be used in one way or another in various parish committees, organizations, or ministries. For example, laymen and laywomen may be called to serve on the parish council or finance committee. Others may become involved in religious education

or take up the work of sharing faith with others in programs of Christian initiation.

Many people feel called to various outreach programs in a parish. These include ministry to the sick or homebound and to those in need of food, clothing, or shelter. Others find that they can serve through involvement with the liturgy. They help to plan liturgies and participate in the liturgical celebrations in their roles as altar servers, members of choirs, leaders of song, musicians, lectors, and extraordinary ministers of the Eucharist.

Some laypeople travel halfway around the globe to serve as missionaries in other lands. Others do mission work in our own country, serving wherever the need is the greatest. Today more than ever before, qualified laypeople are taking leadership positions in dioceses and local parishes. Working closely with the bishop, priests, and deacons, laypeople are putting their talents to work in many ways.

75

◆ On the board draw the diagram shown below. Have three volunteers each write one of the three reasons we say our way of life begins in and revolves around the parish.

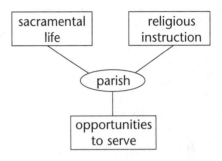

Discuss the young people's chosen ways of service.

◆ Ask the young people to tell some of the many ways Catholics serve others in the parish. Then say, "Draw a star next to the one way of service you think you would be most interested in doing."

If time allows, have the young people do the journaling activity on page 52 of the *Creed Journal.* Volunteers may be comfortable sharing their journal entries for this activity.

FYI Each year on March 9 the Church celebrates the feast of a woman who lived a life of service wherever the need was the greatest. Saint Frances of Rome (1384–1440) was married to a prominent Roman citizen, Lorenzo de' Ponziani, for forty years.

Francis and her sister-in-law served those left poor and hungry by the civil wars then being waged in Italy. When a plague struck Rome, Frances sold her jewels to provide food for those stricken with the illness. After her son died in another plague, Frances converted part of her house into a hospital to care for the suffering children. At her death great crowds of people came from all parts of the city to honor Frances of Rome.

Presentation (cont'd)

◆ Point out that we have, so far, talked a great deal about the apostles. The apostles were disciples, but there were many, many other disciples of Jesus who were not called to be apostles. (*Disciple* comes from a word that means "a learner, a follower".) These other disciples came from every walk of life: They were young and old, learned and uneducated, women and men. Jesus challenged them and continues to challenge the most ordinary people to do his work and to carry on his mission. Ask, "Are you his disciple? What have you learned from following him? What does he expect of you?"

◆ Generate a discussion on the **thought provoker** at the top of page 76. If some young people seem cynical about the opportunities to serve, ask them why. Explain to them that they should experiment with service of others because it's a positive thing that Christ asks of us.

◆ Ask the young people what they think the world would be like now . . .

• if Saint Francis of Assisi had not begun a community of men who followed his example of living a simple life

• if Elizabeth Seton had never founded the Sisters of Charity, who opened schools and orphanages in the United States

• if Benedict had not founded a community of monks who dedicate their lives to praying for all members of the Church and for the whole world.

Help the young people to conclude that religious communities have made great contributions of service to the Church and all society.

In recent times the Holy Spirit has renewed our understanding of the dignity and importance of the laity in the Church. Now more than ever before the laity are sharing in pastoral ministry as team members. It is exciting to see.

While all this is true, we know that the majority of laypeople carry on the mission of the Church each day by sharing the good news of Christ in the workplace. They use their gifts in their occupations and professions to change the world by the light of the gospel. In all they do, they try to bring to their surroundings the love and justice that is characteristic of God's kingdom.

Jesus himself sent disciples other than the Twelve to join in his saving mission and to prepare the way for him. He once sent out seventy-two to many towns. He reminded them, "The harvest is abundant but the laborers are few; so ask the master of the harvest to send out laborers for his harvest" (Luke 10:2).

Discuss some ways that young people can serve the Church in their parishes.

Religious

Although the laity are the largest group of people in the Church, many thousands of Catholics live out their lives in a different way. These are the members of religious orders and communities. How did this way of life come about?

Throughout the history of the Church, certain men and women have tried to follow Christ in a special way. These are people such as Benedict, Francis of Assisi, Elizabeth Seton, and Teresa of Calcutta. So attractive are their lives and relationships with God that many people have wanted to imitate them. Communities developed around these holy people. Eventually the Church reviewed their way and rules of life and approved them as religious orders and communities. Today these communities are spread throughout the world. How do they live, and what do they do? Let's look more closely at this unique way of living the Catholic life.

All religious share in the joy of community life, ministry, and prayer.

76

Evangelical Counsels Religious men and women consecrate themselves to God by vowing to practice poverty, chastity, and obedience. These are known as the *evangelical counsels* because they reflect a gospel way of life. By living these counsels, religious try to follow Christ's example.

• *Poverty* means that a religious man or woman owns no property and tries to live a simple lifestyle. Without seeking wealth or status, a religious gives witness to our total dependence on God and our deep respect for the proper use of this world's goods.

• *Chastity* means that a religious man or woman lives a life of purity as a witness to the kingdom of God. It includes a life of celibacy, which means not marrying. In trying to imitate Jesus in this way, religious want to be free to share God's love with the greatest number of people.

• *Obedience* means that religious men and women choose to listen carefully to God's direction in their lives. Obedience to the Church and to their religious superior means that individual religious are ready to serve God and the Church anywhere.

Community Life The vowed life of religious is not easy, but it is filled with joy. The vows themselves are positive ways of following Christ's example. The close bonds that religious form in their own community enable them to live their vows fully each day. This is what we mean by a community life. The religious community is truly an individual's religious family.

Some communities are made up of vowed men who also become priests. Some communities are made up of vowed women, whom we call religious sisters. Still others are made up of vowed men who do not become priests. They are known as religious brothers.

There are two kinds of priests. A *religious priest* is a member of a religious order or community and professes the vows of poverty, chastity, and obedience. He serves anywhere in the world his superiors assign him. A *diocesan priest* is ordained for a particular diocese. With the bishop he dedicates his life to the care of the people of that diocese. He is not a religious nor does he profess the vows of a religious. A diocesan priest does, however, make a promise of celibacy. He also promises obedience to his bishop.

77

◆ Have a different volunteer explain each of the evangelical counsels. Discuss the way each of the counsels reflects what Christ asks of his followers in the gospel. Explain that in living their vows religious sisters, brothers, and priests are shining examples of what Jesus expects of us in living simply and unselfishly, being pure, and listening carefully to God's direction.

If possible, have pictures of religious showing the varied ministries in which they serve God. Point out that religious work in education, health ministries, legal work, communications, immigrant services, child care, and ministries for abused children and women. They work with the poor and the homeless, the addicted, and the dying. They do all this in Christ's name, and, as Mother Teresa said many times, they do this because they see the face of Jesus in every human being.

◆ Write the term *community life* on the board. Point out that religious priests, brothers, and sisters living in community life hold all their goods in common; they share their spiritual lives with others through the bonds of prayer; they form a special kind of family of prayer and support.

◆ Have two volunteers explain the two kinds of priests as noted in the *Catholic ID* on page 77.

FYI Saint Vincent de Paul (1581–1660) was ordained to the priesthood in 1600 in Toulouse, France. Vincent was ambitious for a comfortable position. He became a chaplain for Queen Margaret of Valois and tutored the children of the Count of Gondi. But Vincent abandoned his life of comfort after he heard the confession of a poor, dying peasant. He dedicated himself to serving the poor and began to work among prisoners and galley slaves. Soon other men joined him, and they formed the Vincentians. With Saint Louise de Marillac, he established the Daughters of Charity to care for the sick, the elderly, and orphaned.

Presentation (cont'd)

◆ Write the word *contemplative* on the board. Point out that it comes from the Latin meaning "to view with sustained attention, to gaze at, to be absorbed." Ask, "What do you think those religious who are called contemplatives 'view with sustained attention' or 'gaze at' or are 'absorbed in'?" The one-word answer, of course, is God. Ask a volunteer to read aloud the final paragraphs on page 78.

◆ Ask, "What is the difference between contemplative and active communities?" (*Contemplative communities separate themselves from the world and devote themselves to a life of prayer. Active communities combine a life of prayer with a life of active service.*)

◆ Invite the young people to work with a partner to respond to the ⁙ **thought provoker** on page 78. Share the results with the whole group.

Conclusion ___ min.

◆ Form four groups. Assign each group one of the items under *Things to Think About* and *Things to Share*. Allow a few minutes for preparation; then have each group report on its topic.

◆ Direct attention to *Words to Remember*. Have the young people find the description of *laity* on page 75 and write it on page 79.

Assessment: If you plan to administer *Chapter 9 Assessment*, allow about ten minutes for its completion.

Active religious communities combine a life of prayer with a life of active service. They take part in all aspects of the Church's life. They sponsor and staff schools and hospitals, serve as missionaries, give retreats, work in parishes, and engage in many other ministries. Wherever there is a need in the Church, active religious are ready to go. You may know of some active communities, such as the Jesuits, Franciscan men and women, the Sisters of Mercy, and the Marist Brothers.

Religious communities come in all shapes and sizes. Some have a long history; some are very recent. No matter what, these communities are one of God's great blessings to the Church.

⁙ *What qualifications do you think a person needs to join a religious community?*

Contemplative or Active There are differences among religious communities. In *contemplative religious communities* men and women dedicate themselves entirely to a life of prayer. They willingly separate themselves from the busyness of the world. They pray constantly for all the members of the Church, but their lives remain hidden from us. That is why they are called contemplatives. In many ways these men and women are the powerhouses of prayer for the entire Church. You may know of some contemplative religious communities, such as the Trappists, the Poor Clares, and the Carmelites.

78

Answers for Chapter 9 Assessment

1. a   2. d   3. c   4. c   5. c
6. d   7. b   8. a   9. b   10. See page 78.

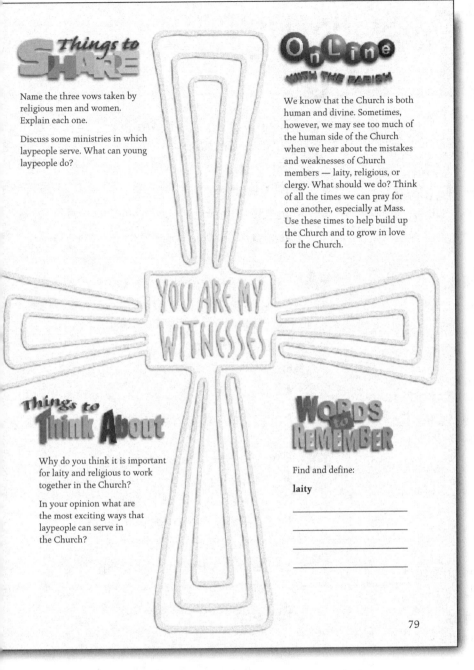

Things to SHARE

Name the three vows taken by religious men and women. Explain each one.

Discuss some ministries in which laypeople serve. What can young laypeople do?

OnLine WITH THE PARISH

We know that the Church is both human and divine. Sometimes, however, we may see too much of the human side of the Church when we hear about the mistakes and weaknesses of Church members — laity, religious, or clergy. What should we do? Think of all the times we can pray for one another, especially at Mass. Use these times to help build up the Church and to grow in love for the Church.

Things to Think About

Why do you think it is important for laity and religious to work together in the Church?

In your opinion what are the most exciting ways that laypeople can serve in the Church?

WORDS to REMEMBER

Find and define:

laity

_____
_____
_____
_____

79

Conclusion (cont'd)

Invite the young people to reflect on the meaning of their Baptism and their corresponding role in the Church by doing the journaling activity on page 53 of the *Creed Journal*.

FORUM Assignment

✔ Read Chapter 10, pages 80–87. Underline in pencil six key ideas.

✔ Complete the handout *The Good Life*. Be prepared to share your interview questions.

Closing Prayer: Ask the young people to listen closely as you read the following story:

A reporter once asked Mother Teresa, the founder of the Order of the Missionaries of Charity, what it felt like to be a 'living saint.' Mother Teresa replied, "I'm very happy if you can see Jesus in me, because I can see Jesus in you. Holiness is not just for a few people. It's for everyone, including you, sir. . . ."

Pray together:

Thank you, Lord, for people like Mother Teresa and others who serve you in religious communities and remind us to strive to be holy.

Evaluation: Do the young people appreciate the dignity and importance of laity and religious in the Church? Do they understand religious community life?

FOR CHAPTER 10

- copies of handout *Upon This Rock*, page 80C
- copies of *Chapter 10 Assessment*, page 87A
- copies of *Highlights for Home*, page 87B

Assessment

1 The life of laypeople revolves around the
- **a.** parish.
- **b.** the diocesan center.
- **c.** the local religious community.
- **d.** vows of poverty, chastity, and obedience.

2 Lay people can
- **a.** minister to the sick.
- **b.** plan liturgies.
- **c.** be missionaries.
- **d.** all of the above

3 _____ means that a religious man or woman lives a life of purity as a witness to the kingdom of God.
- **a.** Poverty
- **b.** Obedience
- **c.** Chastity
- **d.** none of the above

4 Most Catholics live their baptismal call as members of
- **a.** the ordained clergy.
- **b.** religious communities.
- **c.** the laity.
- **d.** organizations such as the Knights of Columbus.

5 The evangelical counsels are
- **a.** faith, hope, and love.
- **b.** the Ten Commandments.
- **c.** poverty, obedience, and chastity.
- **d.** the gifts of the Holy Spirit.

6 _____ is the vow in which a person promises to own no property and to try to live a simple lifestyle.
- **a.** Celibacy
- **b.** Chastity
- **c.** Obedience
- **d.** Poverty

7 _____ is the vow in which a religious promises to listen carefully to God's direction.
- **a.** Community
- **b.** Obedience
- **c.** Chastity
- **d.** Poverty

8 Choose the false statement.
- **a.** There are no men in religious life.
- **b.** Community enables religious to live their vows.
- **c.** Religious try to follow Christ's example.
- **d.** Some religious are called brothers.

9 Contemplatives
- **a.** are engaged in active ministries.
- **b.** dedicate themselves entirely to prayer.
- **c.** do not care about the world.
- **d.** no longer exist.

10 Explain the differences between contemplative and active religious communities.

Highlights for Home

Focus on Faith

As you discuss this chapter, "Catholicism: A Way of Life," with your daughter or son, remember that with the help of Holy Spirit, you are preparing this young person to take her or his place in tomorrow's Catholic Church. It is important to share your appreciation and love for the Church in its rich diversity and beauty. It is important to provide him or her with opportunities to examine the possible ways to live his or her baptismal promises as an adult member of the laity, a religious community, or the clergy.

Mother Teresa wrote, "The young are the builders of tomorrow. Youth today is in search of selflessness, and when it finds it, is prepared to embrace it." Discuss with your son or daughter the many opportunities for service that your parish provides. Some suggestions are given on page 75 of the text.

Conversation Starters

. . . . a few ideas to talk about together . . . .

◆ The Catholic lifestyle . . .
  . . . challenges of being faithful.
  . . . the blessings and rewards of faithfulness.

◆ A religious priest, brother, or sister or diocesan priest
  . . . whom I admire.
  . . . who helped me understand Catholicism as a way of life.

Feature Focus

Catholic ID on page 77 explains the differences between the two kinds of priests, *religious priests* and *diocesan priests*. A religious priest is a member of a religious order or community (Jesuits, Dominicans, Franciscans) and professes the vows of poverty, chastity, and obedience. He serves where his superiors ask him to serve. A diocesan priest is ordained for a particular diocese; he serves the people of that diocese. He does not make the three vows of a religious priest, but he makes a promise of celibacy. He also promises obedience to the bishop of the diocese.

Reflection

Copy the following Prayer for Vocations written by Cardinal Joseph Bernardin. Place the copy where you and your family will be able to read it often.

Lord of the harvest, your word finds a home in our hearts, calls us into community and invites us to generous service of the human family. Bless with courage and spirit your priestly people, called to full participation in the one body of Christ. May many choose to respond in public service to your call offered in Jesus' name. Amen.

THE WHOLE CATHOLIC CHURCH

Adult Focus

In this chapter the young people learn that the Catholic Church's way of life is rich and diverse. They are made aware that within the Catholic Church there are a number of distinct Rites. All Catholics share in common an ordained leadership called the clergy. These are the bishops, priests (presbyters), and deacons who dedicate their lives to the work of Christ and his Church.

The pope and all the other bishops are united in a sacred college. They are the official teachers with full authority—the authority of Christ himself—in the Church. We call them the *magisterium*, from the Latin word for "teacher."

In this chapter the young people also learn about *infallibility*. This gift of the Holy Spirit keeps the whole Church from error—in believing and in teaching—in matters concerning revelation and the deposit of faith.

In all of these ways, the Catholic Church makes Christ visible to the world. The kingdom of God that Jesus preached is the kingdom that the Church seeks to bring about.

Catechism Focus

The themes of this chapter correspond to paragraphs 897–933 of the *Catechism*.

Enrichment Activities

Guest Speakers

- Consider inviting a diocesan priest, a seminarian, or a permanent deacon to speak to your group or to participate in a panel discussion. A good resource in regard to finding guest speakers is your diocesan director of vocations. Make a list of possible guests, and involve the young people in the process of planning and inviting.

- If possible, invite a priest from another Rite of the Catholic Church to talk to the young people about its tradition of liturgy, laws, and customs.

Interviews

Prepare and conduct by regular mail or E-mail, interviews with priests or permanent deacons who serve as chaplains of the following: police or sheriff departments, hospitals or emergency services, professional sports teams, prisons, state or federal legislatures, or the armed services. The young people may want to invite these men to be guest speakers.

Teaching Resources

Overview

To examine the ways the clergy are empowered by Christ to exercise authority in the Church; to explore the rich diversity of the Catholic Church.

Opening Prayer Ideas

Gather in a prayer circle. Read together John 20:19–23. Pause briefly. Offer spontaneous prayers for the Church and its leaders.

or

Gather in a prayer circle. Listen as a reader proclaims Colossians 3:12–17. Have all respond: "Whatever we do, in word or in deed, we will do in the name of the Lord Jesus."

Materials

- Bibles, journals, highlighters

Creed Journal:
For Chapter 10, use pages 54 and 55.

REPRODUCIBLE MASTERS
- handout *Whatever!* page 80C
- *Chapter 10 Assessment,* page 87A
- *Highlights for Home,* page 87B

Supplemental Resources

VIDEO
Papal Spacebridge Youth Forum
Ignatius Press
P.O. Box 1339
Ft. Collins, CO 80522

Whatever!

Whatever you do, in word or in deed, do everything in the name of the Lord Jesus, giving thanks to God the Father through him.

Colossians 3:17

You do not have to wait until you are an adult to help make Christ visible to the world. Begin today. Choose three general ways of giving witness from the list below or write your own. For each general way, write one specific action you will try to do in the near future. Then describe the fruitful results if at least three people followed your example. A sample is done.

- following Jesus' unselfish ways
- worshiping God
- studying Scripture
- bearing the good news
- defending human dignity
- peacemaking

General witness: defending human dignity

Specific witness: not joining in a gossip session about another person

Fruitful results: Gossip sessions end. People are not afraid to do the right thing.

General witness: _____

_____

_____

Specific witness: _____

_____

_____

Fruitful results: _____

_____

_____

General witness: _____

_____

_____

Specific witness: _____

_____

_____

Fruitful results: _____

_____

_____

General witness: _____

_____

_____

Specific witness: _____

_____

_____

Fruitful results: _____

_____

_____

C
H
A
P
T
E
R

10

I am the vine, you are the branches.
Whoever remains in me and I in him
will bear much fruit, because
without me you can do nothing.
John 15:5

THE WHOLE
CATHOLIC CHURCH

Objectives: To examine the ways the clergy are empowered by Christ to exercise authority in the Church; to explore the rich diversity of the Catholic Church.

Introduction ___ min.

Opening Prayer: Invite the young people to stand and gather together to form a circle. Have them make a vine by crossing their arms in front of them and joining hands with the people to their right and left. Ask the prayer leader to stand in the center of the circle to read John 15:5 on page 81. Then pray together:

Leader: Jesus, we ask you to support us, your people, your Church.

All: Jesus, you are the vine. We are the branches. Without you, we can do nothing.

Leader: Jesus, pour into us your grace and life.

All: Jesus, you are the vine. We are the branches. Without you, we can do nothing.

Leader: Jesus, keep us close to you. May giving witness bring forth fruit in the world.

All: Jesus, you are the vine. We are the branches. Help us to remain in your love. Without you, we can do nothing.

Forum: Invite an "editor-in-chief" to lead this discussion in which the "reporters" share with the group the five questions they have formulated to ask about religious life. Have a secretary list all the questions on the board so that the group can see the types of things that interest them. Then the "editor" might encourage the "reporters" to ask these questions of a religious man or woman.

Presentation ___ min.

◆ Invite someone to read the opening paragraphs at the top of page 82. Point out that the Church is one in faith but diverse in the ways that faith is practiced.

◆ Direct attention to page 83. Discuss who the people in the photographs are and what they are doing.

- *Upper left:* Monsignor Hartman and Rabbi Gellman call themselves "the God Squad." During their guest appearances on television, on radio, and in schools and churches, they dialogue with each other and their audiences about respecting the religious beliefs of all people and about the ways these beliefs affect our daily lives.
- *Upper right:* Bishop Moses Anderson, auxiliary bishop of Detroit, is visiting Ghana, West Africa.
- *Lower right:* A deacon is reading the gospel at Mass.

◆ Have the young people share the six key ideas they have underlined in this chapter. Discuss their choices. Then have them highlight those highlighted on your reduced pages.

SOME people think that all Catholics do everything the same way. They think that all Catholics pray at Mass in exactly the same way and follow the same liturgical year. But that is not true.

What is true is that the Church is one in its faith. But it is extremely diverse in the ways that faith is lived and practiced.

Do you know that the whole Catholic Church is made up of twenty-two distinct Catholic Churches in communion with one another? In this chapter we are going to discover that the Church's life is rich and diverse.

Clergy

The membership of the Catholic Church is made up of laity, religious, and clergy. Everyone in the Church belongs to one of these groups. Each group is an important part of our Catholic way of life.

All the Churches of the Catholic Church share in common an ordained leadership called the clergy. These are the bishops, priests (presbyters), and deacons who are empowered by God to exercise authority in the Church. They do this for the service of God's people, each according to his rank in the sacrament of Holy Orders.

The clergy dedicate their lives to the work of Christ and his Church. The priest is the coworker of the bishop in the work of teaching, governing, and sanctifying. Priests, therefore, are never to work independently of the bishop. Rather, they are his representatives in the pastoral care of God's people. Although deacons do not share in the priesthood, as bishops and priests do, they are ordained for a ministry of service.

What about other titles of the clergy, such as cardinal, archbishop, and monsignor? These titles are given to bishops and priests who carry on a special work for the Church or as a special honor. Cardinals and archbishops are bishops; monsignors are priests.

82

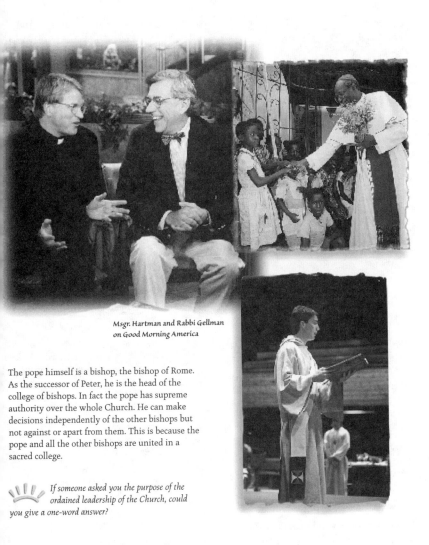

*Msgr. Hartman and Rabbi Gellman
on Good Morning America*

The pope himself is a bishop, the bishop of Rome. As the successor of Peter, he is the head of the college of bishops. In fact the pope has supreme authority over the whole Church. He can make decisions independently of the other bishops but not against or apart from them. This is because the pope and all the other bishops are united in a sacred college.

If someone asked you the purpose of the ordained leadership of the Church, could you give a one-word answer?

◆ Ask, "What does the pope have in common with other bishops, and what sets him apart?" (*The pope is the bishop of Rome and is united with the other bishops in the sacred college. However, he has supreme authority over the whole Church and can make decisions independently of the other bishops, but not against or apart from them.*)

◆ Explain that the official teachers in the Church with full authority are the pope and the other bishops. Then ask, "What special term is given to their role as teachers?" (*magisterium*)

◆ Point out the **thought provoker** on page 83. Give the young people about fifteen seconds to come up with a one-word answer. Share the results. See if there is a consensus.

Just in case...
some pronunciation helps

magisterium . . . maa-jeh-**steer**-ee-um

FYI The term *college of bishops* may seem strange to us because of the American use of the word *college* to mean "an educational institution that students attend after completing high school." However, the word comes from the Latin words *collegium*, which means "a society," and *collega*, which means "colleague."

So the college of bishops is not a school in which bishops are educated. Rather, it is a society of colleagues who are the official teachers of the whole Church.

Presentation (cont'd)

◆ Discuss the difference between ordinary and extraordinary magisterium. (*Ordinary magisterium refers to day-to-day teachings about our faith; extraordinary magisterium refers to the teachings of ecumenical councils and papal pronouncements about our faith.*)

◆ Make sure the young people understand the words *papal* and *ecumenical*. Write both words on the board. Have volunteers define each term.

• *Papal* is derived from the Italian word *papa* for "pope". A papal pronouncement would be one made by the pope. Ask, "What would a papal visit be? a papal blessing?"

• *Ecumenical* means "world-wide, universal, to bring about unity." An ecumenical council would call together all the bishops of the Church to discuss matters pertaining to unity. Ask, "What does it mean, then, to work for ecumenism among all churches?"

◆ Write the word *infallibility* on the board, and ask the group to define it. (*Infallibility is the gift of the Holy Spirit that keeps the Church from error in matters concerning revelation and the deposit of faith.*)

Discuss the ways the Church exercises the gift of infallibility.

◆ Have a volunteer read *Catholic Teachings* on page 84. Make sure the young people understand that the Church is infallible in matters of faith and morals. It does not claim infallibility in all areas of human knowledge.

◆ Read aloud the 〰 **thought provoker** on page 84. Remind the group that ecumenical councils discuss matters pertaining to the unity of the faith. Allow time for the young people to write their ideas in the space provided.

84

CATHOLIC TEACHINGS

About Infallibility

Does infallibility extend to all areas of knowledge? Absolutely not! It has to do only with matters of faith and morals. It has nothing to do with matters of science or other areas of human knowledge. You may be familiar with the story of Galileo. A long time ago the Church misunderstood the work of this great scientist. It mistakenly condemned his scientific teachings about the universe. Today, of course, we know better, and the Church has acknowledged its mistake. This kind of mistake, however, has nothing to do with the gift of infallibility.

Official Teachers

In the Church the official teachers with full authority—the authority of Christ himself—are the pope and the other bishops. They are the official teachers for the whole Church. We call them the *magisterium*, from the Latin word for "teacher."

The teaching office of the magisterium is carried out in two ways. The *ordinary magisterium* is the day-to-day teaching of the pope and bishops about the truths of our faith. Sometimes, however, the pope and bishops teach in a very solemn and formal way. This is called the *extraordinary magisterium*. It happens when the pope gathers all the bishops of the world together at an ecumenical (worldwide) council. Or it happens when the pope by himself makes a solemn and extraordinary pronouncement about our faith.

Jesus promised to be with his Church always, even to the end of the world. He sent the Holy Spirit to teach it and preserve it in the truth (John 16:13). That is why it is unthinkable that the Church, the body of Christ, could fall into error in matters of faith and morality. This is a great gift to the Church.

84

Catholics have a special name for this gift. That name is infallibility. *Infallibility is the gift of the Holy Spirit that keeps the whole Church from error—in believing and in teaching—in matters concerning revelation and the deposit of faith. This is the divine guarantee we have that the Church can never be in error about the truths necessary for our salvation.*

How is the gift of infallibility exercised in the official teaching office of the Church? It happens only in teaching about matters of faith and morals:

• when the bishops, spread around the world in their own dioceses and in union with the pope, teach the truths of our faith with one voice.

• when the bishops of the world, gathered together by the pope in an ecumenical council, define a truth of our faith.

• when the pope speaks to the whole Church on a matter of faith and morals with the full authority he has as successor of Saint Peter. When the pope does this, he is speaking, not as an individual bishop, but as the pastor of the whole Church. This exercise of infallibility by the pope alone is rare.

What a wonderful thing it is to know that the Holy Spirit is guiding the Church.

〰 *Imagine that the Holy Father has called an ecumenical council and that it will begin in the near future. What do you think the world's bishops will talk about?*

A Communion of Churches

The Catholic Church's way of life is rich and diverse. As the people of God, Catholics are one, but this unity does not mean that we are all alike. Our Church spreads across every culture and includes many different peoples.

How did this wonderful diversity come to be? As the first Christian communities were founded during the apostolic age, many developed their own unique customs, laws, and practices. Later the Church spread across the Roman Empire. As the empire split into eastern and western sections, differences among the various Churches became more apparent. The Church of the West became known as the Latin, or Western, Catholic Church. The Churches of the East became known as the Eastern Catholic Churches. ·

The Eastern Catholic Churches should not be confused with the Eastern Orthodox Churches. The Orthodox Churches separated themselves from union with the pope in A.D. 1054 and are not part of the Catholic Church.

Although the Western Church and the Eastern Catholic Churches had many differences, their fundamental beliefs remained the same. Through apostolic succession each had seven sacraments, the threefold ministry (bishop, priest, and deacon), and the same creeds. All of them acknowledged the bishop of Rome, the successor of Peter, as the head of the Church.

Today the whole Catholic Church is made up of twenty-two distinct Catholic Churches in communion with one another and the bishop of Rome. Each of the twenty-two Churches observes one of the Rites of the Church. A *Rite* is a distinctive tradition of liturgy, laws, and customs that expresses the one Catholic faith in its own unique way. There are six different Rites that are practiced by the twenty-two Churches of the Catholic Church.

Most Catholics in the United States follow the Latin Rite. However, Latin Rite Catholics should realize that they can attend Mass (usually called the Divine Liturgy in Eastern Catholic Churches) in any of the other twenty-one Catholic Churches. They may also receive the sacraments there.

Pope John Paul II with a Byzantine Catholic bishop

85

◆ Write on the board *Eastern Catholic Church* and *Eastern Orthodox Church*. Ask volunteers to explain the difference between the two. Then under the first head write: *Part of the Catholic Church; in union with the pope.* Under the second head write: *not part of the Catholic Church; separated from the pope.*

◆ On another part of the board, write *Western Catholic Church and Eastern Catholic Churches.* Have volunteers add the four fundamental beliefs that united the Western and Eastern Churches.

- apostolic succession
- same sacraments
- threefold ministry
- same creeds

The Code of Canon Law: A Text and Commentary (page 26) explains very clearly:

> The universal Church is divided into the eastern and western branches, distinguishable mainly by the different rites they follow in their liturgical celebrations and by their separate administrative structures.

◆ Point out the word *Rite* in the second paragraph of the second column on page 85. Have a volunteer read the definition aloud. Then ask:

- Which Rite do most Catholics in the United States follow? (*the Latin Rite*)
- May Catholics attend Mass and receive the sacraments in any Rite of the Catholic Church? (*yes*)

◆ If any young person in the group belongs to one of the Eastern Catholic Churches or if anyone has been to a liturgy in another Rite, invite them to share their experiences.

Presentation (cont'd)

◆ Allow time for the group to examine the chart on page 86. Stress the unity of the Catholic Church with all its different Rites. Some computer experts in the group might enjoy doing the research suggestions below the chart.

◆ Have a volunteer read aloud "Christ and His Church." After the reading discuss with the group the reasons why we can say that the Church is like a sacrament. Remind them that a sacrament is a visible and effective sign.

◆ Have a volunteer read the *Scripture Update* on page 86. Invite the young people to learn by heart the words from Colossians 3:17.

If you are using the *Creed Journal*, invite the young people to do the journaling activity on page 54.

Then have the young people open their journals to page 54 and read aloud Colossians 3:17. Have them read it again silently.

Then invite them to do the journaling activity on this page as a prayer in action. Allow a few minutes. Then pray Colossians 3:17 together.

◆ Have the young people form four groups. Assign each group one of the four questions under *Things to Think About* and *Things to Share*. Then have the groups share their responses with all.

Conclusion ___ min.

◆ Have the young people find and write the definition of *magisterium* under *Words to Remember*. (See page 84.)

Assessment: If you plan to administer *Chapter 10 Assessment*, allow about ten minutes for its completion.

86

Christ and His Church

Just as Jesus brought humanity the fullness of God, so the Church brings the fullness of Christ to the world. Jesus Christ, then, lives on in his Church. The Church is really like a sacrament; it makes Christ visible to the world. Jesus' mission is the mission of the Church. The kingdom of God that Jesus preached is the kingdom that the Church seeks to bring about. All this reminds us that the Church is necessary for our salvation, for it is there that we meet Christ our Savior.

Is the Church perfect? No, only God is perfect. Will the Church last? If the Church were merely of human origin, it would never last. But if it comes from God, no one can stop it (Acts 5:38–39). After two thousand years, no one has!

Scripture UPDATE

The Letter to the Colossians summarizes what it means to be a member of the Church: "Whatever you do, in word or in deed, do everything in the name of the Lord Jesus, giving thanks to God the Father through him" (3:17).

The accompanying chart lists the names of all twenty-two Churches and the Rites followed by each. It will help you to appreciate even more the beauty and richness of the Catholic Church.

The Catholic Church

Churches	Rites
1. Latin Catholic Church	This Church follows the Latin (Roman) Rite.
2. Belorussian Catholic Church 3. Bulgarian Catholic Church 4. Greek Catholic Church 5. Hungarian Catholic Church 6. Italo-Albanian Catholic Church 7. Melkite Catholic Church 8. Romanian Catholic Church 9. Ruthenian Catholic Church 10. Slovak Catholic Church 11. Ukrainian Catholic Church 12. Krizevci Catholic Church 13. Albanian Catholic Church 14. Russian Catholic Church	These thirteen Churches follow the Byzantine (Constantinopolitan) Rite.
15. Chaldean Catholic Church 16. Malabar Catholic Church	These two Churches follow the Chaldean Rite.
17. Coptic Catholic Church 18. Ethiopian Catholic Church	These two Churches follow the Alexandrian Rite.
19. Syrian Catholic Church 20. Maronite Catholic Church 21. Syro-Malankara Catholic Church	These three Churches follow the Antiochine Rite.
22. Armenian Catholic Church	This Church follows the Armenian Rite.

Try to find out where the homelands of some of these Churches are. For example, most Catholics in Lebanon belong to the Maronite Catholic Church.

86

Answers for Chapter 10 Assessment

1. d   2. c   3. d   4. a   5. b
6. a   7. c   8. c   9. a   10. Accept appropriate responses.

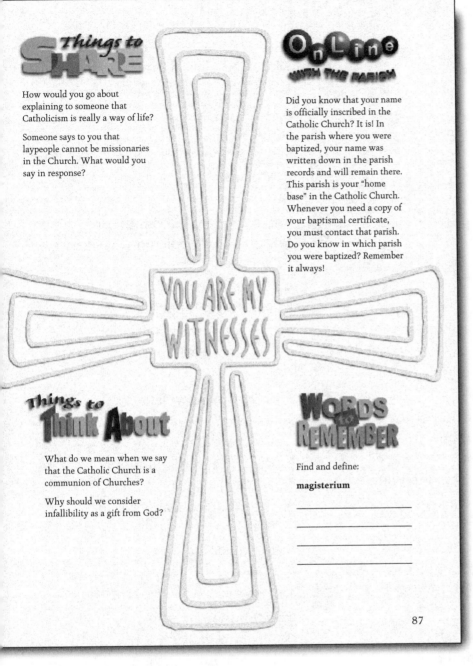

Things to SHARE

How would you go about explaining to someone that Catholicism is really a way of life?

Someone says to you that laypeople cannot be missionaries in the Church. What would you say in response?

OnLine WITH THE PARISH

Did you know that your name is officially inscribed in the Catholic Church? It is! In the parish where you were baptized, your name was written down in the parish records and will remain there. This parish is your "home base" in the Catholic Church. Whenever you need a copy of your baptismal certificate, you must contact that parish. Do you know in which parish you were baptized? Remember it always!

Things to Think About

What do we mean when we say that the Catholic Church is a communion of Churches?

Why should we consider infallibility as a gift from God?

WORDS to REMEMBER

Find and define:

magisterium

_____

_____

_____

_____

87

Conclusion (cont'd)

FORUM Assignment

✔ Read Chapter 11, pages 88–95. Underline in pencil six key ideas.

✔ Complete the handout *Whatever!* Be prepared to share the results.

Closing Prayer: Share the following evening intercessions that are taken from an ancient Byzantine Litany. Have the young people close their eyes and imagine themselves in a peaceful place at nightfall. The response to each petition is "Lord, have mercy."

• For an evening that is perfect, holy, peaceful, and without sin, let us pray to the Lord.

• For an angel of peace, a faithful guide, and guardian of our souls and bodies, let us pray to the Lord.

• For the pardon and forgiveness of our sins and offenses, let us pray to the Lord.

• For the holy Church of God, that God may give it peace and unity and protect and prosper it throughout the whole world, let us pray to the Lord.

Evaluation: Do the young people understand the ways the magisterium is empowered to exercise authority in the Church? Do they appreciate the rich diversity in the Church?

FOR CHAPTER 11

• preparation of opening-prayer volunteers
• copies of handout *Companion on the Way*, page 88C
• copies of *Chapter 11 Assessment*, page 95A (optional)
• copies of *Highlights for Home*, page 95B

Assessment

 1 A diocesan priest belongs to
a. the laity.
b. the magisterium.
c. a religious community.
d. the clergy.

 2 Infallibility
a. means that the pope is never wrong.
b. extends to all areas of knowledge.
c. keeps the whole Church from error in truths necessary for salvation.
d. is not a gift of the Holy Spirit.

 3 The day-to-day teaching of the pope and bishops about the truths of our faith is
a. the extraordinary magisterium.
b. an ecumenical council.
c. the evangelical counsels.
d. the ordinary magisterium.

 4 There is/are _____ official Rites in the Catholic Church.
a. twenty-two   **c.** fifteen
b. two   **d.** three

 5 Choose the *false* statement.
a. The pope is the bishop of Rome.
b. The pope is always infallible.
c. The pope is the successor of Saint Peter.
d. The pope has supreme authority over the whole Church.

 6 Most Catholics in America follow the _____ Rite.
a. Latin
b. Alexandrian
c. Byzantine
d. Chaldean

 7 When the pope and bishops teach in a very solemn way, it is called the
a. ordinary magisterium.
b. communion of churches.
c. extraordinary magisterium.
d. rites of the Church.

 8 The word *clergy* refers to
a. the membership of the Catholic Church.
b. the pope as the bishop of Rome.
c. the ordained leadership of the Church.
d. the magisterium.

 9 The pope is
a. the bishop of Rome.
b. recognized as the Church's leader by the Orthodox Church.
c. separated from the college of bishops.
d. head of the Church in name only.

 10 Explain what these words from the gospel mean to you: "I am the vine, you are the branches." Write your response on the reverse side of this page.

Highlights for Home

Focus on Faith

It is possible for our young people to be unaware of the universality, the richness, and diversity of the Church to which we belong. In this chapter we encourage them to look at the *whole* Catholic Church.

First they explore the leadership of the Church in the ordained clergy, especially the pope and bishops who exercise the full authority of Christ for the whole Church. They are the magisterium.

They learn that the Church is like a sacrament; it makes Christ visible to the world. They also learn about the Eastern Catholic Church, which is part of the whole Catholic Church, and they discover the beautiful variety of Rites through which the Church practices the faith.

Conversation Starters

. . . . a few ideas to talk about together . . . .

◆ What is my understanding of authority in the Church? Does it help me to remember that all authority is given by Christ?

◆ Have I ever experienced a liturgy in a Rite other than the Latin Rite? Would I like to have such an experience?

Feature Focus

Catholic Teachings on page 84 is about *infallibility*. The young people learned that infallibility is the gift of the Holy Spirit that keeps the whole Church from error in matters concerning revelation and the deposit of faith. In this feature they are made aware that this gift of the Holy Spirit has nothing to do with matters of science or other areas of human knowledge.

Reflection

You may want to look at the photo on pages 80 and 81 as you reflect on the words of Jesus in John 15:5. Then use the following prayer or your own words to pray that you, your family, your parish community, your Church make Christ visible to the world:

Lord, help me to carry on your mission of love, forgiveness, and healing. I pray that the Church might be a sign to the world that God's saving presence is at work in the hearts of all people. Amen.

THE CHURCH ON ITS WAY

Adult Focus

*For here we have no lasting city,
but we seek the one that is to come.*

Hebrews 13:14

In this chapter, we explore the ways the Church is like a pilgrim walking in Christ's footsteps in the world. We, the people of God, are following Jesus as he leads us toward the final stage of completing the Church. At Christ's second coming, Christ and his faithful followers will be united forever; the Church will be completed. The choice we make between living for heaven or living for hell will be made known before the whole world on the last day at the last judgment. The young people will consider that they themselves make a free choice for heaven or for hell. They will discover that at the time of particular judgment, they will be judged on the choices they have made in the light of Christ's teaching.

Help the young people to understand that if we try our best to do God's will, to be faithful, the end of our earthly lives will be the beginning of new life full of joy and love. Jesus himself promised: "I will see you again, and your hearts will rejoice, and no one will take your joy away from you" (John 16:22).

Catechism Focus

The themes of this chapter correspond to paragraphs 673–679 and 946–972 of the *Catechism*.

Enrichment Activities

With Hope

Have the young people discuss song lyrics or dialogue from movies or television shows that support or detract from a hope-filled view of the end of time and eternal life. Then have the whole group work together to compose a letter to the editor of a magazine for young people, in which they praise the writers whose work supports the hope-filled view.

Remote Preparation

Invite the young people to make prayer cards with one of the following prayers or the Prayer for the Presence of God on Guide, page 88–89. Explain that they should say the prayer of choice often to prepare themselves for the time when they will see God "face-to-face."

God be in my heart
And in my thinking;
God be at my end,
And at my departing.
(from the Sarum missal)

God to enfold me,
God to surround me,
God in my ever-living soul,
God in mine eternity.
(from an Irish blessing)

Hopeful View

You may wish to show the video *Encounter with Garvan Byrne*. The film is about a twelve-year-old boy who suffered from painful bone cancer. In the film he shares his insights about the meaning of life and his deep faith in Jesus.

The video is available from:
Ignatius Press
P.O. Box 1339
Ft. Collins, CO 80522

Teaching Resources

Overview

To understand that the pilgrim Church is moving toward the last day when Christ will come in glory; to explore the Church's teaching about the last day, final and particular judgments, and our free choice of heaven or hell.

Opening Prayer Ideas

Invite the group to look at the photo on pages 88 and 89. Then all pray together the words on page 89.

or

All proclaim together:
  Christ has died,
  Christ is risen,
  Christ will come again.

Materials

- texts, Bibles, journals, highlighters

Creed Journal:
For Chapter 11, use pages 56 and 57.

REPRODUCIBLE MASTERS
- handout *Life Changed, Not Ended*, page 88C
- *Chapter 11 Assessment*, page 95A
- *Highlights for Home*, page 95B

Supplemental Resources

PAMPHLETS
- "Facing the Death of Friends"
- "Heaven and Hell: Life's More Than A Beach"

St. Anthony Messenger
1615 Republic Street
Cincinnati, Ohio 45210

CHAPTER
eleven

Life Changed, Not Ended

The funeral Mass celebrated for a Catholic who has died affirms that in death "Life is changed, not ended." What do you think that "changed life" will be? Select one answer for each of the following statements.

	Agree	Disagree	Not Sure
1. Time will go slowly.	_____	_____	_____
2. We will look different.	_____	_____	_____
3. We will be reincarnated as other people or animals.	_____	_____	_____
4. We will have to suffer for everything wrong we did on earth.	_____	_____	_____
5. Heaven will be full of energy, love, joy.	_____	_____	_____
6. We will be nothing. Heaven and hell do not exist.	_____	_____	_____
7. Hell is a place of fire and brimstone.	_____	_____	_____
8. Hell is the complete absence of God.	_____	_____	_____
9. Heaven is a place with white clouds.	_____	_____	_____
10. Heaven is happiness beyond our imagining.	_____	_____	_____

Write your own description of your expectations for life after death.

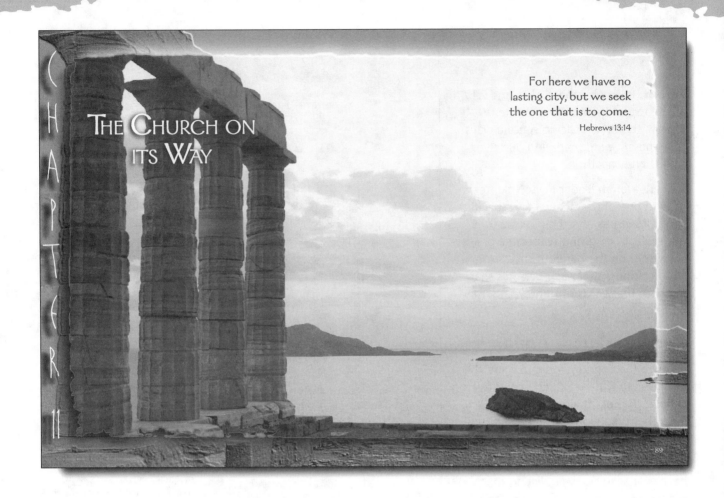

THE CHURCH ON ITS WAY

> For here we have no lasting city, but we seek the one that is to come.
>
> Hebrews 13:14

Objectives: To understand that the pilgrim Church is moving toward the last day when Christ will come in glory; to explore the Church's teaching about the last day, final and particular judgments, and our free choice of heaven or hell.

Introduction ___ min.

Opening Prayer: Invite the young people to look at the photo on pages 88 and 89. Together read Hebrews 13:14. Ask the young people to imagine that they are walking outdoors along a favorite, peaceful path. Have them repeat each verse of the Prayer for the Presence of God.

Through every moment of this day:
    Be with me, Lord.
Through every day of all this week:
    Be with me, Lord.
Through every week of all this year:
    Be with me, Lord.
Through every year of all this life:
    Be with me, Lord.
So that when time is past,
    By grace I may at last,
    Be with you, Lord.

Chapter Warm-up: Distribute the handout *Life Changed, Not Ended*. Allow about ten minutes for the young people to complete the questionnaire. Then ask volunteers to share their descriptions of life after death with the entire group.

Forum: Read together Colossians 3:17 at the top of the handout *Whatever!* Explain that in practicing specific ways of witness we are preparing ourselves for life after death.

Have the *forum* leader invite volunteers to read one of the general and specific ways of witness and the possible fruitful results from giving witness he or she wrote on the handout sheet. Ask all to respond after each person's sharing with the words of Hebrews 13:14 on page 89.

Presentation ___ min.

◆ Invite the young people to share the key ideas they have underlined in this chapter. Discuss their choices. Then have them highlight those highlighted on your reduced pages.

◆ Ask the young people whether they have ever seen signs predicting that the world will end on a certain day or heard a preacher giving a "doomsday" description of the end of the world. Explain that Catholics believe we should get ready for this day not in fear but with hope. Ask, "What do Catholics believe about the end of the world?" If the young people need reminding, have them look at "The Last Day" on pages 90 and 91.

◆ Discuss the last day, the day of judgment. Emphasize that how we spend eternity is dependent on the choices we make about the way we live our lives. Read together Matthew 25:31–46.

WHAT dreams do you have for the future?
What dreams do you think God has for our future?

The Pilgrim Church

From the time of the apostles, the Church has been part of every age. It has grown and developed and spread around the world. It is here, but it is not yet complete. The Church is on its way: It is the pilgrim Church.

Why do we call it the pilgrim Church? The Church is like a pilgrim walking in Christ's footsteps in the world. On this pilgrimage we, the people of God, are invited to go along with Christ. He is headed toward the final stage of completing the Church. That stage takes us to the fulfillment of God's kingdom, when Jesus will bring us home with him forever. This pilgrimage, however, is not a free ride. Between today and the last day of the world, there is a great deal to be done to get the world ready for Christ. He is coming again.

90

The Last Day

Jesus' first coming was at his birth. His *second coming* will be at the end of the world. This second coming is also called the last day, or the day of judgment. The last day will be the end of the world and life as we know it. At that moment the whole magnificent plan of God will be complete. Everything will change. The world we know, with its clouds, mountains, city streets, and country roads, will no longer be the same. All the things we are concerned about now—falling in love, taking a test, getting ill, having fun, even death itself—will come to an end as we know them. Then Christ and his faithful followers will be united forever; the Church will be completed.

When Christ comes, we shall see him for ourselves. What we believed without seeing will then become clear, and we will go on forever with the risen Christ, our brother and our Lord. A timeless, changeless new world will be ours. It seems almost unimaginable, but words such as *time* and *change* will no longer have meaning for us. That's how different everything will be.

For those in heaven there will not be the least chance of being unhappy, lonely, uncertain, or troubled again in any way. What is heaven? *Heaven* is life with the Blessed Trinity forever. It is the state of supreme happiness in which those who have been faithful to God and his commandments will enjoy the beatific vision, seeing God "face-to-face." Jesus himself told us, "I will see you again, and your hearts will rejoice, and no one will take your joy away from you" (John 16:22).

Those in hell, on the other hand, will be miserable for all eternity. *Hell* is eternal separation from God. Hell is the just punishment for those who have rejected God. For those who deliberately choose a life of sin, there is nothing ahead but everlasting misery.

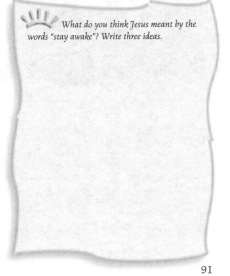

What do you think Jesus meant by the words "stay awake"? Write three ideas.

When will all this happen? Jesus did not say. It wasn't his Father's wish that he make that detail known. How will the world end? We aren't sure. We know only that Jesus put us on alert. He said, "Stay awake, for you know neither the day nor the hour" (Matthew 25:13).

Should we be afraid of this last day and worry that everything will be destroyed? Not at all. God has promised us that it will be the beginning of new life, the likes of which we have never experienced. At his second coming Christ will take possession of creation for his Father and remake it. We read in 2 Peter 3:13: "According to his promise we await new heavens and a new earth."

91

◆ Direct the young people's attention to the photo on pages 90 and 91. Have them imagine that they are on one of the escalators. Remind the group that the Church, which is part of every age, is moving with Christ toward the final stage of completing the Church.

Ask the young people to come up with other images that might suggest our pilgrimage with Christ.

◆ Read the thought provoker on page 91. Have the young people write their responses to these questions in the space provided.

Note: The following activity is optional.

◆ Point out to the young people that for the past ten weeks, they have been traveling companions on the journey of faith. They have helped one another by sharing their insights in discussion and prayer.

Invite each young person to write a note of thanks to the group for sharing and helping along the way. Display the notes where all the young people can read them and appreciate one another's many contributions.

Presentation (cont'd)

◆ Read together Matthew 6:19–21. Ask "What treasures in heaven may Jesus be referring to in this passage?" Have the young people consider what they have studied during the semester. Possible responses include: prayer, the deposit of faith, our ancestors in faith, and the Church.

Encourage the young people to do the journaling activity on page 56 of the *Creed Journal.* Play music softly as they work.

◆ Invite responses to the following questions about an individual's personal last day.

• What is particular judgment? (*On an individual's day of death, Christ judges the individual's choices and determines whether the choice deserves eternal reward or eternal punishment.*)

• How is it our choice whether we receive eternal reward or punishment? (*We choose heaven or hell by the way we live each day. God does not choose for us.*)

• What does death bring for those who have served Christ? (*the end of their earthly pilgrimage and the beginning of eternal happiness and peace*)

• What is purgatory? (*a process of final purification after death, in which those who have died in the state of grace grow in the holiness they need to enter the joy of heaven*)

◆ Read together the parable of the rich man and Lazarus (Luke 16:19–31). Then have the young people form small "dramatic troupes" to prepare modern adaptations of the parable. Have each troupe present its dramatization to the whole group or to another class.

On that day Jesus will come in glory as king and judge, sitting on a throne surrounded by angels. Everyone who ever existed will be assembled before him. Those whom he has placed on his right will enjoy "eternal life"; those on his left will go off to "eternal punishment" (Matthew 25:31–46). The message is clear; the way we live our lives is up to us.

Do you ever think of yourself as a pilgrim? Where are you headed? Who goes with you? What hopes do you have about your destination?

The choice we make between living for heaven or living for hell will be made known before the whole world on the last day, the day of judgment. On the day of judgment, everyone who ever lived will be present together. Then all will know where they stand in relation to one another and to Christ. This is the *last judgment* that will accompany Christ's second coming at the end of the world. It is described with powerful imagery in Scripture.

CATHOLIC TEACHINGS
About Death
Even though death is a time of great sadness, Catholics have a sure hope in the resurrection. Everything we do points to this hope. We gather to support one another at a wake service and kneel at the coffin to pray for the deceased. Our funeral liturgy is filled with the good news of eternal life. We bury the body with reverence in blessed ground. We continue to pray for our loved ones after their death. We believe what we say in the liturgy: "Lord, for your faithful people life is changed, not ended."

92

Our Personal Last Day

Human beings have a limited time on earth. Death is a part of our life; it is a result of original sin. In every person's life there is a "last day," and this last day takes place before Christ's second coming. This personal last day is the day we die.

At the time of our death, we shall see ourselves as we are. We will be judged on the choices we have made in the light of Christ's teachings. By the way we live now, we choose heaven or hell. Free people have to accept the responsibility and the consequences of their choices. God does not choose heaven or hell for any one of us; we choose it for ourselves.

For those who have served Christ, death will be the day they have been waiting for—the end of their earthly pilgrimage and the beginning of endless happiness and peace. Will this eternal happiness start immediately? No. For many there must first be a process of purification, which the Church calls purgatory. *Purgatory* is a process of final purification after death in which those who have died in the state of grace grow in the holiness they need to enter the joy of heaven. We can help the souls experiencing purgatory by our good works and prayers, especially the Mass. That is because the souls in purgatory are certain of heaven, unlike those who have chosen hell.

The day of death is final. On that day, in what is called the *particular judgment*, Christ will judge the choice each individual has made and will determine the eternal reward or punishment that each choice deserves. This choice and its consequence—heaven or hell—is what will be repeated before the whole world at the last judgment at the end of the world.

People of faith should not get nervous at the mention of heaven, hell, and judgment. Heaven actually begins on earth with Baptism and is completed in eternity. Because we trust in God's great love and mercy, the Church reminds us that staying out of hell is not our life's work. Staying in heaven is.

Did you ever think that heaven or hell is your choice to make? What do you think about this freedom you have to choose?

93

◆ Have a volunteer summarize *Catholic Teachings* on page 92. Take time to share the ways the Church shows its respect for the dead and its faith in the resurrection.

• The casket is covered with a white cloth. This symbolizes that the person has been baptized in Christ.

• The paschal candle is lit. It is the sign of Christ's resurrection in which all believers will share.

• The body is blessed with holy water, again a sign that the person is united with Christ through Baptism.

◆ Allow time for the young people to respond to the **thought provoker** on page 93. Invite volunteers to share their thoughts with the group.

FYI Share the following prayer, which Catholics sing or say as they process from the church with the body after a funeral Mass.

> May the angels lead you into paradise;
> may the martyrs come to welcome you
> and take you to the holy city,
> the new and eternal Jerusalem.

How do the words express our belief that for those who have served Christ, death is the end of their earthly pilgrimage and the beginning of endless happiness and peace?

Presentation (cont'd)

◆ Have a volunteer read aloud the second and third paragraphs of "The Resurrection of the Dead" on page 94.

Note: Sometimes young people may be skeptical of anything that cannot be proved scientifically. If you encounter such skepticism, you might respond simply that God's wisdom and plan for us goes far beyond our limited human imaginations.

◆ Read the first two sentences of "A Catholic View," and discuss the Church's teaching about reincarnation.

Then ask, "As a Catholic what is your reaction to those who claim to know when and how the world will end?" (*God is a God of love, not of destruction. We should be full of hope because there will be a new heaven and a new earth.*)

Conclusion ___ min.

◆ Have the group find the definition of *heaven* and write it under *Words to Remember.*

◆ Have a volunteer read *On Line with the Parish.* Encourage the young people to remember to pray for the dead whenever they hear the tolling bell.

Assessment: If you plan to administer *Chapter 11 Assessment*, allow about ten minutes for its completion.

The Resurrection of the Dead

Our profession of faith concludes with our belief in the resurrection of the dead on the last day. Catholics firmly proclaim that just as Christ rose from the dead, so will Christ raise us up. On the last day our souls will be reunited with our bodies. Jesus himself scolded some people who did not believe in the resurrection of the dead (Mark 12:24). Jesus also described himself as the "resurrection and the life" (John 11:25). Several times he even gave a sign of the future by bringing some of the dead back to life.

The resurrection of the body is difficult for some people to accept. After all, the body decays after burial, and some bodies are even cremated. What do we say about this? We respond in faith. Just as Christ rose from the dead with his human body totally transformed, so he promised that we will rise at the end of time with our bodies transformed. How will this happen? Through God's almighty power, which is beyond our imagination and understanding.

What we can say with certainty is that we belong completely to Christ. From the moment of Baptism, we are united with him, both body and soul. Because human beings are not just souls, both the body and the soul should experience the rewards or punishments of eternal life.

A Catholic View

You may have heard someone say, "In my next life, I want to be...." What should a Catholic say to this? The Church's teachings about the last things are definite and clear and come from what God has revealed to us. After our pilgrimage of life on earth is ended, God will not make us live another earthly life or a series of earthly lives. We will die only once and then stand before the God of justice, mercy, and love. That is why Catholics do not believe in reincarnation. The idea is totally contrary to God's plan for us.

94

You may also have heard people who claim to know when and how the world will end. They quote passages from Scripture that seem to say the world will end in complete destruction, with stars and planets falling from the sky. What should a Catholic's reaction be?

As always we turn to the Church to guide us. Just as Catholics see the truth of creation described in poetic terms in Scripture, so, too, the end of time is described in a poetic but truthful way. God is not a God of destruction; he is a God of love. As we already know, there will be new heavens and a new earth. The Church really does have a beautiful and hope-filled view of the end of time and eternal life.

How should our beliefs in the last things affect our daily lives? Do these beliefs frighten you? challenge you? give you hope? Explain.

Answers for Chapter 11 Assessment

1. b	2. a	3. d	4. b	5. a
6. a	7. b	8. d	9. d	10. See page 94.

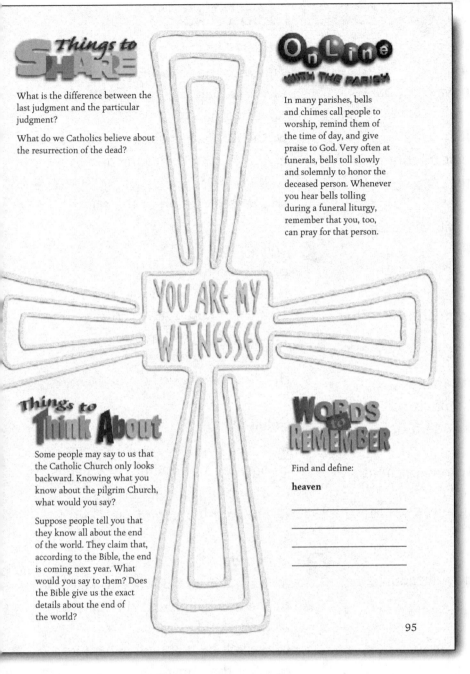

Things to SHARE

What is the difference between the last judgment and the particular judgment?

What do we Catholics believe about the resurrection of the dead?

OnLine WITH THE PARISH

In many parishes, bells and chimes call people to worship, remind them of the time of day, and give praise to God. Very often at funerals, bells toll slowly and solemnly to honor the deceased person. Whenever you hear bells tolling during a funeral liturgy, remember that you, too, can pray for that person.

YOU ARE MY WITNESSES

Things to Think About

Some people may say to us that the Catholic Church only looks backward. Knowing what you know about the pilgrim Church, what would you say?

Suppose people tell you that they know all about the end of the world. They claim that, according to the Bible, the end is coming next year. What would you say to them? Does the Bible give us the exact details about the end of the world?

Words to REMEMBER

Find and define:

heaven

_____
_____
_____
_____

95

Conclusion (cont'd)

◆ Invite responses to *Things to Think About* on page 95. Then ask the young people to share their thoughts on the 〰 thought provoker on page 94.

◆ Form two groups. Each group will prepare a response to one of the questions of *Things to Share.* Bring the groups together for discussion of these ideas.

FORUM Assignment

✔ Read Chapter 12, pages 96–103. Underline in pencil six key ideas.

✔ Ask at least three people of different ages: "Why is Mary so important to us Catholics?" "What is your favorite image (statue or painting) of Mary?"

Closing Prayer: Gather the group in a prayer circle. Someone might lightly toll a handbell several times. Play evocative music in the background. One suggestion might be the movement from Dvorjak's *New World Symphony* (from the spiritual "Goin' Home"). As the music plays softly, read Revelation 21:1–5. Pause at the end for silent reflection. Then all pray together the words from Hebrews on page 89.

FOR CHAPTER 12

- preparation of opening-prayer volunteers
- copies of handout *Companion on the Way,* page 96C
- copies of *Chapter 12 Assessment,* page 103A
- copies of *Highlights for Home,* page 103B

Evaluation: Have the young people explored what Catholics believe about Christ's second coming and our personal last day? Have they understood that the choice for heaven or hell is theirs?

Assessment

1 The Church is called _____ because it is on the way to God.
 a. the family of God
 b. the pilgrim Church
 c. the Church of reincarnation
 d. the body of Christ

2 The final judgment will take place at
 a. Christ's second coming.
 b. a person's death.
 c. the particular judgment.
 d. purgatory.

3 Choose the *false* statement.
 a. Heaven or hell is our choice.
 b. In death life is changed, not ended.
 c. Heaven begins with Baptism; it is completed in eternity.
 d. We can know when the world will end.

4 The process of final purification is called
 a. canonization.
 b. purgatory.
 c. heaven.
 d. hell.

5 A person's particular judgment will take place
 a. on the day of death.
 b. at the end of the world.
 c. at Baptism.
 d. none of the above

6 Which of the following is **not** a Catholic belief?
 a. reincarnation
 b. the last judgment
 c. the reuniting of body and soul on the last day
 d. the intercession of the saints

7 The last day
 a. is to be feared.
 b. will be the beginning of a new heaven and a new earth.
 c. has been given a date by Scripture scholars.
 d. all of the above

8 Hell is
 a. only a superstition.
 b. only for a brief time.
 c. a time of purification.
 d. eternal separation from God.

9 In heaven
 a. we shall see God face-to-face.
 b. there is a timeless, changeless new world.
 c. we will be completely happy.
 d. all of the above

10 What do Catholics believe about the resurrection of the dead?

_____
_____
_____
_____
_____
_____

CHAPTER 11

Highlights for Home

Focus on Faith

In this chapter, the young people explored the ways the Church is like a pilgrim walking in Christ's footsteps in the world. At Christ's second coming, Christ and his faithful followers will be united forever; the Church will be completed.

Today the young people see and hear so many strange things about what happens at the time of and after a person's death. Read over this chapter and discuss with your son or daughter the Church's teachings about death and judgment, and the resurrection of the body on the last day. We want our young people to face the future with hope, not dread, in their hearts. Help them appreciate that they are connected to all the members of the Church in Baptism and faith.

Conversation Starters

. . . . a few ideas to talk about together . . . .

◆ At my death Jesus will say, "Whatever you did for one of these least brothers of mine, you did for me" (Matthew 25:40). Does this give me hope?

◆ My feelings about death . . . eternity . . . the end of the world . . .

Feature Focus

In *Catholic Teachings* on page 92 the young people learn that at the time of a person's death, Catholics show by everything they do that they have a sure hope in the resurrection. We support one another at a wake service. We celebrate the good news of eternal life during the funeral liturgy. We bury the person's body reverently in blessed ground, and we continue to remember the person in our thoughts and prayers.

Reflection

Reflect on "The Pilgrim Church" on page 90. Share your reflections with family and friends. Write a list of things that need to be done to get the world ready for Christ's coming at the end of time.

Respond in your journal to the following:

• Your pilgrimage is not a free ride. Are you willing to do the work required to complete the journey? Write one specific thing you will do this week to earn your place among the pilgrims.

• Jesus Christ is with you on your journey. What words of his in Scripture will bring you comfort and fill you with determination to keep traveling through storms and across difficult terrain?

DISCIPLES FOREVER

Adult Focus

In this chapter the young people will learn that Mary, the mother of Jesus, is a guiding light to the pilgrim Church on its way. On earth her life was an example of the Church's pilgrimage of faith. In heaven she is the image of what the Church hopes to be.

The young people will discover that all the members of the Church are connected to one another in Baptism and faith. They will learn that the communion of saints is the unity and cooperation of the members of the Church on earth with those in heaven and in purgatory.

As you come to the end of this course on Creed, encourage the young people to make the beliefs they have studied an integral part of their lives so that they will be vibrant, generous, and faithful disciples forever.

Catechism Focus

The themes of this chapter correspond to paragraphs 942–976 of the *Catechism*.

Enrichment Activities

Video View

The following videos are available from Vision Video. (See *Supplementary Resources* for address.)

- *Mary: A Word, a Prayer.* Covers twenty centuries of devotion and art honoring Mary.
- *The Holy Rosary with the Pope.* Shows Pope John Paul II with Cardinal O'Connor praying the rosary during the pope's visit to the United States in October, 1995.

The Printed Word

The following pamphlets are available from St. Anthony Messenger Press. (See *Supplementary Resources* for address.)

In *Youth Update:*
- "On Mary: Truths and Connections"
- "Seen Any Saints Lately?"
- "The Rosary's Mysteries Can Be Your Own"

In *Catholic Update:*
- "The Communion of Saints: 'People Who Need People'"
- "The Feasts of Mary"

Overview

To deepen understanding of Mary as a model for the Church; to explore the significance of the communion of saints.

Opening Prayer Ideas

A volunteer reads aloud Matthew 4:18–20. Pause and ask the young people to reflect on what it means to them to follow Jesus.

or

Have several young people invoke the titles of Our Lady mentioned in the *thought provoker* on page 99. All should respond after each invocation, "Pray for us."

Materials

• Bibles, journals, and highlighters
• instrumental music

Creed Journal:
For Chapter 12, use pages 58 and 59.

REPRODUCIBLE MASTERS

• handout *Companion on the Way*, page 96C
• *Chapter 12 Assessment*, page 111A
• *Highlights for Home*, page 111B

Supplemental Resources

VIDEOS
Vision Video Inc.
2030 Wentz Church Road
P.O. Box 540
Worcester, PA 19490–0540

PAMPHLETS
St. Anthony Messenger
1615 Republic Street
Cincinnati, OH 45210

Companion on the Way

Choose a saint to be your friend and companion as you walk in Jesus' footsteps. Then, in the speech balloons, write conversation you share with your "companion on the way."

- In frame 1, talk with the person about the reasons you have chosen him or her.
- In frame 2, discuss one accomplishment for which the person is known.
- In frame 3, tell what's going on in your life and why you need guidance. Have your companion respond.

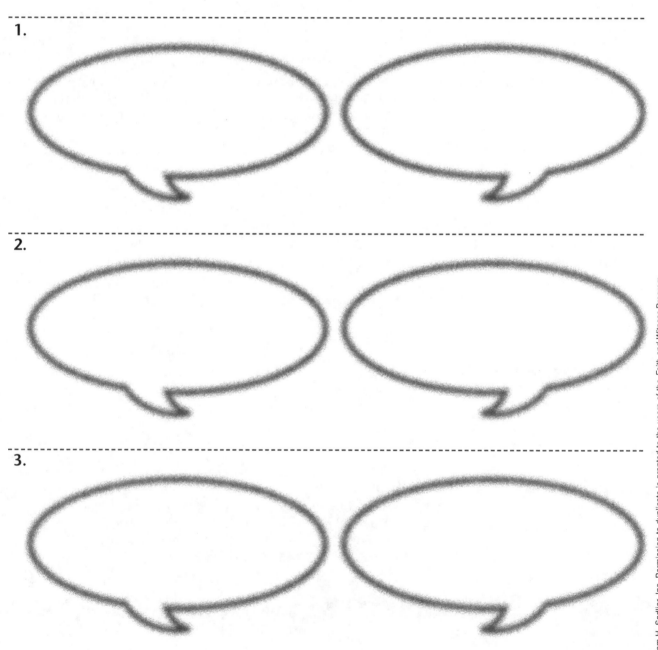

1.

2.

3.

DISCIPLES FOREVER

Come, follow me.
Matthew 4:19

Objectives: To deepen understanding of Mary as a model for the Church; to explore the significance of the communion of saints.

Introduction ___ min.

Opening Prayer: Invite the young people to look at the photos on pages 96 and 97. Use the following script to guide their reflection.

> In the colored photograph, you can see that each rock or stone has a unique shape, varied markings, and different coloration. In the black and white photograph, you see that when placed together, each stone contributes to making a path or a way to walk.

> Let each stone represent a saint, a disciple who answered Jesus' call to follow him, each bringing his or her unique God-given gifts along the way.

> For each colored stone pictured, designate a saint who is special to you, who forms a path or shows you the way as you answer Jesus' call to discipleship. Write each saint's name in your journal.

Have the young people read together the words of the hymn on page 98. Then have a prayer leader read the reflection that follows. Have the young people respond to the questions in their journals.

Forum: Have the young people form small groups to share the responses they received to the questions:

- Why is Mary so important to us Catholics?
- What is your favorite image (statue or painting) of Mary?

Ask, "Do any of these images illustrate an event or main idea presented on pages 99 and 100? in what way?" If time permits, have a representative from each group share its findings with all.

Presentation ___ min.

◆ Ask several young people to share the six key ideas they have underlined in this chapter. Discuss their choices. Then have them highlight those that are highlighted on your reduced pages.

◆ Ask the young people why they think a chapter called *Disciples Forever* would begin with a section on Mary. Perhaps they will recognize that Mary is the first and greatest disciple of Jesus. She always answered his call; she always did God's will.

◆ Point out to the young people that in the Litany of the Blessed Virgin Mary, Mary is called "Morning Star." Ask, "What is the significance of this title?" (*She is a guiding light to the pilgrim Church. On earth her life was an example of faith; in heaven she shows us what the Church hopes to be.*)

◆ Discuss the privilege of Mary that we know as the *immaculate conception*. Write the term on the board. Make sure that the group understands that from the very moment of her conception, Mary was free from original sin.

THE words of an old hymn remind us:

> Whether the road be brief or long,
> Whether silent or full of song
> We follow, Lord, through night and day:
> You are Companion, Light, and Way.

We Christians are pilgrims on our way to fullness of life with God forever. We do not travel alone, however. We have one another. We have the Church. Angels and saints walk with us. The Mother of God protects and supports us. And Jesus himself is our "Companion, Light, and Way."

Do you believe this? How does it help you during difficult times?

98

The Morning Star

A study of the Church and what it means to live a Catholic way of life would be incomplete without mentioning Mary, the mother of Jesus. On earth her life was an example of the Church's pilgrimage of faith. In heaven she is the image of what the Church hopes to be. That is why she has been given the beautiful title of the "Morning Star" in the Litany of the Blessed Virgin Mary. She is a guiding light to the pilgrim Church on its way.

Who is this woman for whom thousands of parish churches are named and whose image we see in millions of statues and paintings throughout the world? Why do Catholics show her such great honor and devotion?

There has never been anyone quite like Mary. From all eternity God chose her to be the mother of his Son. For that reason God gave her the privilege of being free from original sin from the first moment of her conception in her mother's womb. This privilege of Mary is what we know as the *immaculate conception*. It doesn't mean that Mary wasn't fully human. It means that she experienced redemption from the first moment of her life. She was full of grace. This was appropriate because she was to be the mother of the Savior of the world. She would carry God's only Son in her womb for nine months.

How did Mary become the mother of God's only Son? At the annunciation she said yes to God's invitation, and she conceived through the power of the Holy Spirit. Her son was not conceived through sexual relations, as other children are. Jesus was to have no human father, but only his Father in heaven. That is why we call Joseph the foster father of Jesus. That is also why we call Mary a virgin and why Jesus' birth is described as a virgin birth. Mary never engaged in sexual relations at any time in her life.

As we already know, the child born of the Virgin Mary was a divine Person with both a human nature and a divine nature. For that reason the greatest title of Mary is Mother of God. Jesus was not a human person; he was a divine Person with two natures.

And that is why the Church reminds us that Mary must always be seen in relationship to her son. Mary's greatness comes from Christ. The Church's teaching is clear: "What the Catholic faith believes about Mary is based on what it believes about Christ, and what it teaches about Mary illumines in turn its faith in Christ" (*Catechism*, 487).

The Litany of the Blessed Virgin Mary prays to Mary under many titles. They include Mother most pure, Cause of our joy, House of gold, Health of the sick, Queen of peace. Write a prayer using one title, or draw a symbol that expresses it for you.

99

◆ Have three volunteers who have prepared in advance do a dramatic reading of Luke 1:26–38. The readers will take the roles of narrator, Gabriel, and Mary.

Then write the word *annunciation* on the board. Ask, "What happened at the annunciation?" (*Mary said yes to God's invitation to become the mother of God's only Son, and she conceived through the power of the Holy Spirit.*)

Now have a volunteer read the last two paragraphs in column 1 on page 99.

◆ Point out the **thought provoker** on page 99. The young people can respond to this on page 59 of the *Creed Journal,* or they can do the journaling activity on page 58 of the *Creed Journal.* Volunteers may share their thoughts *if they wish.*

Presentation (cont'd)

◆ Remind the young people that the word *disciple* means "someone who follows a teacher, a master, to learn from him."

Invite the young people to name ways that showed Mary to be Jesus' first disciple. They should be able to name the following ways.

• She brought Jesus into the world.

• She witnessed his public ministry.

• She stood at the foot of the cross.

• She was a witness to his resurrection and ascension.

• She waited with the disciples for the coming of the Holy Spirit.

Emphasize that from the moment Mary said yes to becoming the mother of Jesus, she became the first Christian, the first follower of Jesus.

◆ Discuss the Church's teaching about the assumption. Explain that since Mary was always free from original sin and its effects, God chose to have her anticipate the resurrection that all of us one day will experience. Mary was taken, body and soul, into heaven.

◆ Now have the young people respond to the ꜱꜱꜱ **thought provoker** on page 100.

◆ Have a volunteer read aloud the *Scripture Update* on page 100.

The First Disciple

Who knew Jesus better than Mary did? We know from Scripture that she was an intimate part of Jesus' life. She brought him into the world. Like other mothers, she was there as her child grew. She witnessed his public ministry and even stood at the foot of the cross. But her closeness to Jesus did not end there. Along with Jesus' disciples she became a witness to the resurrection and ascension. She also waited in prayerful anticipation for the coming of the Holy Spirit. All these things tell us that Mary was the first of Jesus' disciples. From the moment she agreed to the incarnation, she was a Christian before anyone else was.

Mary cooperated fully with God's grace and remained free of any personal sin her whole life long. She was obedient to whatever God asked

of her, and she followed no one but her son. In bringing Jesus into the world and in living as she did, Mary is a true model for the Church. She gives the example all of us should follow. Because we are the body of Christ, Mary, the mother of Jesus, is the Mother of the Church and our mother, too.

Although we do not know all the details of Mary's earthly life, we can be sure that she was a treasured member of the early Christian community. But what became of Mary? The Church teaches that because of her immaculate conception, Mary was given another privilege at the end of her life. She anticipated the resurrection that all of us will experience. Mary was taken up, or assumed, both body and soul into heaven at the end of her earthly life. This is known as the *assumption*.

Jesus loved his mother very much and knew how important she would be for his Church. When he was dying on the cross, Jesus himself said to John, his beloved disciple, and to us, "Behold, your mother" (John 19:27). Having been taken up into heaven, Mary has not forgotten us. She is still Mother of the Church. She is the mother of each one of us.

ꜱꜱꜱ *Some people have described Mary as the perfect disciple of Jesus. Give examples to show why this is so.*

*Scripture*UPDATE

Mark 3:31–35 and several other Scripture passages refer to the brothers and sisters of Jesus. If Mary was always a virgin, what do these passages mean? The Church teaches us that these passages are "not referring to other children of the Virgin Mary. In fact James and Joseph, 'brothers of Jesus,' are the sons of another Mary, a disciple of Christ, whom Saint Matthew significantly calls 'the other Mary.' They are close relations of Jesus, according to an Old Testament expression" (*Catechism*, 500).

Saint Martin de Porres

Saint Cecilia

Blessed Kateri Tekakwitha

Help Along the Way

Whenever we think of the Blessed Virgin Mary, we should remember that she is the first and greatest among the saints. Who are these men and women called saints? Why are they so important in our Catholic life?

The word *saint* means "one who is holy." It was used in the early Church to describe all the baptized. They were called holy because through Baptism they had been given a share in the divine life. As time passed, however, *saint* was used more often for holy people who followed Christ in extraordinary and heroic ways. For example, the early martyrs, who shed their blood for the faith, were immediately recognized and honored as saints in the communities where they lived.

Eventually an official process was developed to help the entire Church community recognize those who had lived exceptional lives of faith. This process is called *canonization.* How does it work? First the name of a person considered to be worthy of the title saint is submitted to Church authorities.

Then a thorough investigation of this person's life is conducted. When this process is completed and positive results are found, the pope proclaims that person a saint. Now the new saint can be honored by all the members of the Church. We can follow his or her path to holiness.

Are all the saints in heaven canonized? Of course not. Millions upon millions of good and holy people, including members of our own families, have not been officially canonized by the Church but may well be in heaven. The saints who have been canonized are a gift to the whole Church. They have been set before us as heroes and heroines of faith.

The canonized saints are a great treasure. We honor them by remembering them in prayer and by setting aside special feast days to commemorate their lives. Besides this, we name shrines, churches, and other institutions after them and dedicate these structures to their memory. But there is one day during the year when all the saints, both canonized and not canonized, are honored. That day is November 1.

101

◆ Have the young people imagine they are living during the early days of the Church. Ask them to take a minute to greet one another by saying the title *saint* followed by the person's first name. Then ask a volunteer to explain the reason the early Christians called one another "saint."

◆ Have volunteers explain the process of canonization. List the following steps on the board.

• The name of the person considered to be worthy of being called a saint is submitted to Church authorities.

• A thorough investigation of the person's life is conducted.

• If the results are positive, the pope proclaims the person to be a saint.

Then ask, "Why do we consider the saints a great treasure?" (*They are heroes and heroines of faith. They are shining examples to us.*)

◆ Point out the question that begins the second paragraph in the right column on page 101. Stress that any person who has died in God's grace is a saint in heaven. Canonized saints have been named by the Church so that we might have models of holiness to follow.

FYI

Share the following profiles of the saints pictured on page 101.

Martin de Porres was a Dominican brother in Lima, Peru. He cared for anyone who was sick or afflicted.

Cecilia was a martyr in the early Church. She is the patron saint of musicians.

Kateri Tekakwitha was a native American who became a convert to the faith. She was treated with cruelty by her tribe. She escaped and became a very prayerful and caring helper of the sick.

Presentation (cont'd)

◆ A final term to add to the board is *communion of saints*. Ask, "Who belongs to this communion?" (*The members of the Church on earth, those experiencing purgatory, and those in heaven.*) Invite a discussion of what it means to be part of this union.

◆ Have the young people complete the ☼ **thought provoker** on page 102.

◆ Direct attention to "Living as Catholics" on page 102. Emphasize the following points:

• Each day we have an opportunity to make our beliefs as members of the Catholic Church an important part of our lives.

• It is now up to us to share the teachings of Christ and his Church with the whole world.

◆ Discuss *Catholic ID* and explain the meaning of canon law.

Conclusion ___ min.

◆ Take a minute or two to ask for responses for the questions under *Things to Think About* and the first question under *Things to Share*. Then have the group find and write the definition of *communion of saints* under *Words to Remember*.

Assessment: If you plan to administer *Chapter 12 Assessment*, allow about ten minutes for its completion.

Whenever we think about saints, we are reminded that all the members of the Church are connected with one another through Baptism and faith. This includes three groups: the members of the Church on earth, those experiencing purgatory, and those who have already attained the blessedness of heaven. We call this union of all the Church members the communion of saints. The *communion of saints* is the unity and cooperation of the members of the Church on earth with those in heaven and in purgatory.

Why is this communion of saints so important for us? It reminds us that we can pray for the dead and assist them by our prayers. It also reminds us that Mary and the other saints can pray for us, or intercede for us with God. The saints are our brothers and sisters in faith. Through their prayers for us and by the example of their lives, they are powerful friends in helping the pilgrim Church on its way.

CATHOLIC ID

Every Catholic should know that the Church has its own body of laws called canon law. The word *canon* means an "official rule." The canons of the Church are formulated to guide the life of the Church. Questions they deal with include Church administration, the rights and obligations of the faithful, and the correct procedures for Catholic marriages and other acts of divine worship. There are 1,752 canons, or laws, in the *Code of Canon Law*. There is one code of canon law for the Western Catholic Church and another for the Eastern Catholic Churches.

☼ *If you could choose any saint to be your special friend and companion on the way, who would it be? Why?*

Living as Catholics

Our study of basic Catholic beliefs has now come to a close. Each day we have an opportunity to make these beliefs a part of our lives. Our beliefs are so important that they truly identify us as members of the Catholic Church.

Our beliefs give meaning to everything we do. What we believe about the life of grace and our need for salvation, for example, affects the choices we make between right and wrong. Knowing about the Blessed Trinity and understanding the importance of Christ and his Church are the foundations of our sacramental life and worship of God. Our understanding of God, revelation, and faith itself helps us to realize that we can have a personal relationship with the transcendent and living God. All our beliefs, in fact, shape our Catholic life each and every day.

As informed members of the Church today, we stand on the shoulders of those who have gone before us in faith. They have passed on to us the teachings of Christ and his Church and have shown us how to live them in a dynamic way. It is now up to us to share these with the whole world.

102

Answers for Chapter 12 Assessment

1. c	2. a	3. d	4. b	5. b
6. c	7. d	8. d	9. b	10. See page 100.

Things to SHARE

What do you think is Mary's greatest title? Why?

What does your Catholic faith mean to you? What have you learned in this course that has increased your gratitude for your faith?

OnLine with the parish

The Blessed Virgin Mary is so important for the Church that we honor her on many days during the liturgical year. Three of them are celebrated as holy days of obligation. These are: the Immaculate Conception (December 8), Mary, Mother of God (January 1), and the Assumption (August 15). Your parish will announce special Mass schedules for these feasts. Mark these days on your family calendar, and plan to celebrate at Mass.

Things to Think About

What does it mean for you to know that you are a member of the communion of saints and connected with all the other members of the Church, living and dead?

Why is it important for every Catholic to have a deep love and respect for the Blessed Virgin Mary?

Words to REMEMBER

Find and define:

communion of saints

_____
_____
_____
_____

103

Conclusion (cont'd)

FORUM Assignment

✔ Read Chapter 13, pages 104–111. Underline in pencil three key ideas.

✔ Complete the handout *Companion on the Way*. Be prepared to share the results.

Closing Prayer: Ask the final questions under *Things to Share*. Pause for reflection and play music softly in the background while the young people consider their responses. Gather in a prayer circle and pray the Our Father together. Then ask the young people to remember to pray for one another as fellow disciples and pilgrims. Conclude with the words of Saint Thomas More in his farewell before being put to death:

Pray for me, as I will for thee, that we may merrily meet in heaven.

Evaluation: Have the young people expressed a deepening understanding of Mary as our model and guide? Do they appreciate the significance of the communion of saints?

FOR CHAPTER 13

- copies of handout *People Who Bridge the Gaps*, page 104C
- copies of handout *We Walk with Jesus*, page 111A
- copies of *Final Assessment*, page 126
- copies of *Highlights for Home*, page 111B

Assessment

1 Mary's privilege of being free from original sin is called the
   a. assumption.
   b. incarnation.
   c. immaculate conception.
   d. annunciation.

2 At the end of her life, Mary was taken into heaven body and soul. This is called
   a. the assumption.
   b. the incarnation.
   c. the pilgrim Church.
   d. the annunciation.

3 Which best describes the communion of saints?
   a. canonized saints
   b. persons in purgatory and in heaven
   c. the parish community
   d. all the baptized: those on earth, in purgatory, and in heaven

4 The word *saint* means "one who is
   a. catholic."
   b. holy."
   c. a pilgrim."
   d. a martyr."

5 The greatest title of Mary is
   a. Queen of peace.
   b. Mother of God.
   c. Queen of all saints.
   d. Comfort of the troubled.

6 Canon law is the
   a. set of rules for canonization of saints.
   b. rule followed by religious orders.
   c. set of official rules that guide the Church's life.
   d. same for Western and Eastern Catholic Churches.

7 In the process of _____, the Church recognizes saints who lived exceptional lives of faith.
   a. pilgrimage
   b. communion of saints
   c. apostolic succession
   d. canonization

8 Choose the *false* statement. Mary
   a. fully cooperated with God's grace.
   b. is Mother of the Church.
   c. stood at the foot of the cross.
   d. was not a Christian.

9 Morning Star
   a. is a name for Jesus.
   b. is one of Mary's titles.
   c. was the first Native American saint.
   d. will fall from the heavens on the last day.

10 Explain what we mean when we describe Mary as the first and perfect disciple of Jesus. Write your response on the reverse side of this page.

Highlights for Home

Focus on Faith

In this chapter the young people are reassured that they are not alone on their journey of faith. As pilgrims on our way to fullness of life with God, we do not travel alone. We have one another; we have the Church. Angels and saints walk with us. Above all Jesus himself is "Companion, Light, and Way."

Also in this chapter the young people explore the reasons Catholics show Mary, the mother of Jesus, such honor and devotion. They learn that the Church regards Mary as a guiding light to the pilgrim Church on its way.

With this chapter we come to the end of our study of our basic Catholic beliefs for this semester. But as Catholics we never really come to an end of learning about our faith. These beliefs are so important because they identify us as disciples of Christ and members of the Catholic Church. The young people are urged to live what they believe—to put into daily practice the faith that has been passed on to them.

Conversation Starters

. . . . a few ideas to talk about together . . . .

◆ The Blessed Virgin Mary . . .
Her most beautiful title . . .
My favorite Marian devotion or song . . .

◆ Someone in our family who led a saintly life . . .
My favorite canonized saint . . .

Feature Focus

In the *Scripture Update* on page 100, we learn what is meant by the references in the New Testament to the brothers and sisters of Jesus. The term *brothers and sisters* refers not to children of Mary, Jesus' mother, who was a virgin, but to other relatives in the extended family of Jesus and Mary.

Reflection

Reflect on the meaning of the words of the Hail Mary. Say this prayer often during the coming weeks, pausing for a few moments after each line.

Hail Mary, full of grace,
the Lord is with you!
Blessed are you among women,
and blessed is the fruit of your womb,
*   Jesus.*
Holy Mary, Mother of God,
pray for us sinners,
now and at the hour of our death.
Amen.

BRINGING THE WORLD TO CHRIST

Adult Focus

The focus of this chapter and the next is evangelization. The young people will explore and celebrate in prayer ways that we can bring the world to Christ and Christ to the world.

Emphasize that at Baptism we are set apart and consecrated to carry on Christ's mission. Try to convey your own joy and enthusiasm for this baptismal calling. Help the young people to understand Saint Paul's words:

> *For all of you who were baptized into Christ have clothed yourselves with Christ.*
>
> Galatians 3:27

Find ways to help the young people look at the world with the eyes of Christ. Affirm them when they take initiative, and offer words of encouragement when the work of evangelization seems too difficult to continue. Provide assistance for any service project they plan. Be a model of an evangelizer by bringing the good news to them and to others by recognizing Christ's presence in them and in all parts of the human experience.

Catechism Focus

The themes of this chapter correspond to paragraphs 904–913 of the *Catechism*.

Remote Preparation

If possible, hold an "Evangelization Day" or a "Retreat for Disciples." Use Chapters 13 and 14 as the focus of this experience.

Who?

◆ Consider inviting young adult "evangelizers" to speak to your group or to participate in a panel discussion. A good resource for finding guest speakers is your parish or diocesan director of youth ministry or your pastor. Make a list of possible guests, and involve the young people in the process of planning and inviting.

◆ Invite your pastor or another member of the parish-ministry team to address the young people about the importance and need for each person to use his or her unique gifts to share the good news of Christ with the world.

Where?

Try to find a location that is different from your usual meeting place. The place should be conducive to private reflection and group sharing.

When?

Many parish councils sponsor evangelization projects during the season of Lent. You may want to use this break-out chapter and the next for a Lenten retreat day.

Teaching Resources

Overview

To discover that, as baptized members of the body of Christ, we have a responsibility to carry on Christ's mission to the whole world.

Opening Prayer Ideas

Look at the photograph on pages 104 and 105. A volunteer reads Galatians 3:26–27. All repeat verse 27.

or

Offer spontaneous prayers for family members. All respond: "Lord Jesus, bless my family."

Materials

- Bibles, journals, highlighters
- posterboard; construction paper
- biodegradable helium balloons; long string; permanent markers
- brown-paper grocery bags; weights

REPRODUCIBLE MASTERS

- handout *People Who Bridge the Gaps*, page 104C
- prayer handout *We Walk with Jesus*, page 111A
- *Highlights for Home*, page 111B
- *Final Assessment*, page 126 (optional)

 Creed Journal:
For Chapter 13, use pages 60 and 61.

Supplemental Resources

VIDEOS
- *Commitment to Caring*
- *Empty Cup*
- *The Reign of God*

St. Anthony Messenger/ Franciscan Communications
1615 Republic Street
Cincinnati, OH 45210

People Who Bridge the Gaps

Read the following stories, and write a positive ending for each one.

One day Marissa was complaining to her friend Megan. She had spent her allowance and didn't have enough money left to buy her favorite CD. On the way home Marissa thought to herself, "I've been complaining a lot. I've got to stop whining. I've got to stop spending money." Marissa remembered her mother telling her about the self-help book of reflections that she was reading. The author suggested that her readers try to find one thing to be grateful for each day.

Marissa said to herself, "I'm going to try to do that! Maybe I'll talk to Mom. We could check with each other about what we are grateful for and keep track on a special list or in a journal."

Marissa's mom liked the idea, and the two kept to their plan. After a month passed, Marissa's friend said to her, "I haven't heard you with the 'I wants,' and you haven't been complaining. What's up?"

_____

_____

_____

_____

_____

_____

Todd was upset because earlier in the day he had overheard his friends making fun of him for missing a foul shot at last night's game. When his older brother asked what was wrong, Todd explained what happened and said that he felt betrayed.

Todd's brother said, "You know, Todd, you've been a bit of a pain yourself. You're always talking about others' faults, trying to make yourself look good. If you want others to change, sometimes you have to change first."

Todd and his brother made a pact that same day that they both would try to keep: If we can't say anything positive about a person, we won't say anything at all. After the brothers shook hands, Todd asked, "Do you think anybody will notice?"

_____

_____

_____

_____

_____

_____

CHAPTER 13

BRINGING THE WORLD TO CHRIST

Through faith you are all children of God in Christ Jesus. For all of you who were baptized into Christ have clothed yourselves with Christ.

Galatians 3:26–27

105

Objective: To discover that, as baptized members of the body of Christ, we have a responsibility to carry on Christ's mission to the whole world.

Introduction ___ min.

Opening Prayer: If possible, make arrangements to conduct opening prayer outside or in an auditorium or gym. Have the young people form small groups. Give each group thick-tipped, permanent markers; two or three *biodegradable*, helium-filled balloons with long strings attached; a brown-paper grocery bag, and a weight of some kind.

Invite the groups to list on the bags poor attitudes that some young people have. Explain that giving in to these attitudes keeps people from developing the gifts God has given to us. Then have the groups place a weight at the bottom of their open bags.

Ask the groups to write on the balloons God's gifts that help them to be witnesses of God's love to others.

Then have the groups use the open grocery bags to weigh down the balloon strings.

Ask a representative from each group to read aloud the list of poor attitudes that are written on the group's bag. Then read aloud Ephesians 4:20–24.

Have each group take turns reading aloud together the names of God's gifts written on the balloons. Then read aloud the following prayer. Pause at the appropriate places to have the young people repeat the words.

O Holy Spirit, help us to cast aside (*pause*) anything that weighs us down and holds us back (*pause*) from following in Christ's footsteps. (*Pause.*) Help us put on the new self (*pause*) created in God's way in right-eousness and holiness of truth. (*Pause.*) Release our spirits (*pause*) so that we may be witnesses of God's love to others. (*Pause.*)

Then ask the groups to remove the weighted bags and release the balloons into the air to symbolize their willingness to cast away their old selves and to allow God to enlighten their minds and hearts.

Forum: The leader invites members of the group to share their responses to the handout *Companion on the Way.* If you are using this chapter as a basic tool for a day of prayer or a retreat, this *forum* will help the young people to remember that they are not alone in the great challenge of living and sharing the faith.

Presentation ___ min.

◆ Invite the young people to look at the photo on pages 104 and 105. Explain that it shows various groups of young people from different parishes who have gathered for a prayerful celebration during a visit from Pope John Paul II.

Ask a volunteer to read Galatians 3:26–27. Elicit suggestions for symbols to place on badges to illustrate this passage. Have the young people choose their favorite. Then invite artists in the group to design and make a badge for each person to wear during prayer for this session and the next.

◆ Have a volunteer read the introductory paragraph on page 106. Invite the young people to fill out as much of their baptismal records as they can from memory. Encourage them to have their families supply any missing information.

◆ Have the young people share the three key ideas they have underlined in this chapter. Discuss their choices. Then have them highlight the ideas that are highlighted on your reduced pages.

◆ Dim the lights. Ask the young people to imagine that they are in their rooms, reflecting on the day's events. Suddenly they get an idea. They know that God wants them to bring the good news of the gospel to a friend or family member who needs support and reassurance.

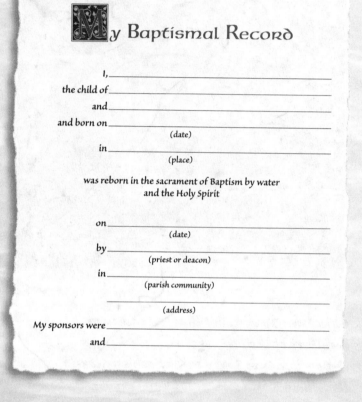

THE day of our Baptism is a day unlike any other. From the moment of Baptism, we are changed forever. As children of God we are set apart and consecrated to carry on Christ's mission. Do you know the facts about your own Baptism? See how much of your baptismal record you can fill out from memory. Then ask your family to help.

My Baptismal Record

I,_____

the child of_____

and_____

and born on_____
(date)

in_____
(place)

was reborn in the sacrament of Baptism by water and the Holy Spirit

on_____
(date)

by_____
(priest or deacon)

in_____
(parish community)

_____
(address)

My sponsors were_____

and_____

106

Chosen by God

When does our responsibility to carry on Christ's mission to the whole world begin? Some people may think that this responsibility begins when we are adults or that it is something for older members of the Church. But that is not true. Recall the story of the prophet Jeremiah.

Jeremiah was a young man when God called him to be a prophet. In response to this call, Jeremiah said to God, "I know not how to speak; I am too young." At this God said to him, "Say not, 'I am too young.' To whomever I send you, you shall go; whatever I command you, you shall speak" (Jeremiah 1:6–7).

God is saying the same thing to each one of us in Christ. As people of faith and as members of the body of Christ, we are appointed right now to share our faith and the good news of the gospel with the whole world. We call this mission of bringing the good news to others evangelization.

Evangelization means bringing the good news to every person and to all parts of the human experience. It means that we bring the world to Christ and Christ to the world. It is something so exciting that when it happens, the lives of people are transformed from within and made new. They begin to see everything with the eyes of Christ.

This does not happen automatically. Rather, it takes initiative, commitment, and hard work. After all, the best witness to Christ and our faith is the way we live our lives. It takes more than good will and intention; we must know Christ and know our faith. That is one of the reasons this course on the creed is so important.

How can you as a young person carry on the work of evangelization? Where will you go? What will you do? Let's begin to explore three areas in which evangelization can happen: at home, in your school and neighborhood, and in the wider world. This will be a journey of discovery. Let us turn to the Holy Spirit and ask him to be our guide.

107

Ask, "How will you respond?" Have the young people write their responses on page 60 of the *Creed Journal.*

Then ask a volunteer to tell the story of the prophet Jeremiah. Ask, "Do you think that *you* are too young to share your faith with others?"

Open the discussion about their concerns. Then ask, "How do you think God might answer you?"

◆ Ask for the definition of *evangelization.* Then direct attention to the photograph on page 107. Explain that when we carry on the work of evangelization, we may feel that sometimes we go it alone. We may feel like the person shown walking across the bridge. The path may sometimes seem shaky and scary, but we should remember that we are guided always by the Holy Spirit and supported by the communion of saints.

◆ Have a volunteer read the final paragraph on page 107. Stress the words *initiative, commitment, hard work, knowledge of Christ, knowledge of our faith,* and *self-knowledge.* Point out that no explorer goes into the wilderness without the necessary equipment. These six qualities are the necessary equipment for an evangelizer.

Note: Choose and prepare leaders for the prayer service that closes this session. See the handout on page 111A.

Presentation (cont'd)

◆ Form small groups to share the good news of Jesus as written in Matthew 5:14–16. Have a volunteer in each group read the passage, and allow about ten minutes for the young people to share their reflections.

Then ask the groups to write a cheer, rap, poem, or song to encourage one another to let their light shine before other people so that they can carry on the work of evangelization.

The following is an example:

> We are light!
> We are energized!
> We don't hide our gifts!
> We evangelize!

Then have each group present its cheer.

◆ Ask the young people about the signs of the times in their lives. Read the last paragraph in column 1 on page 108. Allow time for young people to work in pairs to list the songs, and then invite them to share their choices. Use the questions at the end of page 108 as criteria to critique the songs. Allow plenty of time for discussion and reactions.

◆ Direct the young people's attention to the second paragraph in the left column on page 109. Have the young people highlight the question, "How can your faith become more real in your life?" Allow time for them to write their thoughts in the space provided.

Looking at Ourselves

Evangelization is so important in the lives of Catholics that our recent popes have talked to us about it many times. But they do not want us to go off unprepared. Like Jesus they have urged us to look at the "signs of the times" (Matthew 16:3) to see where God wants us to work in our world, calling us to be a part of his kingdom.

The first people to be evangelized must be ourselves. Pope Paul VI, for example, said that "the first means of evangelization is the witness of an authentically Christian life" (*On Evangelization*, 41). This means that we have to believe and practice what we are going to share with others. Otherwise our witness becomes empty and unbelievable.

What are the signs of the times in your own life? Let's take a closer look. For example, think about the music you enjoy. What are your favorite songs? Write several of their titles in the space above.

My Favorite Songs

Why are these songs your favorites? What do the words of the songs tell you about yourself, what you hope for, what you enjoy? Do the words and feelings of these songs help you to live your faith? Do they make you uneasy about your faith?

108

The answers we give to questions such as these help us to see where faith challenges us. They help us to see where we must allow the gospel and all that we profess about our faith to become real for our lives. Remember Paul's words: "Through faith you are all children of God in Christ Jesus. For all of you who were baptized into Christ have clothed yourselves with Christ" (Galatians 3:26–27).

Do the things you enjoy, such as music, help you to see where you need to clothe yourself in Christ even more? How can your faith become more real in your life? Write your thoughts here.

Family Life

Once we have evangelized ourselves, the first and most obvious people with whom we come into contact are members of our family. Evangelizing, however, doesn't mean that we are going to preach to our family or tell them what to do. What it means is that we are going to try as hard as we can to bring the presence of Christ into our family's life in any way possible. What are the signs of the times in your family's life? Let's take a closer look.

Complete the following statements for yourself:

1. I most enjoy being with my family when

2. The quality I like best about my family is

3. I am most uncomfortable with my family when

4. My family is most uncomfortable with me when

109

◆ Point out that after we have evangelized ourselves, that is, become witnesses to our faith, we look at the people closest to us, our families. Ask, "How do we evangelize—witness to the gospel—in our own families?" To see if all are on the right track, have them look at the questions in the right column on page 109.

Note: If you are presenting this chapter in a day of prayer or retreat situation, you may want to have the young people form small groups to share their thoughts on these questions. You need to be sensitive to the level of trust and acceptance in the group before inviting free-flowing verbal responses.

Point out that the young people's answers to the fourth question will give them a clue about what they need to work on to strengthen themselves to be witnesses to their faith.

Have the young people open to page 61 of the *Creed Journal*. Read aloud the quote from Paul VI. Have a volunteer read the prayer that introduces the journaling activity; then invite the young people to write their thoughts. Play music softly as they work.

Presentation (cont'd)

◆ Explain to the young people that their responses to the last question on page 109 should help them consider more closely the areas in which they need to grow or improve as evangelizers. Have them check off any areas in the chart on page 110 that "ring a bell" for them. Have them look at the qualities they have checked and ask themselves, "How can I do better in developing gospel values in my life?"

◆ Distribute colored construction paper. Explain that evangelizers search within themselves for gifts or abilities they have and can use to bring the good news of God's love to others. Have the young people reflect quietly for five minutes to think of their gifts or abilities. Then have them write these gifts on the construction paper.

Emphasize that everyone should respect each person's privacy while writing.

◆ Read aloud the introduction to the activity on page 111. Give the young people a few minutes to reflect and then challenge them to write the "transformations" they wish to make. Some might be comfortable sharing their responses. They should be received with respect and attention.

◆ Invite the group to be "caption writers." Elicit suggestions for one-line prayer captions for the photographs in this chapter. Encourage the young people to write their prayer captions neatly beside each photo.

In the chart check off the areas in which you think you need to grow or to work harder as a family evangelizer.

— gratitude   — generosity
— joy   — anger
— friendliness   — patience
— helpfulness   — cheerfulness
— enthusiasm   — support
— selfishness   — stubbornness
— jealousy   — prayerfulness
— cooperation   — attentiveness
— responsibility   — forgiveness

Young people who are well trained in faith and prayer must become more and more the apostles of youth. The Church counts greatly on their contribution.

Pope Paul VI, On Evangelization, 72

Look over your list and your answers. This isn't an examination of conscience or a way to find out how bad we are. This is a way to get in touch with our lives. This is a way to be real evangelizers, to bring the values of the gospel home with us.

The signs of the times are there for us to read. The possibilities of being effective evangelizers are there for us, too.

110

Behold, I am with you always, until the end of the age (Matthew 28:20).

Think about some things that need to be changed, or transformed, in you so that you can become a true evangelizer and witness to Christ. For example someone might pray:

Transform my laziness into energy to do your work.

What "transformations" do you need?

TRANSFORM

my _____ into _____
my _____ into _____
my _____ into _____
my _____ into _____
my _____ into _____

Here is a prayer to help you see more clearly how to be an effective evangelizer.

Jesus,
you have chosen me
as a member of your Church
to be your evangelizer.
Help me to
see each day where I can
bring the message
of your good news to others.
Help me to
transform my own life
and so be a witness
to my family.
Amen.

111

Conclusion ____ min.

Assessment: If you plan to administer the *Final Assessment* for Creed Part II, set aside about twenty minutes for its completion.

There is no *Chapter 13 Assessment.*

FORUM Assignment

✔ Read Chapter 14, pages 112–119. Underline in pencil three key ideas.

✔ Complete the handout *People Who Bridge the Gaps*. Be prepared to share your story endings.

Closing Prayer: Begin the prayer *We Walk with Jesus* on the handout on page 111A.

Note: You may prefer to use the following prayer idea.

Gather in a prayer circle. Go around the circle and have each person read one of the "caption prayers" they wrote beside the photographs. After each one has read a caption prayer, have all say together the prayer on page 111.

Evaluation: Have the young people shown a willingness to accept their responsibility to be evangelists? Have they begun to evangelize themselves?

FOR CHAPTER 14

- preparation of opening-prayer volunteers
- copies of handouts *Making Waves*, page 112 and *A New Beginning*, page 119A
- copies of *Highlights for Home*, page 119B
- CD or tape player: instrumental music
- votive candle or substitute
- construction paper, scissors, glue

Walking with Jesus

Note: *If possible, walk two-by-two to the room where the prayer service is to be held. Imagine you are the disciples on the way to Emmaus. Walk slowly and heavily because you are mourning the loss of Jesus. When you reach the prayer place, gather in a circle around a table with an open Bible placed upon it.*

Dramatic reading of Luke 24:13–35 (prepared in advance)

Parts:

• Narrator reads all except the words of the disciples.

• Two disciples alternate parts.

• Jesus

After the reading pause briefly for reflection. Then pray together.

1: Jesus, when our faith is weak, help us to find encouragement in your words in Scripture.

All: Be with us, Lord.

2: Jesus, when we are not sure where we are going, walk with us.

All: Be with us, Lord.

3: Jesus, when we fail to understand the ways in which you lead us,

All: Be with us, Lord.

4: Jesus, when you come to us in others, and we fail to recognize you,

All: Be with us, Lord.

5: When we feel we are alone, help us find you in the eucharistic breaking of the bread.

All: Be with us, Lord.

Sing the chorus of *Here I Am, Lord* or *Companions on the Journey* from *Glory and Praise*.

Highlights for Home

Focus on Faith

The final two chapters of this book engage the young people in an exploration of the challenge to be evangelizers—to live as people of faith and to be willing to share that faith with others.

They are reminded in this session that evangelization takes place first within themselves, and it doesn't happen automatically. It takes initiative, commitment, and hard work to live the gospel values faithfully.

The young people are then asked to think of the ways they are (or are not) being evangelizers in their own families. They are challenged to change the things that need to be changed so as to be better bearers of the good news of Christ. Remember to help them fulfill this challenge with words of encouragement and other signs of support.

Conversation Starters

. . . . a few ideas to talk about together . . . .

◆ Do the songs I listen to help me to begin to look at the world with the eyes of Christ?

◆ Do the movies or TV programs I watch portray Christian values?

◆ A quality I would like to experience more in our family . . .

◆ A quality I wish to share with my family . . .

Feature Focus

The young people are asked to gather information about their Baptisms and to fill in the baptismal record on page 106. This activity affords you the opportunity to share with your son and daughter your own memories of this significant moment in his or her spiritual life.

Reflection

Set aside some private time. In a quiet, peaceful place, sit still in God's presence. Thank him for the many blessings that have come to you through your faith in him. Think of some specifically. Ask God to keep you faithful to him.

BRINGING CHRIST TO THE WORLD

Adult Focus

In this second chapter on evangelization, the young people examine the ways they can practice their gospel values among friends, in their school, their neighborhood, and finally, the wider world. They consider "evangelizing moments" in which they examine specific situations and recognize and express the ways a true evangelizer would respond. They read letters from young evangelizers who share their experiences and their discoveries about themselves and others that they have gained from these experiences.

Finally, in a prayer service they renew their commitment to Christ and their desire to share their faith in him with others.

Catechism Focus

The themes of this chapter correspond to paragraphs 904–913 of the *Catechism*.

Preparation

If you plan to use this session for a day of prayer or a retreat, you might wish to do the following:

◆ Make your meeting place look and feel different from the normal meetings. For example:

• Place the prayer table on which there is an open Bible, a votive candle, and holy water in a central location.

• If possible, avoid harsh lighting. If candles cannot be used, use area lamps or battery-operated candles.

• Have tables and chairs arranged for small groups.

• Have tape deck and/or CD player in place. Have music playing as the young people enter.

◆ To facilitate a smooth transition from one stage of the day to the next:

• Have all needed materials prepared and readily accessible to the group.

• Prepare in advance those who have specific roles to play.

Teaching Resources

Overview

To explore the ways friends can be evangelizers to one another; to recognize that evangelization is the mission of every member of the Church.

Opening Prayer Ideas

Read the story of the Good Samaritan (Luke 10:29–37). Then invite petitions for the needs of the world.

or

Pray together *Come, Holy Spirit* on page 121.

Materials

Creed Journal:
For Chapter 14, use pages 62–63.

- Bibles, journals, highlighters
- construction paper, scissors, glue
- a stone or rock for each person
- a bowl of holy water and a battery-operated candle

REPRODUCIBLE MASTERS
- handouts *Making Waves*, page 112C and *A New Beginning*, page 119A
- *Highlights for Home*, page 119B

Supplemental Resources

VIDEO
Journey to the Mountain Top
(a documentary of the World Youth Day in Denver)
Ligouri Publications
Ligouri, MO 63057

Making Waves

Evangelizers read the signs of the times. They find ways to energize themselves and others to live and witness the values of the gospel. In other words, they make waves!

Choose one wave from the following list, or make up your own. Devise a plan of action to help your "wave" have a powerful, positive impact on the world.

- wave of gratitude
- wave of patience
- wave of charity
- wave of cooperation
- wave of helpfulness

Step 1 Turn the Tide

What will you do each day as part of your evangelization commitment?

_____

_____

_____

Step 2 Stir Up the Waters

What will you do to help your family and friends catch the "wave"?

_____

_____

_____

Step 3 Make an Impact

What special ritual or celebration can you plan so that other groups will notice and want to catch the "wave," too?

_____

_____

_____

BRINGING CHRIST TO THE WORLD

You continue to build your Church with chosen stones, enlivened by the Spirit, and cemented together by love.
Prayer for the Dedication of a Church

Objectives: To explore the ways friends can be evangelizers to one another; to recognize that evangelization is the mission of every member of the Church.

Introduction ___ min.

Opening Prayer: Direct the young people's reflection. Invite them to look at the photograph on pages 112 and 113. Ask them to think about what this photograph "says" to them about the Church and the world. Allow a few moments for reflection. Then encourage responses.

Some of the young people might see the Church as the rock. They might see in the radiating circles of light the love that unites us and energizes us to spread the good news. The rays of light and energy seem to reach out indefinitely suggesting that the message of Christ needs to be transmitted to many people in many places throughout the world. Each of us might be considered one of the rays energized by the Holy Spirit. We are to radiate Christ's light and love. We are called to spread the good news of Jesus Christ in the world. (*Pause.*)

Leader: Now let us pray. (The leader reads Luke 4:18–19.)

All: Here I am, Lord. Send me! Send me in a spirit of understanding and communication.

2: When a friend is in need,

All: Send me to be a support and a strength.

3: When I don't feel like giving up my time for others,

All: Send me to be a generous and willing giver.

4: When I am happy and comfortable in my own little group of friends,

All: Send me to reach out to those who do not seem to belong.

5: When I think I am not old enough, good enough, or ready enough to be an evangelizer for you, Lord,

All: Send me to live my faith with joy, conviction, and hope. Here I am, Lord. Send me!

Forum: The leader now invites as many young people as possible to share their endings to the stories on the handout *People Who Bridge the Gaps*. After the sharing, the leader asks for responses to the questions:

• What gospel values came to light in these endings?

• In what ways were the characters evangelizers?

Presentation ___ min.

◆ Have the young people share the three key ideas they have underlined in this chapter. Discuss their choices. Then have them highlight those that are highlighted on your reduced pages.

◆ Read together the words of Pope John Paul II on page 114. On the board or on flash cards, write *peer pressure* and *peer ministry*. Have the young people complete the chart on page 114. Then direct the young people to describe how each movie and television program shows peer pressure or peer ministry.

◆ Have the young people write their friendship evangelization plans in the space provided on page 114.

Distribute colored construction paper. Invite the young people to write a promise that they will do their best to enact this plan in the near future.

The Church has so much to talk about with youth, and youth have so much to share with the Church.

Pope John Paul II, The Lay Faithful, 46

What do you think you have to share with the Church?

Friends

Having good friends is one of the greatest experiences we can ever have in life. Being good friends means that we wish only what is good for the other person — only what will make that person truly happy.

To help us get in touch with friendship, let's take a look at the way friendship is shown in our favorite movies and television programs.

Look over the answers you have written down in these charts. Are you surprised at your answers? How would you compare these answers with what your faith tells you about friendship? Friends can be evangelizers to one another. Do you see any possibility for evangelization here? Write a friendship evangelization plan.

My Friendship Evangelization Plan

Recent Movies I Have Seen

Names of Movies:

What These Movies Tell Me About Friendship:

Favorite Television Programs

Names of Television Programs:

What These Programs Tell Me About Friendship:

114

School and Neighborhood

Strange as it may seem, the hardest and most challenging place to be an effective evangelizer may very well be in our own backyard. It is always most difficult to evangelize our peers. It may be easier to travel halfway around the world and meet people who have never heard of Christ than to speak with and give witness to him among the people we see and hang out with day after day.

What does this mean? It means that we have to be courageous, imaginative, and skillful in bringing the truth and values of the gospel to this important part of our world. But how do we bring the gospel and the truth of faith to the football or soccer field, to the basketball court, to the mall, to the classroom, or to a Friday night dance? After all, this is the world in which we live every day.

Read the following descriptions, and think about the situations as possible evangelizing opportunities. For each, write one way you would try to bring gospel values to this experience.

Evangelizing Moments

• For many months your parish council has been asking for volunteers of all ages to help start an outreach program to the elderly and the homebound. It is not easy to volunteer alone. What are your plans as an evangelizer?

• Sports have always been important in your school. But lately you and others have noticed a different attitude on the part of many, both young people and adults. Sports and winning seem to have taken over as the most important things in life. What are your plans as an evangelizer?

• The local mall is the place to hang out and meet others. However, the mall security guards have been cracking down in the last couple of months. People were complaining about the noise and rough behavior on the part of some of your peers. What are your plans as an evangelizer?

Look back at what you have written today about being an evangelizer. Are you surprised that evangelization can take place in situations where you might have thought it would not be possible?

115

◆ Discuss the photograph on page 115. Invite the young people to suggest a title or a caption for it. Then have the young people form small groups to discuss and to write their responses to "Evangelizing Moments" on page 115.

Have a volunteer in each group read Sirach 6:5–17. Then have the group discuss the significance of these words in today's society. Ask the final question.

◆ Distribute the handout *Making Waves*. Go over the directions and allow time for the group to complete the three steps. Then ask volunteers to share their plans for making waves.

FYI

Do you think you should be open to making new friends while deepening the friendships you have already made with others? Here is what Father Edward Farrell says about friendship:

Each person who knows my name has a unique way of saying it, calling me, seeing me, hearing me . . . each person uncovers but one of the colors of my rainbow.

Do you agree? What colors do your friends and family help you to uncover?

Presentation (cont'd)

◆ Have two volunteers in turn read the testimonies of the two young evangelizers that appear on pages 116 and 117. Discuss their experiences. Elicit questions that the young people would like to ask these two people about their evangelizing activities. List these questions on the board.

If time allows, this would be an ideal opportunity to have one or two young Catholic evangelizers from high school or college talk to the group about their experiences of sharing the faith.

◆ Distribute colored construction paper. Invite the young people to look at the photograph on pages 116 and 117. Say, "Sometimes obstacles can be stumbling blocks; sometimes they can be stepping stones." Have the young people list on the construction paper people, places, or things that may be stumbling blocks to our work of evangelizing. Then have them list people, places, and things that are stepping-stones in the work of bringing Christ to others.

Ask a volunteer to read Isaiah 40:1–11.

◆ Help the young people plan a way to share the good news of Christ with others. You may wish to do both of the following projects or choose one.

• Have the young people form small traveling troupes of puppeteers to dramatize Scripture stories for younger children. Ask each group to make puppets and props and to write a script for their Scripture skit. Take your acts out on the road by visiting the children in younger classes, at a preschool or day-care center, or in a hospital.

A Young Evangelizer Writes

During my senior year at Georgetown University, one of my Jesuit teachers suggested that I volunteer to work in South Africa after graduation. I imagine he thought it would be a good way to round out my education as a Catholic and challenge me as a person of faith. Although his suggestion sounded exciting, I had some other ideas about my life. My life was filled with many blessings, and I wanted to give something back to my own community in the United States. That's how I ended up spending a year in a large U.S. city far from my home. There I taught young people in an inner-city school.

My experience opened my eyes to a part of life I had never really seen. In an area overrun with gangs, drugs, and violence, the strength and ability of my students impressed me deeply. I started out thinking that I could give something back to the community, but I was the one who was actually taught. Now as a law student I am learning to bring greater justice to the inner city.

Tom Sweeney

116

Another Young Evangelizer Writes

When I was in college, I had the opportunity to visit other countries in Central and South America. There I was shocked to see so many people living in cardboard houses and going hungry. For the first time in my life, I realized just how the poor of the world have to live. As a person of faith and a member of the Church, I knew that I had to do something about this.

After college I volunteered to work with a group sponsored by the Ursuline Sisters. This group is called Ursuline Companions in Mission. For the next two years, I found myself working alongside others in youth and prison ministry and family counseling here in the United States. I even went to Central America and worked in an orphanage in Honduras. Was it easy? No. But these experiences helped to change my life. Now as a teacher I try to share with young Catholics and help them see what missionary activity is all about.

Patrice McDermott

The Wider World

You may be surprised where life leads you as an evangelizer. For some it could even be halfway around the world. That's because the work of evangelization and mission is the work of all Church members, not just the clergy and religious. The Church teaches us that through Baptism we are a prophetic and priestly people offering spiritual sacrifices in our lives and announcing Christ to the world. The Church reminds us that "the faithful exercise their baptismal priesthood through their participation, each according to his own vocation, in Christ's mission as priest, prophet, and king" (*Catechism*, 1546).

Now that you have read about their experiences, what questions would you ask these two young Catholics about their evangelizing activities?

What dreams do you have for evangelizing in the wider world?

How can you prepare to help make those dreams come true?

117

- Visit a nursing home or senior-citizen center. Emphasize with the young people that they should encourage the seniors whom they are visiting to share their wealth of experience. Encourage the young people to be active, attentive listeners. Before your visit help the young people plan a simple prayer service that includes traditional prayers and hymns.

◆ Direct the group's attention to the photo on page 117. Remind the young people that as the church building is reflected on the other buildings, so too are we to be reflections of Christ's love in the world.

◆ Distribute copies of the handout *A New Beginning*. Invite a volunteer to read aloud the words of Pope John Paul II. Stress the gospel values mentioned and have the young people highlight them. Then allow them a few minutes to write their thoughts.

Presentation (cont'd)

◆ Ask volunteers to help you set up two prayer stations.

• The first station: On a table place a stone or rock for each young person. Also have an open Bible there.

• The second station: Place a bowl of blessed water and a battery-operated candle.

◆ Have the young people gather at the first prayer station. Sing an opening song. ("Prepare Ye the Way of the Lord" from *Godspell* would be appropriate.)

Invite the Leader to read the opening prayer and Reader 1 to read the passage from the First Letter of Peter.

Have the young people choose stones from those on the table. Explain that they will carry the stones as they process to the second station.

◆ Ask the young people to process silently to the second station. When all have gathered at the table, invite the leader to begin the next part of the prayer service, the renewing of baptismal vows.

◆ When the young people have finished renewing their baptismal vows, have them take turns dipping their hands in holy water and making the sign of the cross.

Explain that they should keep their stones or rocks as a reminder of their call to be living stones. Sing the closing song the young people have chosen.

If time allows, this would be an excellent time to show the video *Journey to the Mountain Top*, a documentary of World Youth Day. In this video, young people express their faith with great joy and openness.

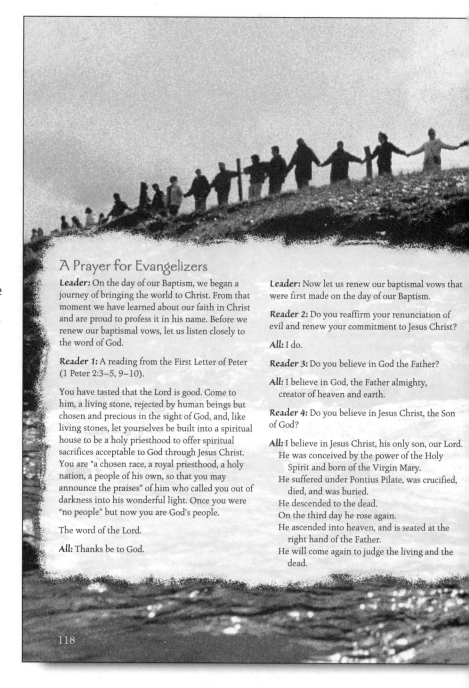

A Prayer for Evangelizers

Leader: On the day of our Baptism, we began a journey of bringing the world to Christ. From that moment we have learned about our faith in Christ and are proud to profess it in his name. Before we renew our baptismal vows, let us listen closely to the word of God.

Reader 1: A reading from the First Letter of Peter (1 Peter 2:3–5, 9–10).

You have tasted that the Lord is good. Come to him, a living stone, rejected by human beings but chosen and precious in the sight of God, and, like living stones, let yourselves be built into a spiritual house to be a holy priesthood to offer spiritual sacrifices acceptable to God through Jesus Christ. You are "a chosen race, a royal priesthood, a holy nation, a people of his own, so that you may announce the praises" of him who called you out of darkness into his wonderful light. Once you were "no people" but now you are God's people.

The word of the Lord.

All: Thanks be to God.

Leader: Now let us renew our baptismal vows that were first made on the day of our Baptism.

Reader 2: Do you reaffirm your renunciation of evil and renew your commitment to Jesus Christ?

All: I do.

Reader 3: Do you believe in God the Father?

All: I believe in God, the Father almighty, creator of heaven and earth.

Reader 4: Do you believe in Jesus Christ, the Son of God?

All: I believe in Jesus Christ, his only son, our Lord.
He was conceived by the power of the Holy Spirit and born of the Virgin Mary.
He suffered under Pontius Pilate, was crucified, died, and was buried.
He descended to the dead.
On the third day he rose again.
He ascended into heaven, and is seated at the right hand of the Father.
He will come again to judge the living and the dead.

118

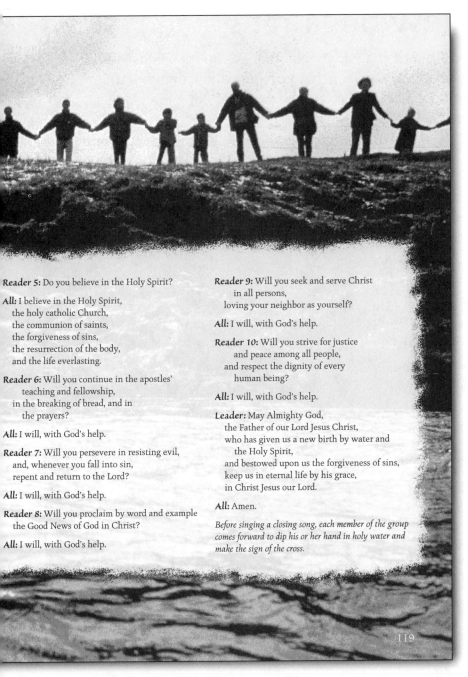

Reader 5: Do you believe in the Holy Spirit?

All: I believe in the Holy Spirit,
the holy catholic Church,
the communion of saints,
the forgiveness of sins,
the resurrection of the body,
and the life everlasting.

Reader 6: Will you continue in the apostles'
teaching and fellowship,
in the breaking of bread, and in
the prayers?

All: I will, with God's help.

Reader 7: Will you persevere in resisting evil,
and, whenever you fall into sin,
repent and return to the Lord?

All: I will, with God's help.

Reader 8: Will you proclaim by word and example
the Good News of God in Christ?

All: I will, with God's help.

Reader 9: Will you seek and serve Christ
in all persons,
loving your neighbor as yourself?

All: I will, with God's help.

Reader 10: Will you strive for justice
and peace among all people,
and respect the dignity of every
human being?

All: I will, with God's help.

Leader: May Almighty God,
the Father of our Lord Jesus Christ,
who has given us a new birth by water and
the Holy Spirit,
and bestowed upon us the forgiveness of sins,
keep us in eternal life by his grace,
in Christ Jesus our Lord.

All: Amen.

*Before singing a closing song, each member of the group
comes forward to dip his or her hand in holy water and
make the sign of the cross.*

119

Conclusion ___ min.

Have the young people return to their places and write in their journals their personal reflections about the reading from the First Letter of Peter and the renewal of their baptismal promises.

◆ Read aloud Matthew 5:14–16. Then read each line of the Prayer of Saint Francis. Pause briefly at appropriate spots, and have the group repeat the prayer words.

Lord, make me an
instrument of your peace:
where there is hatred, let me sow love;
where there is injury; pardon;
where there is doubt, faith;
where there is despair, hope;
where there is darkness, light;
where there is sadness, joy.
O divine Master, grant that I may not
so much seek
to be consoled as to console,
to be understood as to understand,
to be loved as to love.
For it is in giving that we receive,
it is in pardoning that we are pardoned,
it is in dying that we are born to eternal
life.
Amen.

◆ Encourage the young people to share *Highlights for Home* with their families.

Evaluation: Have the young people explored the ways they can share their faith and the good news of the gospel with the whole world? Have they understood the initiative, commitment, and hard work involved in being evangelizers?

A New Beginning

The world is facing a new beginning. We are privileged to be participants in the launching of a new millennium and in claiming it for Christ. Here are the words of Pope John Paul II. Read them carefully.

As the third millennium of the redemption draws near, God is preparing a great springtime for Christianity, and we can already see its first signs . . . people are gradually drawing closer to gospel ideals and values, a development which the Church seeks to evangelize . . . the rejection of violence and war; respect for the human person and for human rights; the desire for freedom, justice, and brotherhood; the surmounting of different forms of racism and nationalism; the affirmation of the dignity and role of women.

Christian hope sustains us in committing ourselves fully to the new evangelism, and to the worldwide mission, and leads us to pray as Jesus taught us: "Your kingdom come, your will be done on earth as it is in heaven" (Matthew 6:10).

Mission of the Redeemer, 86

What are my hopes for the new millennium?

Which gospel values can I help to spread right now?

Do I choose to commit myself to being an evangelizer, a hope-filled bearer of the gospel? To show my commitment, I will sign my name here.

_____, Evangelizer for the New Millennium.

Highlights for Home

Focus on Faith

In prayer, the young people have explored and celebrated ways that we are called to bring the world to Christ and Christ to the world. They have learned that their responsibility to carry on Christ's mission has already begun. They have discovered that the best witness to Christ and our faith is the way we live our lives as individuals, as family members, as friends, and as witnesses in our local communities and in the world.

Help the young people to begin to look at the world with the eyes of Christ. Do this first of all through your own example. Then affirm them when they take initiative. Support their efforts within the family and their circle of friends.

Offer words of encouragement when the work of evangelization seems too difficult to continue. Give example by bringing the good news to every person you meet and to all parts of the human experience.

Conversation Starters

. . . . a few ideas to talk about together . . . .

◆ What are the values of Jesus? What does he ask of us?

◆ How am I living these values? What do I need to change in myself in order to be an evangelizer?

Feature Focus

This entire chapter is considered a special feature. Take time, however, to discuss with your son or daughter the testimonies of the two young evangelizers on pages 116 and 117. Talk about the steps these witnesses must have taken before beginning their missionary work.

Reflection

Gather as a family to share your reflections on a favorite reading from the gospels. Conclude your sharing period with the following blessing:

*May God, the source of all patience and
  encouragement,
enable us to live in perfect harmony with one
  another
in the spirit of Christ Jesus.
With one heart and one voice
may we glorify God,
now and forever.*

BLESSED BE GOD.
BLESSED BE HIS HOLY NAME

Blessed be Jesus Christ, true God and true man.

Blessed be the name of Jesus.

Blessed be his most sacred heart.

Blessed be his most precious blood.

Blessed be Jesus in the most holy
sacrament of the altar.

Blessed be the Holy Spirit, the Paraclete.

Blessed be the great mother of God,
Mary most holy.

Blessed be her most holy and immaculate
conception.

Blessed be her glorious assumption.

Blessed be the name of Mary, virgin
and mother.

Blessed be Saint Joseph, her most chaste spouse.

Blessed be God in his angels and in his saints.

THE DIVINE PRAISES

OUR FATHER,
WHO ART IN HEAVEN,

hallowed be thy name;

thy kingdom come;

thy will be done on earth as it is
in heaven.

Give us this day our daily bread;

and forgive us our trespasses

as we forgive those who trespass
against us;

and lead us not into temptation,

but deliver us from evil.

Amen.

OUR FATHER

HAIL MARY,
FULL OF GRACE,

the Lord is with you!

Blessed are you among women,

and blessed is the fruit of your womb,
Jesus.

Holy Mary, Mother of God,

pray for us sinners,

now and at the hour of our death.

Amen.

HAIL MARY

MY GOD,
I AM SORRY FOR MY SINS
WITH ALL MY HEART.

In choosing to do wrong

and failing to do good,

I have sinned against you

whom I should love above all things.

I firmly intend, with your help,

to do penance,

to sin no more,

and to avoid whatever leads me to sin.

Our Savior Jesus Christ

suffered and died for us.

In his name, my God, have mercy.

ACT OF CONTRITION

Hail, Holy Queen,
Mother of Mercy,

hail, our life, our sweetness, and our hope.
To you we cry, the children of Eve;
to you we send up our sighs,
mourning and weeping in this land of exile.
Turn, then, most gracious advocate,
your eyes of mercy toward us;
lead us home at last
and show us the blessed fruit of your womb,
Jesus:
O clement, O loving, O sweet Virgin Mary.

HAIL, HOLY QUEEN

Come, Holy Spirit,
Fill the Hearts of your Faithful.

And kindle in them the fire of your love.

Send forth your Spirit and they shall be created.
And you will renew the face of the earth.

Let us pray.

Lord,
by the light of the Holy Spirit
you have taught the hearts of your faithful.
In the same Spirit
help us to relish what is right
and always rejoice in your consolation.

We ask this through Christ our Lord.
Amen.

PRAYER TO THE HOLY SPIRIT

I Believe In God,
the Father Almighty,

creator of heaven and earth.
I believe in Jesus Christ, his only Son,
  our Lord.
He was conceived by the power of
  the Holy Spirit
  and born of the Virgin Mary.
He suffered under Pontius Pilate,
  was crucified, died, and was buried.
He descended to the dead.
On the third day he rose again.
He ascended into heaven,
  and is seated at the right hand
  of the Father.
He will come again to judge the living
  and the dead.
I believe in the Holy Spirit,
  the holy catholic Church,
  the communion of saints,
  the forgiveness of sins,
  the resurrection of the body,
  and the life everlasting.
Amen.

APOSTLES' CREED

Glory to the Father,
and to the Son,

and to the Holy Spirit:
as it was in the beginning, is now,
  and will be for ever.
Amen.

GLORY TO THE FATHER

We Believe In One God,
the Father, the Almighty,

maker of heaven and earth,
of all that is seen and unseen.

We believe in one Lord, Jesus Christ,
the only Son of God,
eternally begotten of the Father,
God from God, Light from Light,
true God from true God,
begotten, not made, one in Being with
the Father.
Through him all things were made.
For us men and for our salvation
he came down from heaven:
by the power of the Holy Spirit
he was born of the Virgin Mary,
and became man.
For our sake he was crucified under
Pontius Pilate;
he suffered, died, and was buried.
On the third day he rose again
in fulfillment of the Scriptures;
he ascended into heaven
and is seated at the right hand of the
Father.
He will come again in glory to judge
the living and the dead,
and his kingdom will have no end.

We believe in the Holy Spirit, the Lord,
the giver of life,
who proceeds from the Father and the
Son.
With the Father and the Son he is
worshiped and glorified.
He has spoken through the Prophets.
We believe in one holy catholic and
apostolic Church.
We acknowledge one baptism for the
forgiveness of sins.
We look for the resurrection of the dead,
and the life of the world to come.
Amen.

NICENE CREED

Eternal Rest
Grant unto Them,

O Lord.
And let perpetual light shine upon them.
May they rest in peace.
Amen.
May their souls and the souls of all the
faithful departed, through the mercy of
God, rest in peace.
Amen.

May the angels lead you into paradise;
may the martyrs come to welcome you
and take you to the holy city,
the new and eternal Jerusalem.

PRAYERS FOR THE DECEASED

O Lord, Support Us
All The Day Long,

until the shadows lengthen,
and the evening comes,
and the busy world is hushed,
and the fever of life is over,
and our work is done.
Then in your mercy,
grant us a safe lodging,
and a holy rest,
and peace at the last.

John Henry Newman
A NOVEMBER PRAYER

The Bread Which
You do Not Use

Is the bread of the hungry.
The garment hanging in your wardrobe
   Is the garment of one who is naked.
The shoes that you do not wear
   Are the shoes of one who is barefoot.
The money you keep locked away
   Is the money of the poor.
The acts of charity you do not perform
   Are so many injustices you commit.

Saint Basil the Great
A MEDITATION

Lord, i Believe
In You: Increase My Faith.

I trust in you: strengthen my trust.
I love you: let me love you more and more.
I am sorry for my sins: deepen my sorrow.

I worship you as my first beginning,
I long for you as my last end,
I praise you as my constant helper,
and call on you as my loving protector.

Guide me by your wisdom,
correct me with your justice,
comfort me with your mercy,
protect me with your power.

Attributed to Pope Clement XI
SELECTIONS FROM THE UNIVERSAL PRAYER

Let Nothing
Disturb You,

nothing cause you fear;
All things pass
God is unchanging.
Patience obtains all:
Whoever has God
Needs nothing else,
God alone suffices.

Saint Teresa of Ávila
REFLECTION ON PATIENCE

The Angel Spoke
God's Message to Mary,

and she conceived of the Holy Spirit.
Hail, Mary. . . .

"I am the lowly servant of the Lord:
let it be done to me according to your word."
Hail, Mary. . . .

And the Word became flesh
and lived among us.
Hail, Mary. . . .

Pray for us, holy Mother of God,
that we may become worthy of the
promises of Christ.

Let us pray.

Lord,
fill our hearts with your grace:
once, through the message of an angel you
revealed to us the incarnation of your Son;
now, through his suffering and death
lead us to the glory of his resurrection.
We ask this through Christ our Lord.
Amen.

THE ANGELUS

Chapters 1-7

Circle the letter beside the **best** answer.

1 We call Christ's return to the Father his

a. annunciation.

b. incarnation.

c. ascension.

d. death on a cross.

2 God's overwhelming love and care for us is

a. God's providence.

b. Jesus' resurrection.

c. Yahweh.

d. Jesus' ascension.

3 The kingdom of God

a. is not a place.

b. is among us.

c. still needs to grow in our lives.

d. all the above

4 In the Bible the word *church* means

a. "a people called together."

b. "a sacred place."

c. "a dwelling place."

d. "the popes and bishops."

5 the roots of Church leadership extend back to

a. Jesus and the apostles.

b. the first pope who lived in Rome.

c. those whom Jesus cured.

d. all who were in Jerusalem on the first Pentecost.

Define.

6 actual graces _____

_____

_____

_____

7 laity _____

_____

_____

_____

_____

8 Pentecost _____

_____

_____

_____

_____

9 clergy _____

_____

_____

_____

_____

10 apostolic _____

_____

_____

_____

_____

M I D S E M E S T E R

Explain what Catholics believe about the following:

11 Jesus' ascension _____

_____

_____

12 God's providence and our prayer

_____

_____

_____

13 the paschal mystery

_____

_____

_____

14 the authority and ministry in the Church

_____

_____

_____

15 the Holy Spirit, the Giver of Life

_____

_____

_____

Respond.

16 Why is the Holy Spirit called the *Advocate* or *Paraclete*?

_____

_____

_____

17 What are the essential characteristics of the Church?

_____

_____

_____

_____

18 What did Saint Paul mean by saying the Church is "the body of Christ"?

_____

_____

_____

_____

19 Name one other New Testament image of the Church and explain briefly.

_____

_____

_____

_____

20 Why do we say that the Church is made up of both human and divine dimensions?

_____

_____

_____

_____

For extra credit

Jesus is the source of all authority and ministry in the Church. What does that mean to you?

ASSESSMENT

125

Chapters 8-14

1 Priests are ___ to work independently of the bishop of their diocese.
   a. sometimes
   b. often
   c. never
   d. always

2 Which of the following is not considered an invisible element of the Church?
   a. devotion to Mary
   b. life of grace
   c. the theological virtues
   d. the gifts of the Holy Spirit

3 The word ___ means "one who is holy."
   a. apostle
   b. presbyter
   c. deacon
   d. saint

4 The theological virtues are
   a. faith, hope, and love.
   b. wisdom and courage.
   c. patience and kindness.
   d. joy and peace.

5 The Church's own body of laws is called ___ law.
   a. ecumenical
   b. canon
   c. clerical
   d. apostolic

Define.

6 magisterium _____

_____

_____

_____

_____

7 infallibility _____

_____

_____

_____

_____

8 ecumenism _____

_____

_____

_____

_____

9 chastity _____

_____

_____

_____

_____

10 Rite _____

_____

_____

_____

_____

FINAL

Explain what Catholics believe about the following:

11 heaven _____
_____
_____
_____

12 hell _____
_____
_____
_____

13 particular judgment
_____
_____
_____
_____

14 the immaculate conception
_____
_____
_____
_____

Explain what the Church teaches about the following:

15 reincarnation
_____
_____
_____
_____

16 the communion of saints
_____
_____
_____
_____

Respond.

17 What is meant by the evangelical counsels?
_____
_____
_____
_____

18 What is meant by the visible elements of the Church?
_____
_____
_____
_____

19 Explain briefly what is meant by extraordinary magisterium.
_____
_____
_____
_____

20 Explain why we say that Mary was the first of Jesus' disciples.
_____
_____
_____
_____

For extra credit

Why do we call the Church "the pilgrim Church"?

ASSESSMENT

Answer Sheet for Semester Tests

Midsemester Test

1. c **2.** a **3.** d **4.** a **5.** a

6. interventions of God in our daily lives; urgings and promptings of the Holy Spirit

7. baptized members of the Church who are not religious or clergy

8. Pentecost was the fiftieth day after Passover. For the first Christians this day was the occasion for Jesus to pour out the Holy Spirit upon them.

9. The clergy are the members of the Church who have received the sacrament of Holy Orders.

10. The Church is apostolic because it was founded on Christ and the apostles.

11. See page 11.

12. See page 19.

13. See pages 10 and 11.

14. See page 61.

15. See page 27.

16. See page 35.

17. See pages 52–54.

18. See page 44.

19. See chart on page 46.

20. See page 50.

For extra credit: Accept reasonable responses.

Final Test

1. c **2.** a **3.** d **4.** a **5.** b

6. the pope and the other bishops are the official teachers of the whole Church. We call them the *magisterium*, from the Latin word for "teacher.

7. gift of the Holy Spirit that keeps the whole Church from error—in believing and teaching—in matters concerning revelation and the deposit of the faith

8. refers to the effort on the part of Catholics and other Christians to work toward full unity among all baptized people of the world

9. Chastity means that a religious man or woman lives a life of purity as a witness to the kingdom of God. It includes a life of celibacy, which means not marrying.

10. a distinctive tradition of liturgy, laws, and customs that expresses the one Catholic faith in its own unique way

11. Heaven is life with the Blessed Trinity forever. It is the state of supreme happiness in which those who have been faithful to God and his commandments will enjoy the beatific vision, seeing God "face-to-face."

12. Hell is eternal separation from God. It is the just punishment for those who have rejected God.

13. See page 93

14. See page 99.

15. See page 94.

16. See page 102.

17. See page 77.

18. See pages 66 and 67.

19. See page 84.

20. See page 100.

For extra credit: Accept reasonable responses.

Computer Resources

Flying Colors is a trademark of:
Davidson & Associates, Inc.
P.O. Box 2961
Torrance, CA 90509
(1–800–556–6141)

HyperStudio is a registered trademark of:
Roger Wagner Publishing
1050 Pioneer Road—Suite P
El Cajon, CA 92020
(1–800–421–6526)

Word Cross is a registered trademark of:
Hi-Tech of Santa Cruz
202 Pelton Avenue
Santa Cruz, CA 95060
(1–408–425–5654)

Prodigy is a trademark of:
Prodigy Services Company
445 Hamilton Avenue
White Plains, NY 10601
(1–800–776–3449)
